Take
ACTION!

Take
ACTION!

Successful Australians
share their secrets

YOSSI SEGELMAN

Lothian
BOOKS

Dedicated, with love to Chaya, Mendy & Chanie

Thomas C. Lothian Pty Ltd
132 Albert Road, South Melbourne, 3205
www.lothian.com.au

Copyright © Yossi Segelman 2004

First published 2004
All rights reserved. No part of this publication may be reproduced, stored
in a retrieval system or transmitted in any form by any means without the
prior permission of the copyright owner. Enquiries should be made to the
publisher.

National Library of Australia
Cataloguing-in-Publication data:

    Segelman, Yossi.
    Take action! : Successful Australians share their secrets.

    ISBN 0 7344 0612 6.

    1. Success. 2. Self-actualization (Psychology). 3. Success -
    Australia - Anecdotes. I. Title.

158.1

Produced by Brewster Publishers Pty Ltd
Design by Brewster Publishers Pty Ltd
Typeset in Garamond 12/15 pt
Printed in Australia by Griffin Press

Contents

STRATEGIES FOR LIVING YOUR DREAMS

Contents

Acknowledgements

I am indebted to many people for their assistance with this project. In particular, I am grateful to the individuals who agreed to participate and share their secrets and strategies. They were tremendously generous with their time and belief in me and the project; they are truly inspirational.

Thank you to Pam Brewster for taking the seed of an idea and seeing it flourish, and Lothian Books for publishing Take Action!

To Amanda, Anne, Ash, Melissa and the team at Splash Group, for going that extra mile.

My sincere appreciation to my parents, Dovid and Shoshanna Segelman, and parents-in-law, Yaakov and Toby Lieder, for their continued encouragement, inspiration and shining examples of taking action and living life; also to Dovid Slavin for his guidance and support.

Special thanks go to my dear wife Chaya, for her unwavering belief in me and constant encouragement.

Foreword

Every day we see examples of people who have done great things in their life, but for many the path to that destination is still a mystery. It is this quest for an answer that has driven Yossi Segelman to explore the concept of taking action. This book seeks to demystify the secrets of success, with examples of people that have achieved simply by taking action.

Take Action! adds a fresh perspective to the idea that everyone has the ability to make something great of their life. This book is designed to motivate your thoughts into action.

As for me, I didn't set out to be a champion swimmer, but an accident as a child meant I took up swimming to rehabilitate — an activity that set me on a path for some truly memorable achievements in my life, such as world records and Olympic Gold.

Over the years these experiences have taught me that anything is possible – with equal helpings of self-belief and perseverance.

I have learned that pursuing dreams isn't always easy, and I have faced countless hurdles in my life as a sportsman, but the mind is a powerful thing, and I stayed true to what was important — an unwavering belief in myself.

We all face obstacles on the path to fulfilling our dreams. Only we can decide if these are tidal waves that will steer us off course or simply ripples slowing our progress.

This book's theme, Take Action! is important because it's an encouragement to every Australian, young or old, to find their motivation and then act to fulfill their dreams and aspirations. The stories of the prominent Australians within the pages of this book are remarkable — each contributor generously shares their ups and downs in life, and their secrets and strategies for 'taking action'.

So, let me leave you with one thought before you start: the only person who can make a sustained difference in your life is you; find inspiration, believe in your abilities, don't be put off by obstacles and simply take action!

KIEREN PERKINS

Introduction

I wrote this book to inspire you, irrespective of race, socio-economic or educational background. We can all succeed if we just take action! Over the past five years, whenever I met a person who seemed to me to have been successful in his or her field, I would ask them, 'If there were one or two ingredients that enabled you to accomplish what you have, what would they be?' The response was almost always, 'I believed that I could do it, I took action and just never gave up!' After hearing this for five years I thought, 'Why not emulate and learn from Australians who have overcome significant hurdles to get to where they are today, and be inspired by their vision and tenacity in reaching their goals?'

So I went about interviewing some of Australia's great achievers. They come from a range of industries and sectors, from all walks of life and backgrounds. I asked them the following:

1. What was your overall vision or goal and how, in a nutshell, did you get to where you are today?
2. What was the first step you took towards achieving that goal?
3. What inspired you to take action?
4. What were the initial challenges you faced and what are the challenges you have continued to face throughout your journey?
5. How did you overcome those challenges?
6. What inspired you to stay focused on your goal?
7. How did you balance work, family and other commitments?

8. To share one or two main ingredients that contributed to your taking action and fulfilling your dreams.

9. What would your advice be to someone entering a similar vocation?

10. What quote or line has inspired you to take action?

You can learn from these great Australians. Why reinvent the wheel when these people, who have found their way to the top, are sharing their journey and techniques with you, giving you the opportunity to join their ranks? Laugh and be moved as you read of their challenges and triumphs. These people are just like you and me.

You too can do it! You can make a difference.

Learn some strategies for living your dreams. Here you will find bite-sized, practical steps you can take to change your life forever. Pick and choose what suits you and enjoy your journey to the top!

As John McGrath put it so eloquently, 'Hearing a story about someone who had some initial challenges and overcame them – not only overcame those challenges but went to the whole next level and changed their life – was a life-changing catalyst.'

I hope that through reading this book you too will be inspired to dream and to take action, as these great Australians have. Success is within your reach in the area of your choice; you can create and shape a fulfilled and meaningful life by crystallising what it is you want to accomplish, then adding determination and consistent effort.

Take action, and never give up.

Natalie
BLOOM

Natalie Bloom started her own business at the age of 22. Today Bloom Pty Ltd is a highly successful company manufacturing aromatherapy products, candles, skin-care products and, more recently, cosmetics. Originally based in Natalie's family home Bloom now exports all over Asia, Europe, England and the United States. Natalie's entrepreneurial flair is evident by the numerous awards she has won. These include Cleo's Young Australian of the Year in 1999 and Victoria's Young Australian of the Year Award in 1997. In 1994 she was awarded The Business Opportunities/Optus Young Heroes Award for achievement in establishing a successful small business. Bloom Pty Ltd has received numerous Gift of the Year Awards, designed to encourage innovation and excellence in Australian manufacturing.

I didn't get the kind of job that I wanted to get when I finished college, and after 12 months at a graphic design agency I resigned. The agency that I really wanted to get into was a slick, quite corporate, design studio. I really admired their work, and I always had the feeling that I would end up working there.

I started making greeting cards from home, at the same time doing freelance work for different advertising agencies. I sold the cards at weekends. One lot sold, and that financed the next and the next and so on. A few months later I put together a product, a candle-making kit with recycled paper, sheets of beeswax and essential oils and a candle. I went to the buyer at Myer, showed them the kit and they ordered 5000 sets. I think it was at that moment that I realised I was on to something big. This was at the time when DIY stuff was really popular.

At that time I had absolutely no idea of how to run a business or even what it took to start a business. I will never forget the buyer at Myer who taught me that you had to have an invoice number on an invoice, and how to actually begin to be a vendor or a supplier to Myer. I had to learn all those basic things on the job.

It was the development of the product range that was probably the first step. I couldn't just rely on one product, so all of a sudden I was going to have to develop an ongoing range. The first thing I had to do was think about where the development of the product was going. What was the concept? What was our philosophy and what was it that would make these products sell and make Bloom a brand? So the beginnings were really focusing on the product side of things. I have always said it is the innovation in the product that made the business what it is today. Then it was a matter of financing it and managing all the legal issues that you need to deal with when you are running a business. There were trademark issues and setting up contracts and all those boring things that I hate. And getting staff on board and learning all about tax and GST. All these business basics were not my forte but I had to learn them on the job.

Business management for me was the most challenging part at the beginning, probably because I came from a creative background. But I think I have some inherent business skills through being exposed to business in my family over the years and also with my husband being in business. I obviously did not realise how much business acumen I had had instilled in me. It was just a matter of learning on the job, getting through things and putting my head down and working really, really hard.

The hardest things for me were the legal things. I just thought that once you had your products you could sell them anywhere round the world – but you can't. You need contracts with the people you are working with. The development of those contracts almost destroyed the business because they were so overwhelming. You have to define a distribution strategy or a distribution criterion for distributors to adhere to, for example. It was quite confronting to have to define all those things in order to be able to sell my product on a global scale. The trademark issues have also been really daunting. But I have always sought help when I know that I have needed it.

It was really my passion for design that instigated the business and that has been the thing that has kept me going. My husband Brian, who is a true entrepreneur, was always encouraging me. He said to me, 'I don't understand why you're not starting your own business.' Before he mentioned it I had never really thought about it. He was really the catalyst.

In the early days you don't understand how to say no, and you don't understand how not to get distracted. I was constantly being harassed by people to develop different products under licence or to take on opportunities that really weren't appropriate for the focus of the business, and I learned the hard way, by doing them. They didn't bring satisfaction or financial gain to the business and I learned that you just have to say no. Someone gave me some really good advice: you need to ask, 'Is it really going to make a difference?' I just look at opportunities as they arise now and I ask myself that question. Some can make a difference in terms of your brand positioning or financial contribution, but are they

3

really going to make a long-term difference to the business? Answering that question helps me make decisions and stay focused on the core business.

My parents have always encouraged me and my brother and sister to pursue our own passions in life and careers, and my dad discouraged us from going into his business in the hope that we would find our own paths in life. My brother is a plastic surgeon and my sister is an accountant, so we are all very different.

I am grateful to him for doing that, because my career path would have been totally different otherwise, but I think seeing my dad in business my whole life influenced and encouraged me – it was so exciting growing up seeing a business develop the way he developed his business, which was Portmans.

Sally Browne was a mentor for me in the early days. She gave me a lot of personal confidence. She is a successful fashion designer in Melbourne, whom I did work experience with when I was in Year 10 at school. Coincidentally she became my next-door neighbour, and now we live in the same street. She used to see me running around like a nutcase in the early days, and she would continually reconfirm to me that what I was doing had integrity. She was always sending me little snippets of advice and articles, just bits of encouragement.

I preach all the time that I am balancing, but in reality some weeks you manage it and some weeks you don't. Sometimes I go home on a Friday night and I feel that I am rushing out and leaving work not done, and I get in my car and think oh my God I have neglected my little daughter. You are playing this game all the time. Then sometimes I feel I have a perfect balance. When I see other mothers who are just frustrated, changing nappies all day and having no purpose to their life, I think that is not having a balanced life either.

I think you have to have very good time management and you have to be really disciplined and learn how to delegate. As I said, some days I get that right. You need help and support at home and at work, and a network of people who can make it all work for you. I have someone who looks after Chloe during the day while I am at work, and she can bring Chloe in occasionally if I need her to, which enables me to work but not miss out on the really integral parts of having a newborn child.

But now I make sure that Chloe doesn't come into the office very often. It is distracting for me and for everyone else, so I don't encourage it – but in the early days I was not going to miss out, so either she had to come in or I was at home.

Passion is number one, because if you are not passionate about what you do then you don't get the longevity of success. Discipline and stamina are also important. I also think chutzpah has something to do with it too – it was like, who did I think I was, a 22-year-old, going to New York and selling products to Saks Fifth Avenue? I think I had to have a bit of chutzpah to do that – I had no history, no success rate, but there was nothing stopping me, and what inspired me was that I love what I do.

My advice is to be passionate about what you do. 'Do what you love and love what you do.' There is also Audrey Hepburn's beauty tip, which is, 'For attractive lips, speak words of kindness, and for lovely eyes, seek out the good in people'. I think it is just a pattern of life.

I want to continue growing the brand as a global business and be in a position to create really fantastic, innovative products. I also want to be able to become much more focused on the design and less focused on the business side of Bloom. You need to continually challenge yourself. I think if you are continuously challenged, then you stay focused.

To make it work you have to have integrity in everything that you do – and if you do have integrity, then your team can follow through from that integrity. I also think it is important to give ownership to your team, to encourage them to work autonomously and to be continually challenged. I think that is true about everyone in the company, because if everyone is challenged then they are happy to keep growing as people and growing in business.

Hon. Bob CARR M.P.

The Hon. Bob Carr M.P. is Premier of New South Wales. Bob Carr was born in 1947. He was educated at Matraville High School and studied at the University of New South Wales. Before entering State Parliament, he worked as Education Officer at the Labor Council of New South Wales and as a journalist with the Australian Broadcasting Commission (now Corporation) and The Bulletin magazine. In 1983 he was elected to the Legislative Assembly of the New South Wales State Parliament as Member for Maroubra. In 1984 he became Minister for Planning and Environment in the Wran Labor Government. He also held the portfolio of Minister for Heritage between July 1986 and March 1988. After the Labor Government's defeat in 1988, Bob Carr became Leader of the Opposition and led the Party back into government in 1995. In 1998, the World Conservation Union awarded Premier Carr the Fred M. Packard International Parks Merit Award in recognition of the expansion of national parks achieved under his leadership.

Mr Carr was awarded the prestigious Fulbright Distinguished Fellow Award Scholarship in 1999; he turned his grant into five one-off $10,000 scholarships to teachers of Modern History in New South Wales schools.

When I was 15, one day I got it into my head that I wanted to get into politics. I wanted to be a Labor Party Member of Parliament. Until then I had wanted to be a cartoonist for a newspaper or a Walt Disney animation artist. So I went down and joined the local branch of the Labor Party. I was motivated by a very idealistic view of politics, especially Labor Party politics, and I wanted to be part of it. I wanted to have the honour of representing people, of achieving great things and supporting a great cause.

I think my inspiration towards politics came from my father. He was a train driver, and his father had been a train driver. He had a mainstream Labor view of the world. He was anti-Communist — he saw Communists as hypocrites who simply defended the Soviet Union at every opportunity. He disliked the Democratic Labor Party — he saw them as the Catholics in action in politics. His hero was Ben Chifley, the Labor Prime Minister 1945–49; he too was a former train driver.

So I listened a lot to my father, and started reading a bit about politics, and the biography of Ben Chifley. This was in 1962–63. Chifley had only been voted out in 1949, so it wasn't too far back. He was the last Australian Labor Prime Minister. I settled on a very idealistic interpretation of Labor history.

So at 15, living with two sisters and a brother in a fibro house in Matraville, going to Matraville High School — an ordinary, working-class comprehensive co-educational high school — I formed the view that I wanted to be a Labor Party Member of Parliament to do good and great things, the most noble aspiration one could have.

My family was, I think, bemused by this. However, they saw it as a long-term plan. My mother and father had a lot of common sense. They were down-to-earth people, they weren't flighty. They might have thought that it was a bit unlikely they would have a son who would go into politics, let alone be the Premier. I think they decided to let my enthusiasm run its course.

Some time in mid-1962 I wrote a letter to the Labor Party headquarters at the Trades Hall in Goulburn Street, Sydney. I said I wanted to join the Labor Party and was about to turn 15. I got a reply telling me that the secretary of the Malabar–South Matraville branch of the Australian Labor Party would get in touch with me. I eventually got in touch with him, and one Monday night I went down to their local monthly meeting at Malabar Public School. Imagine a group of working-class adults meeting in a primary school class-room, the president and secretary up the front at the teacher's desk, and a schoolboy in short pants walks in and says he wants to join the Labor Party! I remember the president saying, 'I don't think you're old enough.' I remember replying, 'I know the age is 15. I know the rules. I was advised that the age is 15.'

If I look back now, what lay ahead of that kid going along to join the Labor Party was very many nights of boredom, long nights at the local meetings, and a lot of mistakes as he tried his hand. An enormous amount of learning had to take place, plus discouragements, defeats and blunders, setbacks and mistakes. More seriously, when he thought he was finally getting there, that he had achieved his goal — representing the party that he loved in Parliament — there were further terrible disappointments and setbacks. He thought he had an opportunity of getting to the Senate, but there was a setback, a big setback. His ambitions had to be deferred — but for how long? Ten years. He was prepared to abide by that, to look at not getting into Parliament until he was 40, but in the end he had a breakthrough ... It's very interesting to think back to oneself as a 15-year-old, settling on a vision — quite a personal vision, but also an idealistic one, a noble one. It's like someone making a commitment to a religion or some other career — the law, espionage, the military, whatever. You stay loyal to it throughout, defining yourself through doing it, becoming a better person through doing it, learning from all your mistakes.

If you recognise a mistake, you're saying you can learn something; in fact you have already learned something. Mistakes, considered from this point of view, are a valuable experience, a superb experience. Most of the time you're half-learning things — they are vague in your memory — but a colossal, large-scale mistake will impress itself on you so that you can't forget it, and that's a good thing.

We define ourself by our actions; that's another thing I've learnt. There's no substitute for action. I think it would be very hard to face a life of contemplation, a life of reading, a life of reflection, the life of a pure scholar. I think we crave the world of action, relating to other people, solving problems, waking up each day with a list of challenges. Activity defines us, because it's through activity that we learn things: we learn about ourselves, we learn about society. This job as Premier has been an opportunity to learn about how our society works. It might be the best way of learning about our society, because in the Premier's job you see more of our society than anyone else.

Activity carries you forward. If you're going to live a life of activism, if you've signed up for a life of activity, you're dragged into the next step by the requirements of that life, so if something goes wrong you must trot on. In my job you have to keep talking to the public through the media, and that's a good and healthy thing. Even if you make a mistake, within hours you're on to the next thing, the next problem, the next challenge, but you're facing each one with more wisdom. You need to test what you're learning in the day-to-day world; your learning comes alive if you're using it in a speech to make a point, to hold the attention of the audience.

Otherwise everything you learn is just locked up in your mind and it dies with you.

I overcame those initial challenges at age 15 with plain day-in day-out persistence. I'd go to every political meeting I could get to when I was a teenager. I read every scrap of information on politics that I could lay my hands on. I practised writing at every opportunity — writing letters to the editor, writing articles in the university's ALP club newsletter, in the eastern suburbs Young Labor Association. And I practised public speaking. After a few months in the Malabar branch of the Labor Party I wrote out two motions. I took them along to a meeting, very nervous. Here I was, a 15-year-old, going to a meeting with adults and moving two motions. I increased my confidence by forcing myself to get up and speak at Young Labor and in other settings.

I was just willing myself to become a competent Labor Member of Parliament some time down the track. I regarded any job I had as a preparation, a training ground, for being a Member of Parliament: I knew that becoming a journalist was only a stepping stone, becoming Education Officer of the Labor Council was only a stepping stone, and returning to journalism (this time for *The Bulletin* magazine) was only an opportunity to fine-tune skills that would be useful when I finally broke through in politics.

You have to make your own luck. You have to work at putting yourself into the field you've chosen, so you work hard, you acquire all the skills, you make all the contacts — you become the leader of the university ALP club, you get on the executive of the Young Labor Council, you become the campaign director for your federal Member of Parliament, you become the secretary of a branch, you force yourself forward, you move yourself forward all the time — until eventually you land in a category of people from whom MPs tend to be chosen. Then if there's a stroke of luck, it's a stroke of luck that could well embrace you.

You have to discard a lot that's inessential. For example, there may be something in one of the papers I would consider replying to, but that would take half an hour or 45 minutes out of a day's work, and there are higher priorities: it's a higher priority that I go and visit a government office that was the site of a petrol and fire attack in which one of our public servants died and two were seriously injured.

During the recent bushfire crisis, I simply dropped everything to devote myself to that, but when it was out of the way I was able to resume my visits to key communities in New South Wales to talk about education, jobs, health and the rest of the program that's essential to the government being re-elected in a year's time. In all of this there must be time for maintaining relationships with parliamentary colleagues, opinion leaders in the community and members of my local community.

I am seeing a delegation this afternoon — a tenant group from a public housing estate in my electorate. They have kids who present something of a challenge, kids from a poor background who might be drifting into drugs and crime. I said, 'Well bring them in, let them meet the Premier, I'll talk to them about their future, give them some hope that from a modest background they can do something with their lives.' There's an opportunity for them to come in with their elders and meet the Premier — that's part of my commitment to serving my own electorate. So there are multiple goals, and it's a juggling act. You discard the inessential and return to the major tasks … you have to be flexible.

In a crisis, specifically the bushfires, you need to communicate to the broader community what is going on and what is going to happen. You need to answer their questions:

has there been enough hazard reduction? What will we do with the arsonists? How quickly can we look after the victims? What can we do to help and honour the frontline firefighters? You're obliged to answer these questions, to assure people that they will be looked after. Communication is therefore a very large part of doing the job successfully; we need to carry the community with us through a time of difficulty. In a democracy that's how it works. The public has questions about a crisis; my job is to get the facts and answer the questions.

One has to know how to eliminate the inessential. Time at home is vital. It's part of life; you can't work all weekend, you can't work every night, you won't be at every function or celebration. You need time to reflect and time to read, otherwise you're not adding to your intellectual capital. I would not have lasted the job in leading the Opposition from 1988 to 1995 unless we had taken holidays. Every New Year we went overseas, and for a month we'd travel and see great sites and learn history. I always returned fresh to the awful job of leading a party in Opposition! It's important to plunge into the surf or take a bushwalk, otherwise you'll become like someone on the treadmill.

Mental and physical health are important. I think to be successful you have to have the gift of a steady temperament and reliable physical health. It's as hard to tackle a job if you're prone to serious depression or mood swings as it is if you are prone to a heart ailment.

The second thing is a capacity to communicate, to explain what you're doing and why you're doing it, to be able to marshal arguments.

Third, you have to have the mental equipment to burrow away at problems, to think of solutions and to judge the various options.

An old man on a kibbutz in Israel in 1983 said to me,

'Patriotism grows from the knowledge of your country's history and geography.' I find that the more I see of this community, the more I like it. I saw this city and state blossom during the Olympics. I saw it rally during the terrible bushfire crisis. No one sees more of New South Wales and its people than I do, and the more I see it the more I like it. As a result, I feel the honour of representing it, speaking for it, doing things on its behalf. The more experience I have on the job, the more relaxed I am about its responsibilities, and the more easily I can shoulder these responsibilities.

To someone entering politics I'd say don't give up. Keep training yourself and educating yourself; remember, you're never more effective than when you take up something you really do care about, and when you are sincerely yourself. When I was in Opposition and headed for my second election, I was asked what I would do if I failed. Would I stand for a third time? I said no, and I quoted W.C. Fields: 'If at first you don't succeed, try again, then give up — it's no use being a damn fool about it.'

Strategies for living
YOUR DREAMS

Believe in yourself 100 per cent You've followed your intuition and come up with a plan, you've done your homework, and you know this is what you truly want to do; the final requirement is to believe in yourself — have faith in yourself 100 per cent.

If you believe in yourself totally you will find that you become passionate about what you are doing. When faced with a challenge or an obstacle, you will take it in your stride. You will seek and find solutions to the difficulties you face because you know 100 per cent that what you are doing is correct. Obstacles will crop up — they are part of life — but you will find ways to get around or over them.

If you don't have complete faith in the journey you are embarking on, the first time you are faced with a challenge you will say to yourself, 'I told you so. I knew I couldn't do this. It was probably not meant to be, anyway, and I should never have even tried in the first place.' Your subconscious guides you constantly. It detects whether or not you're truly committed to what you are doing, and when it comes to overcoming these obstacles, if it senses that you are absolutely committed to realising your goal, it will start looking for answers and solutions to the challenges you are facing. But if it detects doubt it will give you that 'you shouldn't bother' type of feedback.

So get clear what it is you want to do, believe 100 per cent that you can do it, and go for it! You will surprise yourself with the solutions that you come up with.

General Peter COSGROVE

General Peter Cosgrove was born into an Army family in Sydney in 1947. After secondary school he entered the Royal Military College Duntroon, graduating in 1968 to the Royal Australian Infantry Corps. He served initially with the 1st Battalion, Royal Australian Regiment, in Malaysia before joining the Australian Reinforcement Unit at Nui Dat in South Vietnam in August 1969. General Cosgrove has commanded the Methods of Instruction Team, instructed in tactics and has been the Commandant of the Australian Defence Warfare Centre at RAAF Williamtown and also of the Royal Military College Duntroon. He was Aide de Camp to the Governor General, Sir Paul Hasluck, and Military Assistant to the Chief of the General Staff. In 1999, as Commander of the Deployable Joint Force Headquarters, he assumed command of the International Forces in East Timor. He was subsequently appointed Chief of Army and in July 2002 assumed the position of Chief of the Defence Force. He was awarded the Military Cross for his service in South Vietnam, and has received several foreign awards. In 2001 he was the Australian of the Year.

When I first started in the military, my vision was constrained by my immaturity. In those days I never saw myself as being a very senior officer in the army because it was unthinkable — I wouldn't know how such people operated and didn't have any idea that I might, by being in the right place at the right time, find myself in such a position. However, the years were kind to me, and now I do find myself a very senior officer.

They say that as you get older your ability to create a vision improves, simply because you have the confidence and the urge to walk ahead, to think of how things should be or might be. As a younger person you need to be persuaded that it's OK for you even to have a vision, that in fact it's desirable for you to have a thought about how your life might be shaped.

The vision I have now, inevitably, is how the Australian army must be shaped to meet its obligations for the nation, not in five or ten years' time, but in 20 years' time. We need to acknowledge that the young people who enter the army today will be leading it in 20 years. They must be the right people, and they must have absolutely carefully focused and appropriate training now. They must be given the right experiences in their first few years in the army, they must be shaped into the character we want in the army, so that in 20 years, when they face very significant challenges — and that is inevitable, even though we can't see now what those challenges will be — they are ready for them.

Objectively I wouldn't want them to fail, and subjectively and personally I wouldn't want it either — their failure in 20 years will be my failure today.

My vision is twofold. First, to create leaders, because the army will rise or fall, succeed or fail through the quality of its leadership. We can accept that the Australians we recruit will be technically competent, that responsible and wise governments will provide enough money for the right equipment, that people will carefully and prudently allocate missions we are able to do — we can accept all that, nothing will change. Our history shows us that we have had a succession of wise and prudent governments. But where we will rise or fall, succeed or fail, is in the quality of the decisions made by leaders and the relationship the leaders enjoy with their soldiers, those who accept the responsibility of standing in harm's way.

So leadership is one focus; the other is the technical proficiency that goes with leadership. A leader without technical proficiency is a formless person. He or she might be an all-purpose leader in certain circumstances — a charismatic individual whose qualities shine out and about whom people say, 'I'd like to follow that person' — but in the military, as in many other professions, there has to be a technical proficiency which can take that leadership ability and give it substance, give it direction and purpose, and give empowerment in a technical sense to the wishes of the leader.

A judge is a leader, but a judge is also an expert lawyer, an expert in the knowledge and administration of the law. In the military, a senior officer or general is by definition expected to be a competent leader, a highly competent leader. In addition, though, that general must be very professional in his or her knowledge of the art of warfare, in the administration of a military force, in the provisioning of a complex organisation to do very unusual things.

When I was a young man, before I joined the army, I think the influences upon me to choose a military career were the example of my father, my grandfather and other relatives who had been in the army; in fact, my father was in the army when I joined myself. So I had role models who seemed to be very decent men, who were model citizens, and it occurred to me that you can be in the army and be a decent person, god fearing, a good citizen, a fine family member. None of these things were excluded by being in uniform. So I joined the army when I was 17.

When I entered the army I joined an institution which

had in its relatively short life — at that stage it had only been going for 64 years — already deeply embedded itself in the national psyche. It had great traditions, many of them based on British traditions. It had a great history; there were legendary people who had been through its ranks. It had great self-esteem, purpose and pride. And I went into an institution within an institution: the Royal Military College, itself a great institution. It said, 'Admire me, love me. I'm an institution, I will care for you. I will change you, but you will be happy with the changes.' That was the sort of mood of the institution.

And I *was* changed. I started as a somewhat immature and quite disorganised young man, who found it very hard to adopt any personal discipline or routine. I changed, over a number of years at the college, to become quite well organised, quite well disciplined personally, and technically I was probably average to above average. I was pleased that I'd been able to flourish in a fairly rigorous environment.

So I had the role model of my parents, plus the changes brought about by being a participant in the institutional life of the army. And then I was commanding troops on operations in Vietnam. I found that I had an aptitude for it. Not a love of war, not a love of violence, but it seemed I could lead soldiers under stressful conditions. Marvellously, for me, I could provide what they needed. I was hugely encouraged by this; it gave me great confidence and a zest to continue doing it.

So there are the three defining factors in my career: the role models, the changes brought about by being in a great and good institution, and the moment when I appreciated that I had some aptitude for the life that I'd chosen.

Over the years, when my military life became quite demanding, particularly on the family, I would always be balancing these demands — the impact on this kid's schooling or whatever — testing this back against the notion, 'Well, you love this work, don't you?' and the answer every time I asked that question was, 'Yes, I still love this role.' But I've been supported and reinforced by a tremendous family who understand how much I love the life. Who've been prepared to put up with a lot because they know that I am a round peg in a round hole. With that in mind, they have sacrificed a lot of the stability that many other families take for granted — there's been an impact on schooling, and on circles of friends made in each new place and then left behind, and just the pain in the neck of packing up the house every couple of years. Plus the frequent absences of Dad from wherever home was at the time. I'd think about all this as I was heading off on yet another round of army duty somewhere. There have been some significant absences, and I can tell you that you feel both grateful and guilty: hugely grateful because the family is allowing you to do the thing you like to do, but guilty because there is a cost.

Everybody must feel as if they are valued in their work, that they are appreciated and promoted and respected by the institution. This applies in the army, but it also applies to any institution or group or cause that people rally to. They must feel valued in the institution. That must be the ambience of the organisation. And then each individual must feel that their particular work is useful, is resourced, that they are valued moment to moment, not just broadly, but particularly, and that's actually part of the leadership transaction. When I say to somebody, 'I need you to do so and so', they must know that I wouldn't ask if it wasn't important, and they must know that I appreciate it. Very often they might be puzzled – why am I doing it? So I must also try to tell them whatever I can about the reasons: 'I would like you to do this for me because such and such will happen if you do.' They must feel part of the team. 'I am helping the boss do such and such, and that's a good thing and he appreciates it.' Of course this isn't rocket science, but it is virtually a mantra with our people. We make it instinctive; it is not some annoying, trivial requirement we impose on people. It is fundamental that people must always feel valued, because sometimes you're asking them to do very tough things.

I am reminded of a tragic situation in the war in Afghanistan, where a soldier was reported to have fallen from a helicopter as it was attempting an urgent departure from where it was being shot at; it went a short distance and at that point it was realised that the soldier had fallen out. And I am told that instinctively and immediately the reaction of the soldiers and their leaders in that damaged helicopter (and another one that was with it) was to return to this very dangerous place to get their friend. They got him back, but he was dead when they got him.

The point was, they said, 'He is a member of our team, he is valued, we will go to enormous lengths and take huge risks to rescue him.' This, to me, is fundamental to the sort of profound value that we place upon each other. Putting service above self, putting the team before the individual, saying that we must take on danger because this is what we do for each other as a team. And we know, in the aftermath, that a large number of soldiers were killed and wounded, all because they said, 'We must rescue our friend.'

This occurs in military forces everywhere in the world on a relatively frequent basis, because it is the foundation stone of military camaraderie, of teamwork; it is the reason people value the team and do incredibly difficult things for the team — because to let down your friends would be unthinkable. To me it is actually a microcosm of patriotism. It is refined patriotism; some may say that it is a building block of patriotism, but I think it's patriotism gone full circle. The patriotic theme is to take on the difficulty of military service in the cause of serving your country or your society or your community. Somewhere in that development you identify a like-minded group who share your values, and then that patriotism becomes an important building block in the relationship you enjoy with your small group, and then the small group who all share these values becomes the core focus of your life at these important and dangerous times.

You could say, and people do, that Australian soldiers tend to shy away from high-flown terms such as 'patriotism', 'service' and 'nation', but that's only because of an innate shyness or embarrassment. The concepts are actually there in abundance: when you hear about Australian mateship you are (especially in a military sense) really hearing a story about a high level of patriotism and a very, very strong bonding between groups of like-minded people who are serving the country, and who acknowledge the importance of their small group as like-minded individuals.

One of the marvellous things about the military is that it's comprised of ordinary people; there are no superheroes, no Supermen and Superwomen in the military. They are people whose deeds would sometimes suggest that, but fundamentally they're ordinary people who manage to do extraordinary things under great pressure. However, because they are ordinary people, they are also subjected to the same sort of pressures that exist in the wider community, and while we try very hard to select people we think will be able to withstand the rigours and stresses of military life, we occasionally make mistakes in our selection — we occasionally find people who have intended to be absolutely perfectly behaved and serve their nation but get it wrong. So we certainly have our share of people who do things which they and the institution are not proud of. But we deal with that. We will never pretend that we are perfect, but we have to try to have perfect intentions.

I've had no special challenges beyond that which any soldier who's in the army for a lengthy period will face, and as I said a while ago, I have to just thank — and keep thanking — my family for their support. The challenges have generally been those ordinary challenges all soldiers face: of separation, isolation from the extended family — the small family will travel to remote places but it won't include grandfathers, grandmothers, uncles and aunties, and that's really sad. It puts a lot of strain on relationships and marriages, and on a soldier's commitment to serve. These are ordinary challenges and people cope with them; and when they sometimes find that the challenges become overwhelming, and they say, 'I have to leave the army, with great regret', we tell them how much we have appreciated their service and we wish them well and we understand that they've made a crucial family decision.

You come to terms with these challenges of separation or isolation, or yet another move, and your family loyally signs up for another spin on the merry-go-round. Then you find yourself waking up in the morning and charging off to work saying, 'Boy, I get another chance to deal with some of the most marvellous young Australians', and that's a challenge in its own right, because you owe them so much every day when you get to work. You owe it to them to be on top of your form, to find out what it is you're supposed to do for them, and to make sure the things they are going to do for you are sensible, well thought out, safe, well resourced – and at the end of it all, you don't forget to say thanks.

I have worked very hard at finding out what people think needs improving and developing new pathways that I believe we should take, and now I do have a vision of what we must do. Now I try to get the right people to help me with the ideas and the details, and then I have to craft messages which I broadcast continually. Sometimes I broadcast across an airspace of two feet, into the ear of a near subordinate. Other times I'm putting out messages in the newspapers or across other media saying, 'Hey out there, I know what we are doing, I know what's wrong, we'll be able to fix some of these things … oh and by the way here's some important jobs you have to do for the nation.' You just have to be out there and hope that you're a person whose message is sought and analysed by the people, somebody whose word is persuasive and trusted.

To a kid just out of school or someone who is looking for some kind of a job for a few years, it is a significant step to take on the challenges and the potential dangers of being in the army. I don't try to over-complicate their lives with information in some sort of nice tight package. I say to them that they've made a tremendously important decision by choosing to serve their nation in the army. I tell them that they have already shown an element of greatness, even though it might not seem that way

I also stress to any soldier, no matter how much that soldier lacks self-confidence, that every person I have ever met has some element of greatness in them. Now I don't know what it is — part of my job is to discover it — and I can't personally discover it in every soldier, but if I imbue my subordinates with the same idea, they then get out there with their people, find out what it is about them that is great and make sure they exploit that. It's from each according to his or her needs and to each according to his or her needs; that's how teams operate. We aim to find in every soldier what it is they do really well, and then they will be part of our jigsaw, and we will say to them, 'Now you are going to do that.' They have already, as I said, exhibited an element of greatness by saying, 'I will join the army', and now we are going to compound that greatness.

When people realise this, they always perform happily and proudly, because they say, 'I am part of the team'; even the ones who sometimes falter feel it and say it. There is patience, persistence, sympathy, a bit of luck, sometimes correction, but very often all the good things rather than the punitive things.

I love any philosophical reference to the core nature of the human spirit, anything that says it's what's inside a person, rather than their physical attributes, that represents the true greatness in the human race. That while we love our athletes, we also love any people who have boundless generosity, or boundless forgiveness, or boundless love, or boundless enthusiasm, and none of these can be measured with a stopwatch.

I think having a balance of humility and enthusiasm is important. Humility helps because you know that you'll never reach perfection in any endeavour. The enthusiasm says, 'I don't care, I am going to keep going!'

Hon. Alexander DOWNER M.P.

Alexander Downer was elected Federal Member for Mayo in South Australia in 1984. He served as Shadow Minister in a number of portfolios before becoming Leader of the Opposition in 1994. He subsequently became Shadow Minister for Foreign Affairs and in March 1996 he was appointed Minister for Foreign Affairs when the Liberal–National Party Coalition was elected to Government. Mr Downer is a member of the National Security Cabinet Committee. Before entering Federal Parliament, Mr Downer held several positions including economist to the Bank of New South Wales (Westpac), and diplomat for the Department of Foreign Affairs. He was also the Senior Foreign Affairs Representative in South Australia and acted as a political adviser to the former Prime Minister, the Hon. Malcolm Fraser, and Political Adviser to the Federal Leader of the Opposition, the Hon. Andrew Peacock from 1982 to 1983. Mr Downer was also the Executive Director of the Australian Chamber of Commerce from 1983 to 1984.

You can be lucky or unlucky in life. There is one most important way you can be lucky — you can be born with privilege. The greatest privilege you can have is parents who care for you and who are really interested in you. Who ask you how you are getting on at school and try to help you, take a genuine interest; a family where there is a real sense of affection and love coming from the parents.

If you have that as a child it is such a privilege. I had that. The second thing I had, and it may be related, is that I worked out at a fairly early age where I wanted to go in life. I think there is an element of luck in that. If you stumble across something that really interests you and you have this idea in your head about what you would really like to do, then you can start crafting your current activities towards that broader objective. I was really interested in issues of public policy and I felt strongly about them. I was the sort of teenager who wanted to throw a brick through the television, not out of vandalism but out of irritation with people who didn't agree with me. That is unusual for somebody of that age, but that is how I felt — I had that 'that's absolute rubbish, I couldn't imagine anything more silly than what you are saying' kind of attitude. So I developed these ideas at an early age.

But nothing comes without hard work. I didn't always work exceptionally hard. A lot of my time at school I worked just hard enough to pass, which was not very hard, believe me. There wasn't much work involved just to pass. But as time went on I gained momentum and when I got into my late teens, when I started to work out what I wanted to do, I began to accelerate my pace of work and commitment.

When I was 16 or 17, I followed politics very closely for somebody of that age and I was especially interested in international relations, so when I was at university I chose courses that would equip me to work in that area and I undertook activities that I thought would help me achieve my objective.

A lot of people go for jobs for status and prestige; that can be very dangerous if you don't work out what you want to do with the job. If you are seeking any position you need to work out before you get the position — even if you might never get it — what you would like to do with the position. In my case

I had a lot of background in foreign affairs: my father was an ambassador and I was in the foreign service myself for six years.

I had a lot of intellectual interest in foreign policy, and I had a view about how Australian foreign policy should be run. I come very much from the so-called 'national interest' school. A Foreign Minister is somebody who obviously is only going to be in the position for a limited period of time. I do this job on behalf of 20 million Australians, and they expect me not to conduct myself as though I was in a university seminar, but to go out and pursue their interests and achieve their objectives. So I need to identify what their objectives are. Have a clear idea of what I think they are. They won't all agree with me, but overall I have an idea of what I think the objectives of Australians are and I follow that, through all the difficulties that arise — the Solomon Islands, the problems with the international criminal court, the Middle East, India, Pakistan, Zimbabwe and so on.

I have a paradigm in my head about how I should be pursuing the national interest, so the amount of energy I put into these issues, the way I handle these issues, is from the perspective of what's in it for Australia — there's a fairly aggressive pursuit of the national interest.

You should pursue a job or an occupation with a view to what you would like to achieve in it. The further up you go, the further up the greasy pole you go — as Disraeli would have said, the more perilous it becomes — and the more out- siders analyse what you're doing. You get up to being the Number Three in a company and an awful lot of people in the company know who you are and they follow what you're doing quite closely. If you become Number Three in the Australian government, it's the same. If you don't know what you are doing, you will fail.

You can't please everyone, so you have to put that aside. I have no idea what all 20 million Australians think, for example. I am not trying to articulate what they think, I am trying to articulate what I think is best for the country. I have to make that analysis. Very few people are focused on foreign policy day in and day out; they just see a bit about it on the news. This gives me an opportunity to take a leadership position. If you know what you are doing you build the confidence of your constituency, be it a political constituency or a business or a legal constituency, whatever it is.

You know one of the reasons I like golf? Golf is difficult; that's why I like golf. I don't find things that are easy so interesting, and being the Foreign Minister, believe me, makes golf look easy. There is so little scope for mistakes, but in golf there is some. If you hit the ball way off left, you hook the ball down the fairway and it goes into the rough, you might have a reasonable lie, and with a six iron you might get it out of there and right on to the green.

As the Foreign Minister it's often not quite so easy. If you go into the rough it can be perilously difficult to get out of it. And the consequences of being in the rough can be rather serious, not just, 'Oh well, that's golf.'

The challenges are one of the things that make it interesting. The fact that it is hard makes it interesting, so when big issues arise I just focus on how we are going to resolve them.

Like all people, I like to go to a restaurant, I like to go to a pub, go to the movies, go to the theatre, I like to do all those sorts of things. I love playing sport, so I have plenty of other activities that I undertake just for fun. And I have a wife and a family, and that's another component of my life.

I live in Adelaide, so I am away from my family an awful lot of the time, but we ring each other up all the time. We have a whole world of our own which nobody else sees. People out there would say they know who Alexander Downer is, but they don't know anything about the world that I live in at home.

My mother is still alive. She and my father were both fantastic, and she still is. My father was a Cabinet Minister in the Menzies Government. He must have gone away like I do, and transport wasn't quite as good in those days as it is now, but I don't have a sense of him having been away from home a lot, even though he must have been. I only have a sense of him saying, 'Hello dear, how are you?'

There is something about enthusiasm for your family that is different. We fight with each other sometimes and all that sort of thing, but there is this notion of enthusiasm for each other, interest in each other, wanting to talk to each other to find out what everyone is doing. I am not wildly social; I am gregarious but I am not wildly social. I would rather just be at home or go and play golf. I mentioned golf before — that's just the latest interest I have. If I go to play golf I'd rather play with my son than with a friend — we have the same sense of humour, we have the same sort of points of reference. A lot of people are not so interested in their own families.

My parents really cared for me when I was a child. I can still feel that so strongly. How they built a whole structure for my life of complete security. I have never wandered around thinking no one loves me, because I know people love me. There are also people who don't like me, who absolutely hate me. Do I care very much about that? You would rather people liked you than didn't like you. But I can cope because I have always had that security of my own family, of my mother, my father, my sisters — and then my wife and my children. The reason why my sisters and I are quite self-confident is because of the security that our parents gave us right from the beginning.

You can go down to a bookshop and buy all those books on management techniques and how to build self-confidence, but honestly, if your parents got you off to a bad start in life by neglecting you, by thinking they had more important things to worry about than you, then you are off to a shocking start through no fault of your own. Parents need to understand that just a little bit better than some of them do. It is a simply immense responsibility you undertake when you have children.

It doesn't worry me particularly that I see letters to the editor absolutely hammering me. It doesn't worry me as long as I feel confident that what I am doing is right. If somebody writes a letter saying how wrong I am it's just another day in the office, and it comes with the territory. This is what is important — my parents, my wife, my children.

Strategies for living
YOUR DREAMS

Create an anchor Have you ever overcome a challenge or fulfilled a goal and experienced the most awesome feeling, as if you were walking on air? Your spirits are sky high, you have fulfilled your goal, and both you and your vision are unstoppable?

When the chips are down the trick is to relive that wonderful feeling you had when you reached the finishing line. Replay in your mind the scene and that unstoppable feeling you experienced, the power and control you felt.

Here is a technique many people use: they select a moment or a stage in their life when they overcame a specific challenge or experienced a great sense of accomplishment. Some people use specific moments of joy with their family. They express the feelings they had at that time on a business card-sized piece of paper or they get a picture that reminds them of that special moment, and they keep the card or picture in their wallet.

So create an anchor. Take a pen and a small piece of card and describe that marvellous feeling of accomplishment, or find a picture which expresses that special moment, and keep it close by. When the chips are down, spend a few moments mentally replaying the scene you have chosen as your anchor. Remember that unstoppable feeling you experienced, the power and control you felt. This process will get you back into, or close to, the state you were in at that time. Then take action immediately, even if you only do something small. If you act straight away you will be able to build momentum and get back on track.

Lindsay
FOX

The son of a truck driver, Lindsay Fox left school at the age of 16 and bought his own truck. Forty-seven years later, Linfox, a private company, is one of the largest transport, warehousing and logistics organisations in Australia, operating nationally and internationally. Starting with one vehicle Lindsay delivered coke and coal for West Melbourne Gasworks and soft drinks for Schweppes. Today 2500 vehicles carry the Linfox slogan. Committed to helping the less fortunate, Lindsay joined forces with Bill Kelty of the A.C.T.U. and together they introduced a national campaign called 'Work for Australia'. This campaign encouraged companies and local communities to generate jobs for the unemployed with the aid of government subsidies and programs. Over 60,000 jobs were pledged through their efforts and they were awarded 'Victorians of the Year' by the Sunday Age. In January 1992, Lindsay was made an Officer of the Order of Australia (AO) for his contribution to transport and the community.

At school I was a disaster. I left school at 16 and I bought a truck for £400. It was a Chevrolet Maple Leaf. I actually managed to convince the guy to accept four quarterly promissory notes to buy this second-hand truck. My next step was to get a licence! I drove that truck transporting coke and coal for the gasworks in West Melbourne and soft drinks for Schweppes.

In 1957, the year I got married, I doubled my fleet and created the slogan 'You are passing another Fox', which appeared on the rear of the two vehicles, creating an illusion about the size of my fleet. At the time I used to park the car out the front and drive the truck. I had two or three drivers, then three became six, six became twelve and it went on from there. Today over 2500 vehicles still carry this slogan in Australia, New Zealand, Malaysia and Thailand.

There was no vision, just an evolution. I guess all the way through I tried to analyse my own weaknesses and compensate for them using other corporations' strengths, so all the companies we dealt with were blue-chip companies that had been around for a long time and were obviously going to be available to do business with us for a long time. And most of those companies we still deal with today.

They all used to run their own fleets of trucks. I told them they wouldn't go to the dentist to get have their tonsils taken out, so why have a store manager looking after the trucking side of the business? Slowly but surely, one by one, they came across.

By about 1965 we had about six trucks working for a hardware company. Then we started with Coles, with one truck on a three-month trial, and with Dunlop. And all those companies used to pay me every seven days, but let me pay them every 90 days. That's when I first realised about cash flow. So all those companies were very important in the growth and development of our organisation, and they really represented people who backed people.

Companies are clinical; it's the personalities of the people who work there that matter and the chemistries of the personalities. I am thankful even today to some guys, such as the manager at my local Commonwealth Bank, Joe Lonigan. Joe used to go out on a limb for me. He would ask the bank

— the head office — for more money for me and they'd knock him back. Then he would send a letter to them, and they would agree to an extra £10,000 worth of credit. This was a corner-store bank manager. And the guys at BP were also vital; they helped finance my first transport depot, which cost £5000. I would transport fuel, which would offset my loan account. All the relationships with these people helped form me, as well as the guys who worked with me, even those who played football with me — they all had personality.

So Linfox was built primarily on relationships.

When I was 21 Dad died. We had to borrow £400 to bury him, and after that there was no one there driving me and helping me. But I think there's an inner fire in your belly that probably develops pretty young. As a kid, I remember we used to collect food for Britain here in Australia after the war finished in 1945. I would go around with my billycart and collect as much as all the kids in my class put together. I guess in many ways, I just harnessed that inner fire over a long period of time.

Until I was 22, I probably worked eight months of the year and spent four months a year on the beach, because I could live comfortably. But then I got married, and I guess the turning point came with the birth of our first child. Then in seven years I think we had six kids. So the need was there to build something as a foundation for the family.

The challenge was to convince people that I had credibility, that if I said I'd do something I would fulfil my obligations. Making people change in any way is always difficult. In those days all the companies were doing things the way they had done them for 20, 30, 40 years, from one generation to the next. So to implement change and to get them to do something different — they couldn't do it. The easiest way was to bring in a catalyst, an outside organisation that specialised in a particular area, and have that company say, 'OK, we don't do it that way.' Then they'd accept it.

So I had to convince customers all the time that what they were doing in transport was different from their main business, and that I was a specialist in transport and would do things a little differently. 'A physician does one job, a surgeon does another,' I would say. 'Would you like your physician to operate on your body? How would you like an ordinary chemist coming in from the street to do a circumcision?' Sitting across the table from them and using logic and common sense. A winner says, 'There ought to be a better way of doing this'; a loser says, 'This is the way it's done around here.'

And it was revolutionary; I was probably the first person to implement contract cartage and distribution. Before that all the transport companies used to operate like taxicabs — you would ring up and call for a truck when you needed one.

I guess some people feel they achieve success just in doing things, just being doers. Some people want to be always the looker, and I always wanted to be a doer.

But every night of the week I was home for dinner with all the family. It was very difficult, especially in the trucking business, but every night I was home. If business interferes with family, sell the business.

You can do anything if you have confidence, and if you build up integrity and people find that you are a person of your word. Most of the things I do are still done on the shake of a hand. I call it the TIL principle: trust, integrity, loyalty.

I've had 50 years' experience now, and it's difficult to think as a novice when you are a veteran. When people have come to me and told me they want to buy a truck, I tell them, 'No, don't be silly — 17,000 people go broke every year doing this.' They think I am trying to keep them out of the industry, and they go and buy a truck and they lose their truck and their house. It was different in the days when we started. In the early days, you could buy a brand-new truck for $5000; today they are $100,000.

Henry Ford said, 'If you think you can or you think you can't, you're right.' If I had been an academic or an economics graduate, I would have got caught up with paralysis by analysis. I would be trying to analyse if there was some opportunity in a situation, but if you're in, you just react — you see things with your own eyes. This is an example of the difference between an academic and a practical person — their knowledge, what they learn by making mistakes.

I just had two fellows retire after 38 years. These people are part of the extended family: they worked for a company of which they are proud, they have educated their kids, they have bought their houses and they have some money in the bank. A lot of energy has gone out over time, and then the people carry the business on, like disciples.

Oddly enough, probably the inspiration that has stayed with me all the way through my life is Monday morning addresses at school, when they would unfurl the flag, and we would stand at attention and repeat, 'I love God and my country, I'll honour the flag, I'll serve the king and cheerfully obey my parents, teachers and the laws'. Those little things at school are very deeply implanted.

And finally — you get out of the community what you put in!

Jeff
GAMBIN

Born in India in 1948, Jeff Gambin was educated in English schools in India and later graduated in entomology at Cambridge University. He also became a qualified chef and obtained a commercial pilot's licence. After years of hard work he became a very successful businessman who owned several top restaurants in Sydney. Today, this ex-restaurateur helps Sydney's poor by providing them with nightly meals and assisting them with finding accommodation and work. All this is funded out of his own pocket, as he came to realise that there is more to life than making money. That was the start of Just Enough Faith. Along with wife Alina, he feeds up to 500 disadvantaged people from the back of his van in central Sydney. However, their objective is much more than just feeding the homeless: it's about giving them hope and helping them regain respect by counselling and, where possible, housing. In recognition of his endeavours Jeff Gambin was recently awarded the Australian Humanitarian of the Year award.

Just Enough Faith came about some ten years ago. I was building a club. I had exceeded my budget — by not a great deal, only about $3 million or something — and the bank manager didn't want to have lunch with me anymore. All I needed at that time was just under $300,000 to complete this building, so I called in a partner. I had a lot of interest — most people wanted to be silent partners, just put the money in.

Eventually I met a guy who said, 'I am in the industry. I'm in hospitality, I've got the cash and I can work along with you.' I thought this could turn out to be a very good marriage, because having a working partner would give me time off. Unfortunately it didn't work out that way.

The first reason was because when you have been running solo for 30 years and then take on a partner it is like a marriage, and it was never ever going to work. I always found some fault with him — it wasn't his fault; really it was mine. But I was totally uncomfortable, so one particular night I decided to take a walk into Martin Place because it was worrying me. I had not been very honest, not only with myself but also with the people around me. I actually didn't like this man. I hadn't liked him from the very beginning but I still took his money.

I took his money to get my venture started, and I was try- ing to come to grips with myself. This is why I took the stroll into Martin Place. It was the middle of winter and I was sitting on a bench; a man walked by and asked me the time. It was about 10.40. It was one of those coldnesses that I was actually enjoying, I was enjoying that cold; my body was feeling real at the time.

I took out a packet of cigarettes and I could see that the guy who asked for the time was what I would consider an old derelict, a drunk with a brown paper bag. He pointed to a doorway and he said, 'Mate, if you go into that doorway you'll be a lot more comfortable.' I looked at him question- ingly. And he said, 'If you go into that doorway, because it is air-conditioned, you get the back draft of the air-conditioning, which is warm.' I looked at him and I had a smile on my face, and the thing that went through my mind was what an innovative guy he was, even though he didn't look that way. He then left.

At least an hour later — I didn't even realise I had been sitting there for that long — I heard the shuffle of feet. I looked back and there he was. He was shuffling, that was the way he walked, and he quivered when he talked because he suffered with gout. He had gout, he had rheumatism, he had terrible arthritis, his lips just quivered, and he had a beard that was not manicured in any way — it was all over the place, with his hair long and all over the place, curly and grey.

He sat down next to me and said, 'Sit in the doorway. It gets bloody cold out here. I said, 'Look, I'm fine. I've got a home to go to,' and he said, 'They all say that on the bench.'

Then he turned his back to walk away. He must have gone about 20 or 30 paces, and he got up to Philip Street, then he turned around and looked at me, and came back. He was carrying this bag — you may have seen them, red, white and blue $2 bags, the bags you get from the $2 shop. He rested it on the bench next to me, opened it up and took out this blanket. I could see it was grubby, then I noticed, most importantly, that there wasn't much else in the bag. I said, 'Mate, I don't need this.' I kept telling him I had a home to go. And he said, 'Look, I know, I know.' I then said, 'What about you?' He started to walk away and at that moment I wanted to say so much.

I wanted to say 'Thank you', I wanted to say 'What is your name?', I wanted to ask him all these sorts of things but nothing came, no words could come out, and then when he got to almost Sydney Hospital, up that end of the street, I managed to sort of yell, 'I will come back and find you.' And he turned around and waved as if to say 'Oh yeah'.

I don't know what I felt — extremely hungry, sad, I think I was crying, I was happy. It wasn't a bad feeling … it was just, if I had to put a finger on it, it was probably a wonderful sensation. The void inside me had been taken away. It was just fantastic. It felt so good because when I was walking back to my club and my restaurant, I knew exactly what I was going to do.

It wasn't a matter of putting it off until tomorrow, it wasn't a matter of 'I'll give it another month'. I knew what I was going to do. I went and poured myself a scotch. I had a good stiff scotch and I just sat there. Then I went to bed. I woke up in the morning and I knew what my day was going to be. I rang my partner up and said, 'Please come in to the office by ten o'clock today. I need to see you urgently.'

He came into my office in the morning and I took my cheque book out, wrote out a cheque and handed it to him. He said, 'What's this?' and asked me why. I said, 'Because I took it under false pretences and besides, I don't like you. That was something I found extremely difficult but I was living with it.' He accepted it and left.

I then kept playing back in my mind about this old chap, and that night I went looking for him. I drove around the city. If any police or security were looking, they would have thought all sorts of things, because I must have circled the inner city I don't know how many times. Many times over, with my car, I just kept lapping and looking and looking.

I looked every night for a while, and then right up at the Mitchell Library, who should be there, standing across the road, but this old chap. I pulled my car up — I parked illegally in Macquarie Street — and went up to him and said, 'Mate, do you remember me?' He looked and I said, 'I've got something of yours', and he said, 'That's alright, mate.'

I said, 'Can you hop in the car and come with me? I'll buy you a cup of coffee.' He said, 'It's OK, it's OK.' I said, 'No, come on, please get in the car, let's go have a cup of coffee.' He looked at my car, he looked at it from top to bottom, and said, 'Where did you knock this off from?' He thought I had stolen the car and it took me another 20 minutes to convince him that the car was actually mine. I even showed him my photo ID, and the rego papers of the car. Eventually he was convinced.

I took him up to my restaurant, and again he said something that stuck in my mind. He said, 'Can you please make the coffee in a big mug?' and he got his coffee in the big mugs that we used to serve the hot chocolates in. I gave him just a black coffee and asked him if he would like something to eat, and he said no. I said, 'You are welcome to anything you want … you want a steak, you want lobster, whatever.'

Then he started telling me that he was a farmer from past Goulburn way. His father had been a farmer, his grandfather had been a farmer, and he had never been on the dole. He wasn't on the dole or benefits because he believed that's what bludgers do. He was a fair-dinkum down-to-earth Aussie.

I asked him, 'How do you survive?' and he said, 'I work my way through.' I said, 'How?' He said, 'I go to the Matthew Talbot and I sweep the laneway there and they let me have a free feed. I go down to the Sallies and then I clean up the front garden and they give me clothes.'

Again I asked, 'Why you don't eat something? Be my guest.' He said, 'No, mate, no. I don't have the money.' I said, 'You don't need money.' I said, 'Besides, you gave me your blanket.' He said, 'Don't worry about it.' He never realised what he had done.

Eventually he did have a meal. I think he started to relax. He had been out there a long time. He started to talk, but he wouldn't take anything for free; he wouldn't accept anything without being able to pay it back some way or the other.

I then offered him a room out the back — it had a little ensuite, a shower and a toilet — and I used to sleep there sometimes. I said, 'Look, please go and get cleaned up,' and he said, 'I can't accept that.'

I just didn't know how to convince this guy — his name was Owen — that I had been wanting to pay him back, that he had already given me everything and I owed him. And Owen wouldn't accept anything, he wouldn't take anything without giving back.

So I offered him a job. He looked at me and I said, 'Would you like work?' and he said, 'Yes,' and after I had said that I felt, my God you just keep doing this. You keep opening your mouth before the brain falls in, because after I asked him if he wanted work I really took in his state. His hands and his fingers were all bent, he could hardly walk, so physically he wouldn't be much good in the kitchen or any-where; he wasn't a fit man. But I had already said what I'd said, and there was a reason why I had to say it, and now I had to make good. He said, 'What sort of work?'

I said, 'I will make you head of security.' Don't ask me why, I just couldn't think of anything else. So I said, 'I will make you head of security', and I thought, 'What have I done?' I had a head of security, he had about 12 people under him. The man said, 'All right', and I said, 'Good.'

All I wanted him to do was to go into that room, have a shower and put his head down. I would feel good that he had a roof over his head. I knew I could provide that, and then when he accepted it, I ran into my office and called David, a fantastic guy who was my head of security, the real guy. I explained to him very briefly what had happened and he said, 'Don't worry, it doesn't worry me, I will just let the other guys know so Owen doesn't feel …'

Owen didn't try to go out and say, 'I am the head of secu-rity.' He had no problems settling in. Everyone loved him. I mean, loved him. I didn't know how old he was but he looked very old.

The next day I sat down with him and told him he could

have whatever he wanted, and I had told everyone, give him champagne if he wants. Anyway, we were having breakfast, and that's when he started to tell me about the real Owen and the other people on the streets.

I brought him some clothes and I went and bought shoes for him from David Jones. He wore shoes two sizes bigger than his feet because of the gout; he had to have them really loose so they wouldn't hurt. He liked this dark green suede, soft, like Hush Puppies.

Up till now I had had stereotypes in my mind. As far as I was concerned any homeless person was an old dero, an old drunk with a brown paper bag and a fag in his hands. The junkie and the bum, that was my total conception of a homeless person. But Owen told me they were doctors, solicitors, chartered accountants, and I thought that this guy was definitely a bit cuckoo.

About a week later we were talking, and he asked did I have cleaners coming in, and I said, 'Yeah, every now and then we have the cleaners come in. They are contracted to clean the restaurant and the club for me.'

Sunday morning, about two weeks down the track, we opened late because we finish very early in the morning on a Saturday/Sunday. I went in there fairly early, around 10 o'clock in the morning.

There were some strange guys there. I said, 'Who are you?' and this man said, 'I'm Arthur, one of Owen's mates.' Then I said, 'Who are you?' to the other man and he said, 'I'm Ron, I'm Arthur's mate.' I asked Owen, 'Have these guys been staying the night?' and he said, 'No, no, no, they came here to work.' I said, 'Oh no! What do you mean work?' 'If it's all right, all the money you are paying the cleaners and everything, you won't have to pay to clean up. My mates can do it.'

This man made my eyes open all the time. I looked

around and the place was bloody spotless, I mean spotless. It wasn't just swept and left, it was swept, mopped, they had taken the chewing gum off the floor. You know how clubs have chewing gum? I went behind the bar and nearly fell over, because I saw as soon as I walked past that the mats were up and on the bar itself – it was a hug bar that went around — there was a pile of money. One dollar coins, two dollar coins, fifty cents, and one or two $5 bills. I said, 'What's this? Owen, what is this?' He said, 'That's your money', and I said, 'What do you mean, it's my money? Where did it come from?'

He said, 'The deal is this. Anything that falls on this side of the bar (meaning behind the bar) belongs to you, because that should have gone into the till and obviously someone has made a mistake and it has fallen. But anything on the public side belongs to us.' I said, 'OK, that's a fair deal, that's fine.' There was over $130 in change on the bar.

Later I got to know Ron and Arthur and they told me about their lives. Ron had been a seaman. I'd be busy all day but I looked forward every day to getting together with these guys just to hear the stories. I don't read much, I've never had time to read much, but I could listen to these guys for hours.

Anyway, I said about a month or two into it, 'I want to do something', and they said, 'What?' I said, 'I want to help the homeless, I want to help these friends of yours, all these guys of yours. How do I go about it, what do I have to do?' They said, 'Oh, you'll just be like all the others.' 'What do you mean, I'll be like the others?'

They explained: 'You keep saying you understand' — which I did; I thought I understood, and when they would tell me something about someone or something I would say, 'Yeah, I understand.' They said, 'But you don't, you can't. It's impossible, because you have never been there.'

Hang on, there's a bit of truth here, I thought. I could

imagine it but I could never really understand it. I could make an assumption. I then said, 'Chaps, I really want to go and feed the homeless, do something.' They said, 'You can't', and I said, 'I am going to.' They said I had to do an apprentice-ship first. I said, 'You take an oath with me that you will never disclose, unless I ask you to, who I really am.' I put my affairs in place and walked out in a pair of jeans and sneakers with these four guys. I went down to live on the streets.

I remember sleeping in the building at the corner of Hunter and Philip Streets on the floor. I had to sleep on some cardboard, just some box flattened out, and boy your bum gets sore, your hips get sore, your back is sore. I didn't realise there were so many muscles in the human body. It was cold — it was still winter — and I bore it for as long as I could. I visited the Salvation Army and Foster House — if you got up and got there in time you could grab a cup of tea and maybe a slice of toast. I asked for a shower there and they said, 'Sorry, you can't have a shower because you are not a resident in the building.' I said, 'That's OK.' I then went to the Matthew Talbot, which was run by St Vincent De Paul. I lay down there and I had lunch there.

Then I noticed the void. In business I never liked to imitate, copy or provide a service that was already was there, and that was probably why I was so successful over the years. And I wasn't going to do anything different in this area from a business perspective, but I found a void.

I asked myself: Why were these people on the streets? People were on the streets because they didn't have a purpose to wake up to in the morning. They didn't have a reason to be. They just didn't have any faith in themselves, and I thought, 'You have to have faith in yourself before you can have faith in God or in any deity.' That's my belief. You don't need a lot of it, you just need enough!

People think it was deliberate, but it was never meant to be deliberate. This is just how it panned out. I said, 'OK, let's go.' They said, 'How are you going to do it?' I said, 'We are going to be the biggest and we are going to be the best. This is the business side of me coming out, but there is also another side — we are going to be the fairest, the most loving, and the most giving. And we are going to get the biggest results ever. You see that junkie, you see that gambler, you see that drunk? If they don't want to be that way we can change it.'

I think these guys gave me strength because they believed in me. They believed me, and they said, 'OK, how do we go about it?' I said, 'This is how we go about it. Me being in hospitality, I know all the restaurants. I know most of the little takeaway places, and even if I don't know them they know me because I have won 11 gold plates in my time at my restaurant.'

So I went to Martin Place, to all the little places that serve lunch and then close at 3 or 4 o'clock. I introduced myself to all of them, and one would say, 'Well we close at 3 or 3.15, so you be here at 3.25.' I made up a roster. I said, 'Arthur, you and Ron hit Wynyard and start your first pickups.'

I bought half a dozen of those little striped bags — exactly the same kind that Owen had had, but the big ones. And I went with Arthur and Ron and introduced them to all the shop owners. I also bought half a dozen extra-large dust jackets, grey ones, and had their names put on them. The guys put them on and you literally saw the spring in their step — I noticed that bounce.

In the morning they would wake up, and Ron wasn't interested in a flask of wine. He would say, 'I've got work to do this afternoon, Jeff. How can I drink? I can't go up to these people smelling of booze.' I thought, my God, it's all happening.

The first day we fed about 20 people and of that 20 we took about two or three off the streets. I put them in the Sydney Private Hotel, the Central Private Hotel. I paid for them to get off the street, and next thing they were not in their rooms — they were back on the streets because that was their choice. But for me it was, hang on, everyone has to get off the streets. I was doing my apprenticeship.

A radio station I had never listened to rang me up — it was the morning crew, Wendy Harmer and Paul Holmes, at 2-Day FM. Anyway, they rang up one particular morning and said, 'We would like to talk to you', and I said, 'Fine.' Someone had told them what I was doing. They thought it was fantastic, and I got the usual accolades and stuff, and then people started ringing and wanting to be volunteers, of course. Knee-jerk reactions, which I have since learned about. You get hundreds of people, you get more people wanting to volunteer than I had people who needed feeding. But in time that dwindled.

One of them happened to be a woman called Alina. She worked in the Piccadilly Arcade, which wasn't far from where I was feeding the people, and she would come over and give us a hand and serve the soup. After we got engaged Alina said, 'You were raised near the roof top of the world it's appropriate that we get married on Centrepoint Tower.'

So I hired the whole tower and we sent out invitations to people all over the world — her family, my family — and we filled it. It was 1998, and it had rained — and you can check this — for 63 days, every single day prior to 29 August, but on the 29 August, our wedding day, there was not a cloud in the sky and it was 25ºC. On 30 August it started to rain again, and it rained for another three weeks. One of the beliefs that we had, even if it was superstition, was that if it was raining it would be bad luck to get married. I kept telling her,

'Alina, honey, if it rains we will still have a fantastic party, we just won't take our vows,' and she agreed to that. I woke up and saw, when I opened the blinds, that there wasn't a cloud outside.

I was pushed right into the corner now. She rang me up and said, 'You thought you were going to get away with it, didn't you?' And it was the most beautiful wedding and reception and everything after that, and my best man was Owen.

Since then we have taken more than 1100 people off the streets and put back in school more than 120 kids. Kids that people said would never make it, they have got their school certificates, got their Duke of Edinburgh Awards, we have three or four now at university. We have kids from the streets who have gone to Antarctica and that are now doing exploration in the Philippines.

We have reunited around the world about 62 families and put in excess of 800 people back to work. Success rate? If we get under 80 per cent success rate we are not very happy.

We have had a lot of disappointments and challenges. There were a lot of questions that were asked which I didn't have the answers for. But almost every day something good happens, something positive happens. To me positiveness is when someone gets a job or someone has made an effort to get off the streets, where someone has made a pact to get off drugs. That gives me strength; that is when I know I am winning.

That is what keeps me online, keeps me focused all the time. The moment you lose faith in yourself you cannot achieve. When you have that faith in yourself you can achieve just about anything at all. Then have faith in your god, because how could you possibly pray to somebody or something when you don't have any faith in yourself?

I think that in history all the people who went out and did something had faith in themselves. You have to have faith.

49

It is like a guy who says he is walking on hot coals. How can he do it? He has faith in himself, what the mind can achieve. But only you can do it for yourself, no one else can.

Strategies for living
YOUR DREAMS

Don't let your relationships slip into neutral Bertrand Russell, the British philosopher, said: 'The last thing you're likely to find someone saying on their deathbed is: "I wish I had spent more time at the office".' But many would have given anything to spend more time with their loved ones.

Many of those I interviewed for this book have compromised on family and relationships for a time, but they agree that although it is tremendously difficult to find the balance between work and family, it can be done. There are always going to be times when you need to compromise — I am typing these pages on my laptop computer at 4 a.m. in order not to have to give up family time later on this evening, for instance — but if there is communication and support from your partner and your family, it is all possible.

I have found that most people say it's their family that gives them strength, and that is the foundation to build on and succeed in their chosen field. Many will say that the most cherished moments of their life have been those spent as a family — on holiday at the beach or just sitting round together.

Spending an hour with your wife or partner is also invaluable: it gives you an opportunity to reconnect, just the two of you. Go somewhere fun, or just go out for a drink or a meal — and switch off the mobile phone. Don't rush through life without uttering more than a few sentences beyond what is required to run a household every day.

Don't let your relationships slip into neutral; you and your family need to connect, to nurture each other and to grow together.

Graeme
GOLDBERG

With 37 years' experience in the hospitality industry Graeme Goldberg has hosted a number of world-famous (and some not-so-famous) guests. Graeme has played piano side by side with the late actor and comedian Dudley Moore, as well as overseen the needs of former President Bill Clinton and his entourage of staff and secret service personnel. Other guests he has been host to are Madonna, Tom Cruise, Nicole Kidman and John Travolta. Graeme's commitment to work safety is evident, as he has won a prestigious individual WorkCover Corporation Safe Work Award for his outstanding efforts to promote and encourage a healthy and safe work environment. He was also named South Australia's 'Responsible Officer of the Year' for 2001. Former Vice President of Stamford Hotels and Resorts Worldwide, Graeme Goldberg is a self-made man.

I grew up in post-war London when rationing was still in force. Everything I had was second-hand, to the point I thought it was a trademark. I was convinced there was a big store in the West End of London called 'Second-hand'. I suppose that is why I appreciate everything that I have now, because I basically had nothing.

I remember vividly my first day at school — five years of age, a little bit frightened, away from my parents, on my own for the first time. I even went there on my own — I wasn't taken or collected. When I settled into the classroom, the first lesson was called Divinity, which some schools call Religious Instruction or Christian Education; when the teacher got up to start the lesson, the opening preamble started, 'As you are all aware, boys and girls, the Jews killed Jesus.' Even at five I knew I was in trouble!

When the bell went for play break, I had six boys around me who wanted my blood for killing Jesus. I didn't even know who he was and I denied the charge emphatically. But they pushed and pushed and I was placed into the category of 'He who protests too loudly'. So I thought I would have to give an inch to save my skin and I admitted to throwing some stones at his donkey, but I didn't put my hand up to murder. Academically I wasn't challenged, but I sure could fight and after a few tussles, which resulted in a broken nose, stitches over my right eye and a couple of bruised ribs, they boys left me alone.

Everyone in life has to have a mentor and my mentor was my father. He was smart, funny and bigger than life and I loved him dearly. He was a boxing promoter and made a lot of money and lost a lot of money. But you would never know by looking at his face. My father knew everyone and that's one of the traits that I wanted when I grew up. I remember very well when I was a child, we went to the seaside for a weekend, miles and miles away from where we lived. The weather wasn't good so the beach was deserted — just one man walking along the foreshore and my Dad knew him. I was blown away.

He was a real cool character, nothing really ruffled him and he had such a quick mind. I remember when I wanted to buy a car when I was 16 and I needed him to guarantee the loan. I just had to have the car — the thought of the freedom of it. To have a car parked outside your house and you could go wherever you wanted to go. I could smell the excitement of it and I asked Dad for the loan and he said on three conditions:

1. He wanted me to get out of the kitchen of the hotel that I was working in and work out the front of the hotel. (He wasn't in the hotel business, but he obviously knew that if you make it in life, you make it from the front not the back.)

2. He wanted me to help Mum around the house a bit more, clean up my bedroom, which was basically covered with pictures of the Beatles, complete with old socks on the floor.

3. He wanted me to have my hair cut.

Number one was easy. I spoke to them at work and they were going to make me a waiter in the restaurant. Two: I cleaned up my bedroom, took down my pictures, put my socks in the laundry basket. But three was difficult. I didn't want to have short back and sides because as a teenager you wanted to look like everyone else and your hair was a bit of statement, let alone fashionable. So I went to him and said, 'I'm being transferred at work to a different department, I've cleaned up my bedroom, I'm helping Mum with the washing up, but I'm not having the short back and sides,' and he said, 'That's the deal.' God, I wanted that car, but he was unmoved and then I had a flash of brilliance.

He was sitting in the lounge room on his favourite chair, reading the paper and I said, 'Dad, I want the car — my bedroom is clean, I'm helping Mum, I've got the work issue addressed, but I've got to keep my hair. I think you're being unfair. Even Moses had long hair.' He put down his paper, looked me in the eye and said, 'I know, he had very long hair and that's why he walked around the desert for 40 years instead of driving.' I knew then I'd never be able to beat him. So I cut my hair and bought myself a Ford Prefect.

I don't think I really had a vision or a goal, I just took one step at a time and basically I mean that — one step, cemented the step, felt comfortable with the step, then took another. Basically like how a child starts to walk or an adult who has to learn to walk again after some accident or affliction.

As I am self-educated, I knew that to compete with the people around me, I had to be worldly and understand the issues of the world. I wasn't well read, so I read. I wasn't versed in great conversation, so I talked. There were a million issues I didn't understand, so I listened and I was never ever frightened, even to this day, to ask 'What does that mean?' It is always best to put your hand up and ask the question as opposed to not asking the question and always remaining ignorant.

I came from a family of high achievers. I was the second youngest and there was a big age difference between me and my older brother and sister. What they had, I wanted too and, more importantly it seemed to me, they had the respect of their peers — something my father had too — and I wanted that.

I always felt in the early days that my London accent was a hindrance, that my accent sounded common or working-class. But now I know how stupid that is, for it's not how you say it, it's what you say. Look at Michael Caine.

Sometimes challenges can be attributes. What you see as an impediment is sometimes a strength. Everyone in life wants to be different, hence what they drive, how they cut their hair, what they wear. I've got it all built in — I'm six foot seven with a Cockney accent. I've got to be unique — can't be too many of me around. I use my height and accent now as a major tool — people remember me, which sometimes is embarrassing because I don't remember them.

I'm in a very fortunate position and business, a business

that is continually changing, and I am lucky enough to be in a position to change it. I do not exchange my time for money — I have to add value. My business has to be stronger for my input at the end of the day. I have to contribute something. Not just do my job within my job description — I have no job description. I always take stock during and at the end of the day because at the end of the day, I report to only one person — the man in the mirror, for he is the one that I cannot con and cannot trick.

Everything in life is balance and if you have to get out the scales, then you're not a balanced person. One must know when to give, when to take, when to work, when to play. I think one does keep score or some kind of record, but it doesn't have to be in graph or chart form. I do things out of necessity not because of a time of day. I eat when I'm hungry, I sleep when I'm tired, I go on holiday when I'm weary.

As I came from nothing each step I take is taking me further away from nothing to a place called something. Secondly, although both my parents are no longer with me, I feel their presence and I want them to be proud of me and I don't want to let them down. I also have a beautiful wife and two wonderful children and I can see the respect in their eyes and I wouldn't do anything in the world to extinguish that.

To those wanting to enter the hospitality industry I'd say, make sure it's for you, talk to people in it, do some work experience. It means long hours, weekends, and keep in mind that when everyone is partying you're serving them. Make sure you like people and you're a team player and if you still like the idea, then start at the bottom and work your way up and enjoy every step from the basement to the penthouse. For if you shortcut it and you do not learn your trade properly, somewhere along the line you'll be faced with questions or problems that you don't know how to address and therefore, when that happens, you will lose the respect of your team and that won't do your esteem any good either.

My favourite inspirational quote is 'Shoot for the moon, even if you fall short you will be amongst the stars' and my favourite work expression is 'In like a lamb, out like a lion'. It is something that I've practised for many years in work, friendship and family. For if you go in like a lamb, you usually come out a lion. But if you go in like a lion you more often come out like a lamb.

Ray
HADLEY

Ray Hadley grew up in the western suburbs of Sydney. He has been named Australia's Best Radio Sports Broadcaster for five of the past ten years. The radio industry awards are known as the 'Rawards' and Ray's most recent win came for his coverage of the Sydney Olympics. Ray's career highlights include commentary on the 2000 Olympic Games held in Sydney, the 1992 and 1996 Olympics, 13 successive Rugby League grand finals, including the last game at the SCG and the first game at Stadium Australia. Ray was awarded a Medal of the Order of Australia (OAM) in the Queen's Birthday 2002 Honours List for service to Rugby League Football as a broadcaster, and to the community, particularly through fundraising for charitable organisations. In 2002, after 19 years with Radio Station 2UE, Hadley accepted an offer to work with rival broadcaster 2GB.

As a kid growing up I wanted to be successful, but I didn't know at what. I grew up in a country area and the western suburbs of Sydney. I came from working-class parents: my dad was a butcher, my mum a factory worker. I was an above-average student. I had a feeling from a very young age, from as young as I can remember, that I was going to be successful at something. I had no idea what it was going to be. I guess my original goal was to be successful, but I didn't know at what.

What inspired me? I don't know, it's just always been there. It's a strange thing; it's like something's guiding me. Through my career I've worked particularly hard, but I've also had a lot of luck. It's all about checks and balances — you know, sometimes people may have dreadful tragedies in their families, and the next generation might have some success in things.

I lost my father when I was 19. I thought that was the end of the world. He was a great man and a great friend. I started to question the meaning of life — when someone who means a great deal to you drops dead at 45, it makes you think. But even through that period I used to wish he was still alive because he would be proud of me eventually. It sounds stupid. I haven't spoken about this issue to many people but I always had this focus that I was going to be a successful person. I didn't mean that I was going to be wealthy, but I was going to be successful in whatever I did — not just successful, but the best. My focus was to be the best in what I did, and that has remained with me all the time.

Yet you need to learn not to be put off by anything.

I left school with a very poor pass in my Higher School Certificate. I thought about teaching, but I didn't want to be a teacher. I always had this propensity to describe things; I was always mucking around pretending to be a sports commentator. Kids play with trains or pretend to be sports commentators like a little dream. People pat them on the head and say, 'You're going to be a sports commentator! Good boy!'

Anyway, I thought, 'Maybe this is what I can do. Maybe I have an ability here, something that I know about.' So I started to look in the paper for jobs as a trainee sportscaster. There were none. They didn't have courses in 1972 like they do now for journalism, where you can get a cadetship. I saw a job one day for a trainee auctioneer. Auctioneer? Using my voice? Yes, that's what I'll do, so I got the job. I did become quite successful, but I realised after having done it for seven or eight years, that it was not the thing I was going to be really successful at.

The first day that I worked at 2UE with Gary O'Callaghan in 1981, I thought, this is it. It sort of dawned on me — broadcasting, this is what I'm going to do. They put me in a helicopter — I'd never been on the radio before — and asked me to describe what was happening, and I did. I did it to the best of my ability — my limited ability at that time — and when I came down they all shook my hand saying that was fantastic, that was great, and I thought, jeez, I am good at it! I didn't know I was good at it, but all these experts said, 'That was fantastic for your first attempt!' and that was great. I thought, 'This is what I can do!' From then on I became even more single-minded in my desire to achieve, because it was then that I discovered what I wanted to do. It took till I was 23 or 24.

When I started broadcasting I just knew I had to be good at it. I had to be the best at it. Initially it was to be the best sports broadcaster; I guess I eventually want to be the best broadcaster that I possibly can be. I think what kept me going in 1980–81 was a group of about 15 people, my age or younger, who had the same ambition — to be a sports broadcaster, specifically at that stage in the racing industry, which is what I started in. I guess our ambition at the time was to attain full-time employment in that industry.

I'm currently the only one left out of the 15, because over a period of time everyone had to make sacrifices: girlfriend, money (there was none — we did it just for practice and people took advantage of that). They knew we were young and ambitious and they wanted to give us the opportunity but they didn't want to pay us for that opportunity, so between 1980 and 1985, when I became self-sufficient doing what I was doing, all those other people fell away because they couldn't sustain their lifestyles. Some people ask me if I feel that in that period, 1980 to 1985, I missed out. I say no, I just worked really hard for a period of time.

I'm still single-minded, but I now have a wife and four children, so I have to be single-minded about them to a certain extent. I think in order of importance, at that period it was career, career, career; now it's my wife and children — depending on which day it is it's either my children then my wife, or my wife and then the children, because you have to try to divide your time — and then just slightly behind is my career. My children changed my perspective on life. I feel really fulfilled now that I have healthy and happy children. I matured a bit. If I had felt 20 years ago the way I do now I probably would never have achieved my goals, because as you get older your view on life changes; it's just the way things are.

I determined earlier on, when I was given the opportunity to do the John Laws show, that there was no one in broad-casting who could do a range of things. I decided that this would be my niche in the industry: there were specialists in all areas but no one who could do everything. There will never be another Alan Jones or John Laws, but if you can do every-thing at a level just below those people, and do it consistently over a whole range of things, you become a most valuable asset to the radio station. You gain a reputation for being a person who could do pretty much everything, no matter what changes came about in that radio station. When 2UE used to call the races, back in 1980s, I was a race caller, then I did Rugby League, then other things; if I had been just a race caller my career would have finished in 1986, when the station stopped calling races.

I'd say that in the early part of your life, before you have relationships and children, you need to not be discouraged or scared to sample other things, within the framework of what you're doing. If you're working for an office as an accountant and the boss says, 'Why don't you have a crack at sales?', you should do it, because if you're an accountant who can also sell, or a salesman who can be an accountant, or an IT expert who can also sell, then when they look to chop heads they will say, well he does sales, he can chair meetings, he's a genius on the computer and he's a chartered accountant, so we'd better keep him because he can cover for a lot of people. In many ways this decade is about specialisation, but I say no, get a taste of everything.

What challenges have I faced? Having no money was one. I came from a very poor background, and you always think you're going to move above that. I was having a look at something last night at home — when I finished auctioneering in 1979 I was earning $27,000 a year. When I got my first full-time job at 2UE in 1983 I was earning $19,500 a year, so I had lost $8000 a year! I wasn't doing it for the money, obviously, but there were times when there was just no money. I couldn't afford to feed myself and clothe myself. You don't start off on the road to success, to get money, but when you're not eating all that well and not wearing nice clothes you start thinking that it would be handy if apart from being successful you were well rewarded, too. That's part of wanting to break that cycle of poverty, so to speak. That's a very important motivating factor.

When my dad died there were only debts, no money. There was nothing, no legacy or anything like that, so I started from behind the eight ball. That was a motivating factor. I figure it's the dream of every parent that their children should have a better life than they had, and I was starting to think in

1983 that I was going to have it worse than my parents financially. I thought, 'This is dumb. I've gone from a full-time auctioneer to a full-time radio announcer and I'm earning $8000 less. That doesn't make sense.'

Then I thought about the big picture and about becoming successful. I looked at the people around me at 2UE who were being particularly well rewarded, and I thought, 'That's another reason to be successful — if you're a successful broad-caster you get well rewarded.'

I kept setting the bar a bit higher, probably every six months. I'd get somewhere and I would say, well, the next ambition is to do this. Sometimes they were fanciful, un-obtainable, and that's where luck plays a role. I'm a great believer of fortune being a part of this. I haven't seen too many lazy people have a lot of luck! Fortune comes in many disguises; you know the old thing about you make your own luck, well there's a certain synergy to that, but sometimes you can work really hard and have no luck. I'd hate to say to people, 'If you work real hard you'll get lucky', because sometimes poor blokes work really hard their whole life and they have no luck, their lives are beset by personal tragedy, so I wouldn't want to say there's some sort of greater being looking down and saying, 'He's worked hard — give him a bit of luck.'

But I think I've been lucky. In the industry I'm in I've worked really hard, and in 1991 I was in England and I got a call from John Brennan saying, 'What date are you due back?' I say, '16 December.' He said, 'Good. You're doing the John Laws show on 18 December.' Even as ambitious as I had been, that was something I had never even contemplated. I'd been listening to John Laws when I was in school. It was a bit bizarre. I thought, 'This will be a bit of fun', and then when I started doing it in 1992 I really enjoyed it. It was great. 'Imagine getting paid to do this, this is great fun,' I thought.

All of a sudden I had gone off at a tangent because an opportunity was given to me that I wasn't expecting. I think that was the best thing that happened to me; if you covet something, you want a particular job or a particular thing and it doesn't come, it can fill you with bitterness and disappointment.

So if something comes from left field and you're totally shocked and blown away by it, hang on a sec — maybe you should push the bar a bit higher now. Reassess yourself. I think there has to be reassessment for successful people; if you're honest with yourself, the best assessment is self-assessment. People you respect can give opinions, but the way to handle it is for you to assess how you're going, and if you're really honest with yourself you know when you're going well, if you're working hard enough, or if you need to lift it up.

I look at it every six months. Some people may need a three-month interval, or even a three-day interval. Whatever timeframe it is, you have to set that timeframe, particularly if you're not an organised person to start with. You might need to make weekly goals. I guess it's the same as being a recovering alcoholic — one day at a time. You overcome each day. And extend yourself: don't set a goal that you know you can achieve. Set a goal you *don't* think you can achieve, because you'll try a bit harder. It's like Tim Forsyth coming into the Olympics. He knows his personal best is 1.95 m — he can do that in training nine times out of ten — so he enters the competition at 2.10 m, because he knows that to get that he has to push himself. Pick what you think you can do and tack a bit on.

Hard work, forsaking everything else, is another important thing. This is something that disappoints me with young people in the media these days. If someone said to me, right, we want you to be at the airport at 6.15 a.m. to meet Jana Pittman and interview her, and at 9.45 p.m. we want you to interview Kostya Tszyu as he comes back in, I'd say 'Great!'. I look at it as opportunity but some of the people I deal with now say, 'Jeez, I'm starting at six, finishing at ten — it's a long day', and I say, 'Yes, it is a long day, but do you want to be successful?' Think of most blokes sitting in a pub or blokes driving council trucks or buses: if you say, right, your job today is to interview Jana Pittman at 6.45 a.m., at ten o'clock they'll say, 'How good's this!'. As soon as someone shows any hesitation, I know I must look somewhere else.

I noticed that the most successful radio broadcasters I came across in the early part of my career were hardworking. The other thing I noticed was that if you're pretending to be someone you're not, you'll never ever be successful. You simply have to be yourself and trust in yourself. You'll find out in a relatively short time whether or not you're suitable for radio: if people don't listen to you, it means you're not striking a chord with them, you're not being yourself; if they are listening, it means you are striking a chord with them, and that only happens when you are being yourself.

I laugh when I think things are funny — sometimes I laugh inappropriately. Sometimes I cry. I quite often cry on the radio: I cry about things that worry me. I had a little girl with cystic fibrosis call me recently. She's going to die, and she was ringing me to say goodbye. I get emotional just thinking about it. That's the way I am. I have all the shortcomings that everyone else has: I have anger, I have frustration, and people have to be tolerant of me as I have to be tolerant of people. Unfortunately, that tolerance only comes with age. Most of us are fairly intolerant of each other when we're young; as I've grown older I've become more tolerant. When I was young I would go like a bull at a gate, race in and get it done, but as I get older I find there are other ways to approach things. I still get angry within myself. One of the frustrations for people who are ambitious and single-minded is that they can't understand why everyone's not like them, why the copy girl, the sales clerk, the bloke in customer service are not like them and don't share their zest for getting it right.

People who are launching themselves into being successful need to understand that as ambitious as they are, not everyone's like them. Also, you need to accept the fact that you're never going to do everything perfectly; you'll probably think you are at the time, but as you get older, if you live long enough, you realise that you haven't done it perfectly.

I balance work and family with the help of a very capable wife; she carries an enormous load in the family. I'm leaving here now to drive to Wagga Wagga for a charity faction that a mate of mine talked me into doing to raise some money for Camp Quality. I left home this morning, Friday, at 2.30 a.m. and I won't be back till Sunday morning, so she's charged with looking after four children this morning, getting them off to school, sporting events, etc. Without her, I'm gone. Finding a partner I love and who is also a great person is my greatest achievement. Again, I don't get that right all the time, but I work on it and try to do it. I have excellent children (their ages are from four to 12) and a wonderful wife.

I always try to learn something from successful people. People I work with said to me don't let this period pass you by — enjoy your children now because before you know it they'll be at school, matriculating from university, away from home, married, then bringing the grandchildren home. So I try to do that as well, and because of my wife I've done that fairly successfully, for the last six or seven years particularly. I've changed my outlook, and I try to spend a lot more time with the kids than perhaps I would have thought I could.

I don't care how busy you are, there should always be time for the family. It won't be apparent when you're 23 or 24, but it'll become apparent later on that you should be setting time aside for them. My career was first for a long period of time, when I didn't have a family, but that priority has changed now, as it should.

Honesty is another important thing. First, with yourself. Different people handle things differently, but I like to be upfront with people, tell them what I think. That can work to your detriment, because not everyone likes you being upfront. Everyone has bosses; even if you're the chairman of BHP you have bosses — they're called shareholders. Some people have a boss called the wife. You can't make decisions independent of either the shareholders or your family; everyone's answerable to someone in some way, shape or form. You want respect from your bosses. You earn that respect and then, if you're honest enough, you tell them what you really *really* think. Bosses are great at saying 'Tell me what you really think', and then when you do, they don't really want to hear it. It's hard to accommodate that, but if you always tell the truth — as long as it's not going to really hurt someone, it's not of a personal nature — and tell people exactly what you think of what they're doing in a professional sense, you'll always end up in front. Honesty and hard work will get you there; being straightforward and to the point.

A great line? I actually saw one at the swimming pool which I thought was really good: 'Failures should be looked upon as simply the beginning of another opportunity'. I don't know where the quote comes from, but it's a pretty important one. You can't all succeed all the time, but if you let failure be failure as it's described in the dictionary, well, you're going to be a loser; if failure is merely the start of another opportunity, though, it passes very quickly.

Strategies for living
YOUR DREAMS

Don't just accept the status quo Of course we have to conform with the social norm society requires of us in many ways, but the uniqueness of human beings is our ability to extend our cognitive processes, our visions and aspirations far beyond the 'square' most of us think within. Thomas Edison, the man who gave us electricity, was often asked why he didn't find a regular occupation, and was told thousands of times that he would never succeed in his quest to create the light bulb. Obviously the people who told him that were wrong. He persisted in doing what he wanted to do, what he believed he could do, and succeeded eventually.

The people interviewed in this book did not always conform, and they did not always think the way most people think. But they did set goals and standards for themselves, and they did work hard, even though they were often swimming against the current, against the tide. Like Edison, they persisted, and they achieved their dreams.

There are hundreds of stories of people who succeeded in fulfilling their vision — some of them also changed the way the whole world does things or sees things. Are they smarter than the rest of us? Not necessarily. The vast majority of those who are successful are average people who have an above-average attitude. They have the 'Why Not!' attitude — they are strong enough to leave their comfort zone and take action ... the rest is history.

Peter HALAS

Seafolly was founded in 1975 by husband-and-wife team Peter and Yvonne Halas. It has grown into a swimwear empire, producing more than two million articles of clothing per year. In March 2003 Seafolly announced a partnership with international sportswear giant Nike Inc., to design, manufacture, market and distribute Nike Swimwear in Australia, New Zealand and Asia. Despite this success, Seafolly has remained privately owned and is 100 per cent Australian.

I migrated to Australia when I was 17. I came by myself from Hungary in 1957 — the uprising had been in 1956. Having come here by myself and having experienced war, fascism and communism during my 17 years in Hungary, I just wanted a secure place, somewhere where I could see my life through. I guess that is what I found.

Australia was purely a place which was far away from the troubles of the world; that was probably the motivation behind coming here. The challenges were not having a complete education and not speaking any English — finding my feet and learning the language and making enough money to put food in my mouth.

My parents had some friends here who sort of helped — you know that first helping hand is the most important thing in your life. They found a job for me in a warehouse where they did not need my linguistic skills, and from there on I found that on a day-by-day basis I just progressed.

My vision was really to establish some kind of a foothold and some security; it was totally accidental that I even got into the fashion business. I certainly wasn't trained for it — I was purely looking for a job, and a job offered itself, and it just happened to be in the fashion business.

My vision for a business didn't exist until much later, probably not until the 1960s, and this company was officially started in 1975. But I had been involved in the industry from the early 1960s. Again, I think the original thought was just surviving and making enough to look after my family and myself — by that time I was married and I had two children.

So once we went past the first stage – we had a home, we were OK, we were not going to starve, and the kids could go to school — that was when the business vision came in.

It wasn't a straight line. There were lots of ups and downs, but I was a very hard worker and I think I have some intelligence, and when you put the two together you can't have a bad outcome, really.

I made some good choices. I made a very good choice in my partner. I was 20 when I proposed to my wife, and she was 18, so it was very much a lucky thing that it worked out like it did — we now have been married for more than 40 years. I think choosing the right partner was probably the most important thing in my life. Not having parents, siblings, or relations here of any kind, I think that I had a foothold with my wife; her family had been here a few years by then.

People talk about long-term ambition but I don't think I had that. I went step by step, and each day — or each year, or each period — I went to the next step, which to me was just a logical extension. By making good choices at different times the business grew.

I think I have a good name in the business because I am an honest trader. People are good to me and I am good to other people.

The biggest challenge in the beginning was to survive. People say if a small business can survive the first two years it is probably going to be OK — but we would look out of the window sometimes at night, wondering if they were going to repossess our car because we didn't have enough money to pay the hire purchase on it. A couple of times the landlord was going to put us out because we were not paying the rent on time and things like that. Once you have survived these early difficulties you have invested an awful lot in that business, because if you worked for someone else those problems wouldn't come up.

Once you jump you can't scramble back up. Perhaps it was because I didn't have academic training — I had no choice but to enter business. And when I worked for other people — which was for a very short period of my life, maybe a couple of years — I always felt that I could do better than my bosses were doing. So that was probably the reason I went into business – it seemed so easy.

I was working for a company that was not doing things the way they should have been done, and I said to my wife, 'Look, I think we could do a lot better.' She always supported me, and that was really a very important factor, because she could have said, 'How are we going to pay the rent? How are we going to pay the hire purchase instalments? How are we going to live?' But she didn't; she said, 'If you think we are doing the right thing, let's do it.' She believed in me and gave me strength. So we took the plunge, and once you take the plunge you just keep going.

I must say we had lots of challenges. It's not a highway that you drive down! You make a few mistakes — we made plenty of mistakes. One of the very big turnarounds in this business was when my son joined us. This was quite a few years ago, but he really became an active partner about four or five years ago. I think the fact that he has youth — and he doesn't have the same background as me, obviously — means that he is more at that point of thinking, 'Hey, I have a vision and I want to make this into whatever'.

We were doing different things within the business, but when he came in he said, 'Let's just do one thing really well', so we jettisoned lots of ideas that were running concurrently and we focused on one thing. And in the four or five years since then the business has moved on in leaps and bounds.

The other thing is that we have a very, very loyal team of people here. This business is about 28 years old now, and there are people who have been here since we started the business; we have lots of people who have been here for more than 15 years, and lots for more than 10 years. They have always supported the business. We always managed to involve them and they have always supported it.

When we first started, when it was a struggle, the main focus was survival. As the business stabilised we were able to slow down and employ people to do things we had been doing ourselves. My wife was involved in the business up until a few years ago and now my son is. So I have got more time on my hands than I had ten years ago.

I was working seven days a week, I worked sometimes 18, 19 hours a day. I look back now and I think that if I had gone to university I could have spent more time with my children and perhaps not have been in an office pushing a pen. I am not sure, but I think there were certain sacrifices made in those early years, which had to be made if I wanted to get to where I got to.

I don't think it was a conscious decision; it was survival,

and we just had to do it. I don't think we sat down and thought about it — if we do this then we can have that, and if we do that we can't. We just did it. I think the first 10 or 12 years were pretty tough.

The major ingredients are perseverance, some intelligence, hard work and respect for people. I always maintain that it doesn't matter how you do business — as long as you do it with integrity and honesty you will eventually win.

Wendy HARMER

Wendy Harmer is Australia's best-known comedienne. She is a veteran of the Edinburgh, Montreal and Glasgow-Mayfest festivals and has worked extensively in London, America and Ireland. In 1990, her show Love Gone Wrong received a 'Pick of the Fringe' award at the Edinburgh Festival and subsequently transferred to London. A former political journalist, Wendy is the author of two plays, and three books for adults. She has also written a children's series, the first book of which, Pearlie in the Park, was published in late 2003 by Random House.

Wendy was the host of the ABC TV series The Big Gig, co-starred in the critically acclaimed World Series Debates with Andrew Denton in 1993–94 for ABC TV and in 1990 she had her own TV chat show, In Harmer's Way. Wendy also hosted the Logie Awards in 2002. In 1993 Wendy joined Sydney's top-rating radio station 2DAY FM to lead the Morning Crew, which has rated No. 1 on FM radio for the last ten years.

There was a very interesting and different philosophy I heard from Jerry Springer, the talk show host. He said that you are born with 99 per cent of your destiny. I guess that is really true. We are lucky: being able to talk about being successful, living in the era that we are, the country that we live in. A lot of other people, who also have 99 per cent of their destiny given to them at birth, are born in a third world country — maybe they are born in a refugee camp or they are born with a disease.

But for those of us who are born into this time and this place, we already have the most extraordinary luck. So whatever happens, whether life is going well for us or going poorly, we should always go back and touch that stone and say, 'How much do I already have?' and that should really buoy us.

The fact that you have an opportunity to think about what you want to do and make something of your life is an extraordinary gift. That is what I always try to remember: the fact that I have any choice at all is an extraordinary thing.

Having been born with a cleft palate, I couldn't really speak very well as a child, so that was a bit of a driving force for me. I wanted to learn how to articulate and how to formulate my thoughts and how to be heard and be respected, and from that I guess the megalomania took over! It was such a humble kind of dream in the beginning. I guess it was about being able to be loved or be heard and express myself. It just evolved, really. So what do I end up being? I end up being on radio, so I guess it evolved from the small, humble beginning of wanting to be heard and understood to getting into a larger and larger and larger arena.

I have this philosophy: I never bite off — never try to chew off — anything bigger than my head, really, so what I always try to do is get a task and break it down into little pieces so that it can be done. As an example, when I was asked to write a libretto for the Australian Opera and Baz Luhrmann was going to be directing it, I thought, 'My God, how can I ever do this?' But then I just broke it down. I pretended it was a script for *Neighbours* with some tunes. So I wrote the first bit and saw how that went, and before I knew it the whole thing had been done. If I had sat there before this monolith of a task I never would have been able to do it.

I always wanted to be a journalist, so I studied journalism. I was lucky enough to be invited to be a journalist — I've always had that kind of luck. Then one media job led me through to another media job. I've always had this philosophy: I have plan A, B, C and D, and while I am working on plan A, I am also working at a lesser rate on plan B, but I also have plan C, D and E activated, so I never do one thing at a time. I am always anticipating the end of what I am doing and I am thinking about what I am going to do next, and there is always an overlap period where I am doing two things at once.

I always have my antenna out — my little antenna, testing the atmosphere to try to feel what is in the zeitgeist, what is in the ether, what is the big idea that is coming up next. And that has stood me in extraordinarily good stead. I read a lot, I sample a lot, I listen and I watch very widely. I try to never rest on my laurels, but always to look out for what is next, what is round the corner, and to keep moving, like a shark, I suppose. You have to keep moving ahead.

My motto is, 'I don't have to do this for a living.' I never feel forced into doing what I do; there is always some kind of a fallback position. I am extremely disciplined about what I do and I work very, very hard. I never believe people when they say, 'I would really like to write a book, but I can't find the time' or 'I would really like to become a poet but I can't find the time'. I never wait for the muse to visit me because I started out as a journalist and at the end of every day you had to have written 10,000 words. I make a rule for myself: I never get up without finishing something. I never start something unless I know what its ending is. And every project that I do, I try to make sure it has a purpose. Usually that is to say something, to make a point that expresses a part of me, or says something which I want to say.

The other thing I do — and this is a really important thing for me as an artist — is I put what I want to do in one basket, what I really want to do, then I put what the market wants in another basket, and then I try to find a point in the middle where those two things overlap. I try to find something that I want to do personally and which the market wants, and that is where I apply myself.

For instance, I might like to do a rock opera about the life and times of Madonna, but then I look at the market and think, 'Well, Madonna is really out of fashion,' so I don't do it, because I am going to be doing it for no reason. But if I still want to do a rock opera, I'll look around and see that Britney Spears is really in fashion, so I'll write about Britney Spears. I'll still enjoy the experience, but I will tweak the idea so that the market will want it.

There are so many people who write things that are really within their hearts. They follow their dreams, but no one wants to know about it, and they end up publishing a little thing just for themselves. And then there are so many people who are working at the other end of the spectrum, perhaps on television, making rubbish they wouldn't watch themselves; they are just serving a market, and they get no personal pleasure from it. So I always try to find the middle line, something I am going to adore doing and something people would like to hear, and then I have my project.

My father was an English teacher and he taught me logic and reason from a very early age. It was his big pet subject, I suppose, and sometimes that means that I can be a little narrow in my thinking, I am not a very surreal or off-the-wall kind of person. I really enjoy the process of decision making, and behind everything I do I like to see the inherent logic, I like to see the research. I don't go out and hire a research company; I just read for myself and I think pretty carefully about things. I also try to have a very thorough self-criticism mechanism — which can get out of balance.

I try to evaluate what I do and be open to criticism. That can be dangerous for a performer — you can take too much criticism on board or you can take not enough, and it is a very cyclical thing. You are always in flux there. Sometimes you feel really good about yourself and you become incredibly arrogant — I always say the down-side of success is arrogance. But on the flip side of that, failure can lead to depression and self-doubt, so somehow you have to walk a line where you are successful but you're open to criticism, and you are stable but with some self-doubt. It is a really hard balancing act!

If you have many plans, you can always say, 'I don't have to be doing this for a living, I will go to plan B.' So I always feel very wealthy because I have lots of ideas – for me that is like having money in the bank, and I always feel I will never be poor. I never ever cared about money. It has just come because I have enjoyed what I am doing. I absolutely haven't ever worried about money or looked at it or cared about it. I am shocking with money. My bank manager looks at my bank account and says, 'Are you kidding me? Where is your investment property? Where are your shares?' and I reply, 'I am too busy having a brilliant time and loving what I do.' Money just seems to flow through my house like a river — sometimes it's in full flood, sometimes it's a trickle.

This is where I think the idea of following your dream is wrong. I think that is incorrect advice. Follow your dream with a few provisos — first, see if your dream is actually going to pay off, because you can follow your dream and end up living in the middle of your dream in poverty. I have lived in poverty. I had that as a child and it ain't fun, so I was never going to starve in a ghetto for my art. What I am always looking for is where my art, or my dream, is going to turn into a lifestyle that I can enjoy. It sounds hard-nosed but it's really important to put things into perspective.

So I would advise people to make a pretty old-fashioned list, really. Just say, 'What is it that I would really like to do?' It might be own a vineyard, to have a small winery business, it might be open a boutique, it might be write a book, or run a day-care centre. And you go, 'OK, which one would I like to do the most?' Then you might look at where you live, what the traffic is going to allow. Just look around the area: you might find that where you live there is no possibility for a vineyard at all, because the area is completely developed already, or the weather is wrong — whatever. Then you might go down the list to 'open a boutique', and say, 'That's not really possible either', so you look down your list to 'write a book' … 'What if I went to a vineyard in Italy and sat there for a year and wrote a book?' You know people love travel books, so you think, 'Let me go and see what travel books are around. I know there was that book called *A Year in Provence*. There were some books about Tuscany, but has anybody written about a vineyard, maybe? No, they haven't. So I will go and do that.'

I didn't expect to end up in radio. I started out as a journalist, but then I went into TV and radio. It has actually been a slow evolution, but what inspires me from moment to moment, I guess, is the psychological need to prove myself, and the joy of being able to realise a concept. It is about being master of your destiny, I suppose.

The challenges in life, for me, are about control, about having control over one's ideas. If you are working in media, there are very few places where you can put together an idea and realise it. That is why you will find I have mostly worked in the area of live work — live television, live stand-up comedy and theatre and live radio. My issues are about control — they don't really let women take control very often, so I am always looking for a place where I can control what I do, and I am always looking for the process where there is least interference, so when I work on stage I direct myself. I am always looking for the cleanest, purest process, the one which gets me in front of the public with the least interference. Obviously the control issue is very important. So although I like working in partnerships, I pretty much have to be in control of my own product.

Every single day, the personal challenge, I would say, is being female in a man's world. I mean, nearly every time I have gone out and done something I have had the headlines 'First Woman to ...', so I think the challenge is breaking those taboos.

When you are performing there is a high level of criticism about who you are and what you do, so every time you perform there are people who like what you do (more or less) and those who don't. Especially in the Australian media, you also have the challenge of reinventing what you do, being fresh and being new.

There is no real formula. I am determined and a hard worker. I think I am one of the hardest working people in comedy, because I have a very high level of self-discipline. I listen to what I do. I have the ability to analyse what I do. I guess it is about application. Not that I don't know how to have a good time, but when it comes to work, I have a quick mind, I am really determined and I have an enormous capacity for actual work, because I love it.

Balancing work and family is working terrifically well at the moment. I have been doing breakfast radio for a long time — it is my eleventh year — and I earn enough money for my husband to stay home, so I have a full-time at-home husband and I am also able to afford a nanny. I get to work at 5.30 a.m. then I get home at 10.30 or 11 in the morning and am in bed at 8 p.m. every night now — I am really disciplined about that.

It took me a long time to find a husband and have the kids — that is just the way it worked. I couldn't find anybody who was … I mean, let's face it, I was always going to be the money earner in the family, I think. When I first met my husband, he said — pretty much almost the first night we met — 'I am a good 2IC (second in command).' I am a first born and he is a second born, and so that is how we work it. He always wanted to be the guy behind the scenes — but as we all know, the power behind the throne is always in charge!

A lot of career women make our relationships late in life and have children late in life — it is one of those things we are asked about a lot. It is a bit chicken and egg, really, because while people point at us, saying that we are obsessed with our careers and don't make time to meet men and so on, a lot of the time the men that we meet are intimidated by us and not actually up to the mark, so there are not many men who are available. I didn't need to meet the big career guy. I was never looking around for the big high-status man, but to find some-one who is comfortable being with a high-profile woman — that is really difficult.

My whole career looks like kind of a mess, but there is one unifying theme — I've had all these ideas I have wanted to express, and I have just found the best medium to express them at the best time. That is where the plans come into it, but the plans don't come from nowhere; they come from me. So I would say: get to know yourself, get to know who you are and what it is that you have to offer as a person — what it is that you think and you feel, and what you believe people would like to hear. Have endless curiosity and enthusiasm for new ideas and never sit still, never be satisfied with what you have achieved. That sounds as if you need to be a Type A obsessive person, but it is also a realisation that life is short and you want to do everything. Think of what you want to say and what you want to communicate to the world and then find the best way to say it. That is what my whole life is about.

There is a great saying 'These circumstances will change — this situation cannot last.' It's a good one to remember.

When I had Drew Barrymore sit down in front of me and say to my listeners, 'You know, girls, it is really easy — all you have to do is follow your dreams,' I thought, this is coming from Drew Barrymore, who was born into one of the greatest acting dynasties in Hollywood! You know it is an American thing — 'follow your dreams' — but when people say, 'Follow your dreams', you have to have the right dreams.

Strategies for living
YOUR DREAMS

Enhance your mental and physical wellbeing Where is your energy going? Do you have enough energy left over for what is really important to you?

- For a while I just didn't stop for a second during the day. From the moment I woke up, I did not take a minute to catch my breath. As you can imagine, that totally wore me down — no one can last long that way. During your day, take time out to stop, to recharge yourself. If you really do have to eat lunch at your desk, close the door for a few minutes, hold the calls, give yourself some time out to reinvigorate yourself — it's time well spent.

- Don't neglect your body. What good is the mind if it resides in a body that is in poor health and weak? Get a good night's sleep, eat healthy food — eat everything in moderation, but eat more fruit and vegetables and drink lots of water — think positive thoughts and exercise regularly. On exercise — most people find it hard to make time to exercise regularly, even though they want to. It just becomes another 'should' instead of a great way to get more energy.

- There are also things that can drain your energy. Financial issues, relationships that don't live up to your expectations or unresolved conflict with family and friends, for example, all drain energy. Any step you take towards resolving these outstanding issues will release energy. It doesn't matter what the result of your action is, as long as you take action. It's the storing up of anger, guilt and confusion that will drain you; moving forward always lifts your energy levels.

So start now, take a step towards enhancing your wellbeing — and feel great!

Gerry
HARVEY

Gerry Harvey is an entrepreneur, one of Australia's best-known retailers, a family man, a breeder of racehorses and Chairman of Magic Millions, the thoroughbred sales company, and the co-founder, Chairman and major shareholder of the Harvey Norman Group, a nationwide high-profile retailing business with annual sales of about $2.5 billion and more than 150 stores in Australia, New Zealand, Singapore and Britain. Gerry's drive and ambition stems from his childhood when he experienced the best of both worlds: he attended private schools until his parents lost everything and became broke pensioners and then had to live in a garage no bigger than an office with a concrete floor and a tin roof. He knew that he preferred the world of the wealthy and this gave him the ambition to be successful. Today, Harvey Norman is one of Australia's most successful retailers.

When I first started, more then 42 years ago, I just wanted to get into business on my own. I knew I liked selling; I had been selling ice creams and vacuum cleaners and so on, but I did not have any specific goal. I started my own business — my goal was just to be in business. I had one shop, and then the opportunity came to open a second shop, and I then started to get a vision of how many shops I could have. We became a publicly listed company in 1972, and by 1982, 20 years later, there were 42 shops and we were doing about

$240 million turnover per year. We were probably the biggest retailer of our type in Australia at that time. Our shares multiplied in that ten-year period about 15 times, so we were regarded as the success story of the 1960s and 1970s. Then Grace Brothers took over the business. They sold it three weeks later to Alan Bond.

I started up again straightaway, but this time I wanted to change the structure of the business a bit. But again I went into business with the view that I would open just one shop. I thought that would do. I opened one, and then six months later I opened the second one. We went public in 1987, and in the next 12 years we multiplied our share price by 100 times. So the shares in the first business went up by 15 times, but the shares in the second went up by 100 times — it is ten times as good a business the second time round.

You have to put that down to the fact that you spend from age 20 to age 40 learning about business, then from 40 to 60 you are a little bit wiser, and you know how to move quicker and smarter. I constantly try to be better at what I do and my belief is that I am wiser now than I have ever been. But when I look back on some of the things I did 20 or 30 years ago, I know that I did some really groundbreaking things that other people had never done

I've spent the last 40 years trying to get better at what I do. Now I look at it and say to myself, 'I have done that for 40 years, and if I can live for another 20, what can I do then?' That occupies my thoughts a bit because I don't really want to retire.

My vision for the future is to try and make Harvey Norman a worldwide company and to try and emulate what we have done here in a lot of other countries. That may or may not be possible. I think it is possible, in the next 20 years, to formulate some sort of a plan that will dwarf anything that we have done in the past 20 years.

I spent some time in Melbourne with Mark Besen, the owner of Sussan, the clothing chain. I don't think he is 80 yet, but he is getting close. He has a personal trainer and he comes to work every day. I said to him, 'You are an inspiration because your mind is still fine and you still look after your body.' That's where I want to be if I live that long.

I have always done that, ever since I was a kid. You look at people 30, 40 or 50 years old and ask yourself, 'Do I want to be like him or him or him?' There are those that have got it right because they are getting a lot more out of their time on earth.

People say to me now, 'When you started in 1982 you said you would just have one shop and that was it. Now you have got all these shops. How do you explain that?' Well, obviously I can't just open one shop and stop. I just can't. I didn't have any choice because I am just that sort of person. I did it once and I did exactly the same thing again. There was no plan. You open one shop, then two, then you open three then five. It just keeps going. Now there are 150 and it is still going. In a few years there will be 200.

I nearly went broke a couple of times in my early 20s; that would have been disappointing but it wouldn't have mattered. I would have bounced back — I have no doubts about that. I know exactly what I was thinking then. Everything went into focus. I went up several notches immediately when I was about to go broke. I remember it very clearly. I knew it could happen but I believed that it wouldn't because I could save it and do it. I had that belief that if it did happen it would be an injustice. I worked 16 hours a day, seven days a week to stop it — I did nothing else. I did all things possible to make it happen. You would have to call that focusing.

One thing I realised very early is that the most important ingredient in nearly any business is the people. If you associate with a certain type of person and you walk through the right coloured door then you have a life that is vastly different from your equal who took a different path. Maybe it is the fickle finger of fate that sends us in different directions. You see a lot of people who show such enormous potential and they have such great talent as kids. Their eyes are alive and alert and their dreams are there, then when you see them 10 or 20 years later they're off the track and all that ambition and light in their faces has disappeared.

I think it has everything to do with who you associate with. If you don't have the opportunity to associate with the right people in the area of your dreams then it is going to make it difficult for you to ever achieve those dreams. If you want to be a great artist or a singer or a piano player and you spend a lot of time with very good people in that area, then there is a fair chance you will probably make it. You look at great sportspeople and you see how many of their kids are great sportspeople too. Jack Nicklaus is probably the greatest golfer of the last century and one of his kids is running sixth in a tournament at the moment.

I was born into a reasonably wealthy family and they went broke and we lived in a garage for years and years. You see a family living like we did today and you would say they were the poorest family in Sydney, without any doubt. So having mum and dad as invalid pensioners living with no money, maybe that had some effect, suffering those hardships as a kid. I always said to myself it would not happen to me. I was dead certain I was not going to rely on the government to support me because I saw what happened to people. My father was a man who did not have to be like that but he did not have drive. He was left money. He did not make a lot of money and when he did he drank it and wasted it.

You can't make it to the top of any field unless you have

determination and a will to succeed — you just can't do it. It does not happen without that.

You also can't be single minded about anything you do because you will lose balance; I don't know anyone who is completely single-minded about anything who doesn't lose the balance. You can still work an 80-hour week and have that balance, it is a matter of how you do it. People talk about quality time and that sort of thing. You have to have an eye on things so you can see if there is a problem. Then you spend less time on this and more on that. You just balance your time a bit better. I don't think it follows that you have to spend 16 hours a week with your kids, or six, or any particular time. You can be spending three hours a week with your kids and it might do the job better than the guy who spends 36 hours with his kids. It's all relative.

Probably the most important thing you can do is try to understand the human race — to try to figure out what makes us all tick. If you want to do business you have to always be onto what appeals to people. Can I sell this? Can I buy this? Can I do this? Can I put a shop there? You've got to understand what they want. You try to understand people and you think, 'If I can do this in Australia can I do this in Slovenia or England or Japan?

Justin HERALD

In 1995, at 25, Sydney high school dropout and former Kmart management trainee Justin Herald got sick of being told by people that his attitude was poor, and decided to cash in on his disarming personality. He decided to start his own business. He had enough money to buy four blank T-shirts and have them printed with his logo. He sold those shirts and now his company, Attitude, has sold over 150,000 units. The Attitude brand currently sells in over 1800 stores throughout Australia. Today Justin runs his own businesses, is a motivational speaker, consults to other businesses and the Taxation Office and is the focus of much media attention. Justin released his first business/motivational book in April 2003.

At 25 I had $25 in my pocket, and it got to the point where I had to say to myself, 'Either it is someone else's fault that I am here or it is my fault.' I came to the conclusion that it was my fault that I only had $25. That being the case, it was my responsibility to get up and get to where I am today.

First I had to eat, which meant I had to get off my rear end. My ultimate goal was success, but my own level of success — not based on what other people believe. I wanted success based on the fact that I was happy with what I was doing.

I thoroughly appreciate it when people come up and say, 'You know, you have done really well' — I like that, but if I don't think I have done really well, I won't take it on board. I am a very hard taskmaster. I am my biggest critic. I think we need to have that sort of level of honesty with ourselves: we are all pretty big when things go well, but when things don't go too well we need to say to ourselves, 'Why aren't I unreal right now?'

A lady in my father's church said I had an attitude problem and I didn't think I did. She still thinks I do, to this day, and I don't think I do. When someone says you can't do something, to me that means I am going to go ahead and do it. I wanted to prove her wrong. Back when I started, the word 'attitude' was always followed by the word 'problem'. You have an attitude problem. Now 'attitude' is a buzz word, a positive word. I always knew it was — my attitude is my attitude. Attitude problems are third-party things, your view of where you think I am at.

I have a slogan: 'It is none of my business what you think of me'. People have their own opinion of me but ultimately I don't want to hear that. I just want to get on with getting on. If it's negative I don't allow it into my life.

I had $1.25 in my bank account, and I was sick and tired of having nothing. I was paid really well in the job I had, but I used to spend all the time. The biggest lesson I have learned with Attitude over the last seven years is not how to grow a big business, not how to come up with fantastic products — it is how not to go back to having $1.25 in my bank account. Too many times people don't let life teach them lessons. They are waiting for a knock on the door to come and for someone to say, 'Here is the lesson that you need to learn.' I learn lessons every day.

I had to borrow $50 from my younger brother to start the business, which I have never paid back. I could only make four shirts — I actually had to scam my way through the printing because I ran out of money. I needed $680 and I only had $50. I said, 'Look, if you stay with me I will stay with you and I will grow your business,' so the printer decided to do everything for free except for buying the four blank T-shirts — he printed the shirts for nothing. On the back of the shirts it had 'In the end it's all a matter of attitude' on the front it just had 'Attitude'!

I was expecting the idea to last a week but I sold those shirts, then made six more, then twelve, then twenty-four. I had never borrowed money, never had an overdraft, never done a business plan, never done a profit and loss statement. I had never done anything that you are supposed to do as a business. I knew how to sell well and I knew that what I had the public liked, and that meant I could sell it even better.

Then in 1997 Philips contacted me. They wanted to licence my business's name to put on stereos. Had I not been open to opportunities, I could have missed that boat big-time. It is something I love talking about now — how things will come your way if you are not closed off. I could have said back in those days, 'No, no, no, I only sell T-shirts', but if I had done that I wouldn't be sitting here at 32, retired.

So Philips came along, and they did an Attitude stereo — it was the biggest product they have ever launched in this country. And then other companies came to me and said, 'We want to use your name on our products.' Now Attitude has 180 products worldwide. Only one of them is clothing, my original dream, so sometimes your dreams will become bigger than you and bigger than you think you are going to be.

We all have dreams, and you have to grow with your dreams; you have to allow your dreams to grow, otherwise you won't achieve anything you want — you will limit yourself to what you could have achieved in the first place.

I still have plans for what I want to achieve. But something may come along that may take me off that path. Call it destiny, call it karma, call it the plan of God, call it whatever you want to call it. I have been taught through my whole life that there are plans. We are supposed to be on this planet for a certain reason, and I believe that I need to be the best me that I can be. That means I have to start thinking outside the square. You are not successful until you are helping other people reach success; otherwise you are just telling yourself you are.

Entrepreneur — I hate that word. I had a guy sitting next to me on a plane the other day and he said, 'I am an entrepreneur.' I thought, 'Hey, you are an idiot! You are putting a label on yourself, and if you can put good labels on yourself, you need to put the bad labels on yourself as well.' The biggest mistake a lot of people make is building yourself up into something that you are not. A lot of it is fake; it is false and it is one-dimensional.

Success for me was selling my first T-shirt, so I reached success pretty quickly. Selling my hundred thousandth T-shirt didn't make me feel any better. If I need to go 'Look at me, look at me' then my success isn't having the effect that it should be.

I couldn't stand the kids at school whose Mummy and Daddy were rich; they used to get stuff and go 'Look at me, look at me' and I'd go, 'You've got nothing — someone has given you that.' There is no level of appreciation for something that has been given. What inspired me was my need to be better: be a better husband, be a better father. The only way I could do that was to get off my rear end.

I deal in a world where there are no ethics, there is no integrity — I wasn't expecting that. I was expecting people to be nice — your yes is your yes and your no is your no! But it doesn't work like that in the business world.

People who come and see me and who have great ideas

and passion inspire me. My younger brother Dean inspires me, my father inspires me. He is the most ethical man I have ever met. I get inspiration from my 12-year-old daughter. What inspires me also is the fact that I inspire people. There is a saying: practise what you preach; I have another one: preach what you practise. For me, my boat gets floated when people come up and say, 'Wow — thank you so much! You're the bloke they talk about, and when I read your book you're the same bloke, and when I speak to you, you're the same bloke.' I am inspired by that because I am trying to stay as normal as I humanly can, so if I can do that, it's great.

Now, at age 32, I have achieved all these things that I never thought I could. My dreams and goals are huge — and one of them was retiring at 32. When I was writing goals down I threw that one in, not expecting to do it. When you do achieve those sorts of goals you realise, 'Wow, this stuff actually works — writing goals down and aiming at some-thing does work!' That is what my next book is all about — this stuff does work. It is about change: things that you have to change every day on your way to success. I want to show people that just because you have reached some level of accomplishment in your life, whether it be what I have done, or getting up in the morning, whatever it is, never think you have made it, because the day you do is the day you have to start all over again. I don't want to start all over again.

I had no money, so cash flow was a big challenge at the beginning! I also had a lot of doubters around me. Not so much my friends, but retailers and people who all of a sudden thought they could tell me how I should or shouldn't be run-ning the business. People from the church and friends of friends would say, 'That won't work, Justin.' Having that constant negative input was something I really struggled with. So I have surrounded myself with like-minded people. Not yes-men; I make sure I don't associate with that sort of person. I do a thing called a spring clean (my wife does it in our home all the time), but I do it with my friends and business associates as well. If you are not adding any value to me in a positive way and I am not adding any value (it is not a one-sided thing) to help you to get to where you want to go — then really we are not going down the same path in life. We are going in different directions, so ultimately one of us is going to lose out, because it is going to be draining on one of us, and I don't want that.

I want to achieve more than I have yet achieved. Once I achieved what I did, I sat back and thought, 'How did I get here?' Then I thought, 'This is how I did it, but I also know how I did not do it.' Now when I come to all my new businesses, I use the same principle.

All my friends own their own businesses. They are not my friends because I am elitist, but because we all understand what is required in our day-to-day lives, and how hard it is in our personal life, because we have got our families in the middle of it as well. People who work for someone else say, 'Oh you never come out, Justin'; they don't understand about how hard owning a business is.

When I first started my business I had three goals. One was to upset the lady in my dad's church — I did that the first day. The second was to have a nice car, and the third was to retire at 32. I worked on the car. In life, if you have nothing to aim at, you will always hit nothing. Some people said, 'This is a stupid thing to talk about, Justin, a car is a stupid goal', but I have had 11 cars in the last six years. I could say 'That's stupid' about other people's goals, too.

I needed something tangible to aim at — I didn't want to use money as my goal because it is not tangible, and I didn't want to use success as my goal because it is not tangible either, and it can come and go every day; I had to have something that I could reach out and touch. With every decision I make in my business — whether it is do I need to buy some more stock, or do I need to visit this customer, or do I need to buy a pencil — the question at the top of my head is: 'Is this going to take me further away from my goal or closer to my goal?' My business has to operate so that for every decision I make, I can see the results straightaway — that is where focus is.

People say, 'Stay focused'. How do you do that if you have nothing to aim at? How do you know you are focused? As soon as you start seeing what you could lose, and start seeing that you are getting further away from what you want to do, your focus changes quickly and your decision-making changes quickly, so I found it easy to stay focused. I was not going to fail. I had a no-exit clause.

I was driving a Mini when I started, but I have a BMW M3 now. The garage has just given me the new 7 series, worth $320,000, to drive to see if I like it. I love fast cars and every time I sit in that car and I go 'Wow!' Just sitting in that seat makes me appreciate the effort that was required to get to where I am now.

Family, work, then other commitments — that is the way I do it. I am not going to work my bum off for my family and never get to see them. I know guys who have not sat down with their kids for six to ten months because they are too busy working for their futures. They won't have a future, because their kids will not know who they are. When I was growing up, my dad was all over the world, doing what he had to do. I don't begrudge that, that was his calling, but what I did take from my growing up is that I want to make sure that my kids can come to me at any point. I now work from home, because I have a two-year-old; unless I am away speaking, I am at home 24 hours a day. When I started my business I would take my daughter to school every day and I pick her up. So that means nothing happens after 3 p.m., or if I have a meeting after 3 p.m. I pick her up, take her home and then go out. Some people say, 'That is too hard.' I wanted to make sure that I set the structure of when my business was going to end from day one.

The reason I went into my business ultimately was to have a life that would fit my life. I did not know if it would be possible, but the first thing I said was 'mini goal, mini dream'.

My daughter is extremely important to me. What is the point of Daddy being on TV the whole time and her saying, 'How unreal you are, Daddy, you are not in my head.' I don't want her to ever think that. And as a 12-year-old girl, she wants her dad to be around as much as possible — wants to impress me as much as possible, which means I have to impress her as much as possible. She would be my biggest critic. I care what Jade says about me, and now I have Brook, our two-year-old, and I have been able to experience that whole process again. It is totally different this time, but I have the opportunity to do that, and it is all right for me. My family is the reason I do things. So they're my gauge. My business may not be around here in ten years, but my family will be and I have to make sure that in ten years they still like me.

You have to be passionate about what you do. Passion, I believe, is the fuel for your dream. Not having passion is like starting a car and trying to drive as far as you can without filling the fuel tank up. You won't get very far, and you will be miserable and you will blame everybody. Passion is what drives me. If I am not passionate about something I will not do it. I have better things to do with no passion than working really hard. If I leave my attitude in neutral and wait for the first person I come across to set my attitude, I am going to be

dictated to by other people. That might be great while things are going well, but when things are not going well, will those same people who are dictating where I should be going be the ones getting me out of it? No! That will be me, and if I've let them affect me I won't know where the hell I am.

Too many people in life are waiting for everything to come their way. They are waiting for the car to drive up beside them, someone to pick them up, put them in and push the accelerator, and if they get to their dreams and goals they wonder why they don't appreciate what they have.

Anyone who is starting their own business has to make it happen. You will have bad times, but you need to appreciate those bad times, because then you will know what it is like being in those bad times, which means you don't want to go back there again. You have to let life teach you stuff. If we want to be different tomorrow we have to change who we are today. I have to change every day — my thought patterns, my attitude, my focus, everything about who I am has to change.

'A bend in the road is not the end of the road unless you fail to make the turn.' You drive along a road and all of a sudden there is a bend. Most people will say, 'Hang on — this wasn't planned — I didn't have this in my grand plan!' But it is there, so what are you going to do? At the Olympics I watched the hurdles. When the athletes run, most of the time some of them knock some hurdles over. I have yet to see one of them stop and say, 'Hang on, everyone, come back here. Let's start again, because I knocked one over.'

Life is a race; some people finish it really quickly, some people don't finish it at all, but most people will knock over hurdles — the problem with most people who knock over hurdles is that they think that knocking over hurdles is the end of their goal, the end of their dream. It isn't; it just means you have knocked something over and slowed your progress.

There are three things you can do with hurdles: you can

go over them, which is the easy way, you can go under them, or you can go through them. With any of these you are going in a forward direction. If you don't do that, if you turn around, you are to blame for stopping yourself getting where you want to.

So have a plan — write down your goals and dreams because these are your benchmark. Never give up, have passion, constantly spring clean your friends, and check daily where your attitude is.

Strategies for living
YOUR DREAMS

Find a mentor Don't be embarrassed to ask for help, especially when you are starting out on your own — starting out can be extremely intimidating, and it's easy to give up when things are not going as planned or expected.

Find someone whose advice you would value, and ask to speak to them. You'll be amazed how accessible and helpful these people are. But you must be prepared to take the advice you are being given. If you don't take their advice — without offering a good explanation — the person who gave it may feel that you are wasting their time. You may not get a second chance. If you do follow their advice, though, you may be starting to build an extremely strong and valuable relationship.

Many of the people I interviewed were very happy to advise and mentor others who are keen to learn. They are more than happy to share their experience in order to help someone else achieve their goal.

Marcia HINES

Marcia Hines was born in Boston, USA, in 1953 and developed her vocal skills as a member of church choirs, gaining her first solo spot at the age of nine. In her early teens she was a sought-after rhythm-and-blues-singer fronting groups in her local area.

She came to Australia at 16 to co-star in Hair, and she liked Australia so much she stayed. During the 1970s she became one of Australia's most successful female performer/recording artists, being Australia's No. 1 Female Recording Artist in 1975–79 and No. 1 'Soul' Recording Artist 1976–79. Her achievements include being named 'Queen of Pop' in 1976–78; being the No. 1 Selling Local Artist in 1977 and 1978; the No. 1 Concert Attraction 1976–79; and 'Entertainer of the Year' in 1979. Marcia also hosted her own variety show. She continues to perform throughout Australia and to maintain a high profile in the entertainment industry.

I was very fortunate to have had a mother who told me that I was capable of doing anything, and I still believe that I am capable of doing anything. My mom, her upbringing, and the people that surrounded her all had an impact on me. My mother was of West Indian heritage, and from a great family. The kids were great. They were well loved and were encouraged in everything they did. And my mother was the youngest of 13, so she got an avalanche of love.

I knew I was going to sing when I was about five. I sang around the house, and I sang whenever there were workshops in Boston. But the real step was when I got through the audition to do *Hair* in 1970. I was 16 and bullet-proof — so why wouldn't I? I knew I wanted to sing, and I had a chance to do *Hair* in Boston. But when my friends suggested I go for the audition for Boston, my answer was, 'Why be stuck in Boston? I don't want to be here for the rest of my life, I want to see the world.'

As they say, the rest is history. I came to Australia and stayed for a while, and then I was asked to do another production, so I did that, and then work filtered in. You learn as you go, and I got some great chances to work with some outstanding Australian musicians and every chance I got I would try to grab it. Probably my biggest early challenge was not being too frightened to get on that plane and leave my mother behind in Boston — that was a big one. And then I suppose coming to Australia and finding out that I was pregnant was another big one. But I was always taught that you have to be responsible for your behaviour, so I was. I think that if I hadn't had my daughter, I would not be the person that I am now, because kids keep you really honest.

I don't look for challenges — and I don't look for the negative side of things. I am a bit of a hope junkie, so I look for the positive. I believe that if you look for the negative you will find it.

I knew that things would work out in my life. It was not hope — you don't hope that you are going to get food, you don't hope that you are going to stay fit. You go out to work to get food; you go out and exercise to stay fit. There is proactive hope and there is the other kind of hope.

I was taught from a very early age that no one owes anybody anything and I was also taught never to envy anything I saw that anyone had, because you don't know what people have done to get what they have. If you want it, then you go and work for it, and be happy for anyone who has what they have.

My mother died in May 2003. She was a very spiritual woman and obviously a very, very strong part of my life, and she died in my arms. I watched her practise everything she ever preached about death, dying, fear and going home, so I had a great role model. And now it is kind of spooky, because I have to take over where she left off. That is what happens when the matriarch dies.

But that is how I learned to be who I am. I think children are amazing — they learn by example. We all learn by example, and we are all responsible for bringing up everyone's child. We should give every child that we come into contact with so much positive energy, and just tell them that they can do it — if they are not good at maths, OK, they will be good at something else. It is so important to believe that. Mind you, when I blew it as a kid, I was told; it wasn't as if I was any type of golden child, but when I did succeed, or when I did have something in mind, my mother would usually say, 'Well, what's stopping you?'

You have to put what is real into perspective, and what is real is your family. You have to work, but at the end of the day you leave the troubles of work behind, and you try, if you can, to come home to the reality of your family. It can be done, but you have to want it as well.

What I do I love. I love to perform, and I love to move people with this incredible gift of the voice. It has made me just want to love and be loved in return. I believe that love is truly all there is — that sounds really hippy dippy, but I really do believe that if you give out positives you get them back as well.

There are times when I think, 'OK, I'm not going to leave

the house today because I'm not in a nice mood. I need to stay home.' When people walk up to me in the street, I know how fragile they are because they are coming towards me, doing something they are not sure of. If I am not in the mood to deal with the public I stay home.

Love is the thing. What I see when I see people I really like is that they are so lovable, they are so real. I try and keep it real, I suppose.

There is a great line from Michael Caine: he said, 'Work with the difficulties.' I am a great believer that if you get lemons, you make lemonade. Everybody has down days. My career goes up and down, and the greatest thing about the down bit is that you appreciate what up is. The best thing about down is that you are waiting for up. The most important thing is just to believe. It is bad today, but there is tomorrow. And it's not what happened to you — it's how you feel about what happened, what you do with it, that's important.

I work spontaneously — I suppose that is the right word. And setting goals is just not the way the music industry works. I knew that I wanted to remain in this industry and I have been able to sustain a career. I have been very blessed in that I have had the same manager for my whole career and we have always seen it the same way — I am not here in transit and then gone. I am here for quite some time, and I plan to continue to learn and get better.

People have said to me my whole career, 'Marcia, can you do such and such?', and I will say 'Yes'. I don't know that I can do it, but if it is within the realm of what I do, it means I can learn. I will call someone who is better at it than me and really hope that they are kind enough to share some of their knowledge, and then I will learn to do what it is I said I could do. If I say I can do it, I can probably do it, but not as well as I would like to, so I study a lot.

Surround yourself with people who wish you well and with people who are more than happy to share their knowledge. I believe that knowledge stored is wasted knowledge. Knowledge shared is what knowledge is supposed to be. And I try to believe that most people really do mean you well.

It is an incredibly enchanted kind of life I have lived so far, and it is far from over. And I love what I do — I just adore it. Doing it well is all about focus. It is all about knowing that you must stay focused and keep your eye on the prize. I learned some of that during the Olympics in Sydney. I was privileged to be around some of the athletes, and to watch the Australian guys focus — even if a building had fallen in front of them I am sure they wouldn't have seen it. You go inside; you go into that really good quiet place where you know you can find peace.

Lisa HO

Lisa Ho is one of Australia's most popular fashion designers and manufacturers. She studied dress design in Sydney and initially sold her garments at Paddington Markets before she established her Lisa Ho label. Lisa was one of four fashion and costume designers approached to create original costumes for the 'Arrivals' segment of the Sydney 2000 Olympic Games opening ceremony. Today she has opened signature boutiques and her label is also stocked by major department stores and boutiques throughout Australia.

I wanted to be independent and live a happy life, and in order to do that I felt I had to be self-sufficient.

Basically I went straight out of college and worked for someone else for one year, then I started on my own. It was very small to begin with. I was young — naïve, I guess — and it was hard. It was challenging, but it was always fulfilling; I achieved something small to start with, then grew steadily over the years. That meant it wasn't so scary. If you are starting from nothing, there is only one way to go.

I was very serious about what I wanted to achieve, but not daunted by the size of the whole project. I think if you look at the whole project, it can put you off. You have to tackle one small area at a time. A friend of mine — someone who had been in the rag trade for a long time — gave me some good advice. When in the early stages I got panicky and thought things were too much for me to handle, he said, 'Just think of your workload, and divide it up into lots of tiny piles rather than one mountain. Get one pile done and then move on to the next, then the next, and you'll get through it.' And that's what I did. It is just being highly organised and having priorities.

The initial challenges were coming up with an idea, then coming up with a product that people found desirable and pushing myself forward to sell the product. Then I had to face the reality of having to produce and manufacture, and I had to learn about all the aspects of that.

Now it's about making sure all the arms of the business are running well. That the staff and levels of staff you have are correct, that you are meeting your targets, and that the product is still as creative as it could be. That you are still exciting the customer and that you are collecting your money!

It takes an enormous amount of energy, but you have to keep moving towards your vision and never give up. And also, never say 'no' and never say 'never' — plough through it and be brave about it. Never doubt yourself and be tenacious if you believe in what you are doing.

I have a lot of people that I rely on now. I try to identify who has good judgement about people, who has good skills, and then I can confidently delegate areas to them. You have to trust in their ability because you really can't do it all. If you do, that's when you burn out. You always have to be approachable. You always have to understand how people around you are feeling. If you have a happy team working with you it is much more productive and the environment is pleasant to work in.

At the age I am at now, I want balance, so I am not looking to conquer the world. I have a family and I have a business and I want to keep all of that on track. I think you have to be really true to yourself and be honest, and say, 'Doing this gives me a lot of pleasure' or 'This doesn't give me a lot of pleasure'. If you can stick to what you enjoy doing, it isn't a chore.

I don't take on too many commitments outside work, because I have a young family. I know I have to give a certain amount to my business, but then I want to spend as much time as I can with my children. I will not go out every night of the week socialising. Family always comes first; the career is second. Until I had my children I felt differently. I put all my time into my career and into my work, and I found I got to a point where I felt a bit empty. I think as you get older, you feel that there is something more out there. You think about your own mortality. I thought, 'There are things I want to achieve and get done in my lifetime, so I'd better get cracking at some of those other areas.'

I think it is important to be tenacious and stick to what it is you want to do. And see it through. I hate it when people start things and then stop. Never giving up might mean that you start something and it doesn't turn out the way you thought it was going to, but you have to see things through and you have to get to the finish line.

If you believe that you have the ability to work in the fashion field, polish up your skills as much as you possibly can. Don't be afraid to work, and take on — when you are young — as much work as you can handle

Work hard, have integrity, be true to yourself, be honest.

Strategies for living
YOUR DREAMS

Fix your eyes on where you're going Rabbi Mendel Futterfas
who spent several years of his life in a Soviet labour camp, related
that when Stalin died and the government eased up the pressure on
the camps, some of the inmates decided to have a celebration. One of
the prisoners claimed to be a tightrope walker. He found a long thick
rope and stretched it between two buildings about three metres off the
ground. A crowd gathered around. The man removed his shoes and
gingerly climbed up the ladder to the rope. He moved onto the rope,
took a few steps, lost his balance and fell. But he knew how to fall and
didn't hurt himself. He waited a few seconds and climbed up again. He
kept trying, and eventually he started walking, and then dancing from
one foot to the other. Then he got to the end, turned around, danced
back to where he started and climbed down, amidst the applause and
cheering of the crowd.

Afterwards he was asked how he could walk on such a thin rope
without falling off? After much prompting he finally revealed his secret.
'I fix my eyes on where I'm going,' he said, 'and never even think
about falling. The hardest part is turning around because you lose
sight of the goal for a second. It takes a long time to learn to turn around!'

Once you know what you really want and once you've crystallised
your goal and course of action, lock on to your target — your goal: fix
your eyes on where you're going and then keep focused on it and
never even think about falling. You may stumble and you may fall, but
as long as you quickly refocus on where you're going, you will get there.

Akira ISOGAWA

Born in Kyoto, Akira Isogawa left Japan in the mid 1980s to explore the world and discover himself, and immigrated to Australia in 1986. Today Akira is one of Australia's most innovative and renowned fashion designers and his work has earned him an international reputation. He enrolled in fashion design in Sydney and was strongly influenced by Japanese designers such as Yohji Yamamoto, and Comme des Garçons as well as the Eastern philosophy of Zen. In 1993 he opened the Akira Isogawa boutique in Queen Street, Woollahra, Sydney, and unveiled his first Autumn/Winter collection, 'Not Made in Japan'. Akira presents his exquisite collection twice a year in Paris and three times a year in Sydney. His clothes are stocked in boutiques in London, Paris, Milan, New York, Tokyo and other cities throughout Europe, the United States and Asia.

The original goal, the vision and picture that I had when I opened my store in 1993, was to make beautiful things — in this case, clothing — and to have them worn by a lot of people internationally.

Fashion to me as a child didn't have much importance really, but as I grew up, especially in high school, I became self-conscious and I started looking at how other people dressed. That's when I began to get involved in fashion — but before that, I recall that I used to enjoy drawing and was good at it.

So when I opened my store, I had a vision.

But time was a problem. There was never enough time. I always wished there were another two hours in each day so I could make more designs or have time to sleep — finding enough time was a major challenge. Also finance. I would have hired somebody to help if I had had sufficient capital.

I overcame these challenges by not being so opinionated about things and just surrendering to the fact that these problems existed, but regardless of that, I would just do it anyway. That was my attitude.

Just do it, before you really think about the problems. Just do it. Problems disappear when you're in action. They're no longer problems, they're not there any more, they disappear.

Once I decided that I would like to be a fashion designer, I then took it as a destiny, and that thought — that it was my destiny to be a fashion 'designer' — allowed me not just to push to the limit but also to go where there were no limits any more.

I didn't find competitors. I couldn't find anyone that I could identify as a designer in Australia. I had a one-man operation, and I didn't see other designers doing what I was doing. I guess that was a great advantage. I was very versatile, too: I could be in the shop within a minute if I had to. If a customer needed me I would rush out and there I would be in the store, and if the customer needed something to wear in two days' time and she was passionate about my work, then I was able to accommodate that need, and so on.

My family were not artistic. I felt different from the rest of my family; it felt like I didn't fit in 100 per cent. That's why I left Japan. I appreciate and am thankful to my family, especially to my parents, it's just that we had different values — they knew that as well.

I have a great deal of respect for my family and now they

respect my designs. They used to question my designs; they would say 'Who is going to wear this?' and so on. However, especially since I started to express my respect towards them, it has all changed. If you respect others you will be respected.

What would I say to young Australians? When I was younger I was quite arrogant, and now I can see some people out there — especially teenagers — who are so sure of themselves. This is a very positive attitude but an arrogant attitude, one I find not very attractive. I am not that old yet, I am still young and have a lot to learn, but I feel that learning not to be arrogant is an important lesson.

To someone entering the fashion industry I would say confidence is great, but it's good to be humble at the same time. If you're humble, people around you will in fact support you. That's what I realised: humility is most important.

Balancing family and work? Family comes first. My mother passed away two years ago and I realised then the importance of being in touch with people who are close to me.

These are the three steps that I have always followed:

1. Discipline: start work at a certain time and stay till the end, and make sure to take a lunch break otherwise you won't last long. You also need some time for yourself. Discipline is most important.
2. Assurance: reassure yourself that your vision is still there, because if it is no longer valid, you won't be able to succeed.
3. Integrity: this is also really important. 'Integrity' is a most important word for me. I try to live by it.

My favourite and much-loved line? Since I was in school one of my hobbies has been calligraphy. I took lessons and practised a lot and I used to have to choose a word to expound on. 'Peace' was a word I chose often; in Japanese it is *Nintai*, which also means endurance: perseverance with endurance, persistence and determination.

Alan
JONES

Alan Jones has had a varied career, beginning as a schoolteacher —
he was head of English at the King's School, Parramatta, at the age of
26 — and later becoming a speechwriter and senior advisor to the
then Prime Minister, the Right Honourable Malcolm Fraser, in
1979–81. He turned to sport, coaching Manly Rugby Union team in
1983, and was selected as Australian Rugby Union Coach in 1984.
Alan coached the Wallabies until 1988, and with victories in 91
matches, he is one of Australia's most successful Rugby coaches.

He is also regarded by many as one of Australia's most gifted
public speakers and was invited to deliver the 1985 Australia Day
Address as Guest of Honour of the Australia Day Council in Canberra.
In the same year he was awarded the Rostrum Speakers' Award as
their Communicator of the Year and was chosen by the Confederation
of Australian Sport as Australia's Coach of the Year. In 1989, Alan was
elected to the Confederation of Australian Sports' Hall of Fame in
recognition of his contribution to Australian Rugby.

In 1985, Alan Jones was recruited to join Radio 2UE as their
morning radio host and established himself in the competitive world of
radio. In 1988, he moved to the breakfast shift, and achieved the
largest breakfast audience and the largest radio audience in Australia.
In 1989, Alan was honoured by the Variety Club of Australia as their
Australian Radio Personality of the Year. Alan has also been awarded
the prestigious award of Australian Radio Talk Personality of the Year.

In 2002 he moved to Radio 2GB to host its breakfast shift; along
with 2GB commitments, Alan makes daily editorial comment on the
Channel 9 Today show.

I come from a very humble background in the Queensland
bush. My parents had nothing, there were no schools nearby,
so we went to boarding school — my parents didn't have
money, but that was the only way I could get educated. They
said that was the way out of the kind of privation that distance
imposed upon people in Australia.

I worked hard in school, because my mother told me to.
My mother was the scholar, and my father was the farmer who
had no education, no parents and no money, which is a pretty
tough sort of way to start. My mother encouraged me to read,
and then because I thought it was a laudable vocation and she
had been a teacher — she was a teacher for the deaf and dumb
and they were rare in those days — I became a teacher. I hope
I was a good teacher, but a sort of glass ceiling was imposed:
you knew you had to be a teacher for 15 years before you went
to the next step. It was all too slow for me.

I met then Deputy Prime Minister Doug Anthony, whose
son I had taught. He encouraged me to go to Canberra to
work in politics, so I went to work for him. From there I won
the opportunity to go to Oxford University, where I did some
postgraduate study. I came back and worked for the Prime
Minister, Malcolm Fraser.

I had always coached sport successfully. When I moved to
Sydney some of the players I had coached as schoolboys said
I should coach Manly (the Rugby Union team), who had not
won a premiership for 33 years. I said I couldn't, I didn't have
time, but in the end I did. We won a premiership in the first
year of my coaching grade football. I was then selected as
coach of Australia and we went to Britain in 1984. Everyone

said there was no hope, that we were no good, but I was determined to win. One of the ways of promoting the team and making people understand what we were trying to do was to be available to the media, so I was available to the media at all hours, no matter what time of the night or day. That 1984 tour became the most successful tour in Australian rugby history — we won the grand slam, which no Australian side had ever done (and which hasn't been done since either): we beat England, Ireland, Wales and Scotland.

When I got home this fellow from Radio 2UE came to see me. He said, 'You were just magnificent communicating the message while you were over there. We'd like you to join Radio 2UE.' I said, 'You have to be kidding!' but I went over to see the station. This was on a Sunday afternoon. They were terribly enthusiastic. I didn't know what I was doing, but they said, 'You're on air Monday week.' So I had this new job. I had been on leave from the New South Wales Employers' Federation; I left that job on a Wednesday and started on air the following Monday. That was 18 years ago, and here I still am.

All I do is work hard. I enjoy what I am doing. If you do your homework you'll pass the exam, and I did my homework. We have the biggest audience in Australia — we haven't been beaten in a survey in ten years. We've broken every record in radio, and won 79 surveys in a row. All that is a consequence of hard work. That's all it is.

A lot of people depend upon me: I am a vehicle for providing information. I am reasonably independent, but I have a responsibility to other people. There are other things I have which are a spin-off: I live in this most beautiful apartment, for a start. I live well. I have a lovely place in the bush, I have a lot of opportunities to share, so I have to be sensible. I'm not stupid in that sense; I rationalise — I hope objectively, intelligently — and don't dwell on the downside. The downside is getting up at half-past two; the upside is I do very well. Compared with how other people live and the difficulties they face, I have nothing to complain about. If I'm tired, I stumble over and sit down and have a look at the Harbour Bridge.

I think my mother, my parents, were very powerful influences in my life. My mother used to say the only thing that comes without hard work is failure, and that's true. My father taught me to never forget where you come from — while you don't have to always be looking down the ladder to see where you've climbed up from, it is important to understand that there are other people on the climb and you might have to sort of hold out a hand and help them up. He was very strong about not forgetting where you've come from, and always said that if you've risen to a position of fame and you can help others, you should.

I hope I'm a good sharer. I think there's no virtue in living like this or having a farm if you don't share. I also have a place on the Gold Coast, and I like other people to stay there. There is no virtue in acquiring things unless you're prepared to share the benefits of them, and sharing gives pleasure to others, especially young people who are battling — that's the influence of my parents, I think. I have no difficulty helping a lot of people. I call myself a porter on the railway station of life, really — I'm just trying to help people lighten their baggage a bit, carry a bit of baggage for them, lighten their load.

My parents were very much like that, constantly preached that stuff. They were very good people. Both my parents died without ever having a holiday, but that wasn't important in the scheme of things; other things were more important — family meals were important, sharing was important, giving people credit was important, telling people they were appreciated was important. My parents were strict, and they were firm — there was the strap and all that stuff — but there was the carrot as well as the stick. They were very good people.

I was lucky, because I don't think there were any challenges for me in being a teacher. I think that's a part of me, though, and I'm still teaching now, I'm just using a different format. People know that the Alan Jones program is about Alan Jones's views, and I express those views. I'm reasonably widely read and I think I'm fairly catholic in my interests — I can talk about the soprano Renée Fleming one minute and then about the short-course swimming championships in Moscow the next. I think I touch a lot of people because of that breadth of interest.

The challenge I faced is the medium. I did move into several different mediums — from the classroom to the political office first. That was tough. I was the senior advisor to a prime minister, so I was writing about foreign policy, which is pretty tough stuff. I was virtually shoving stuff in his mouth, but he had the final say — Malcolm Fraser never uttered something he didn't agree with, so we would work on the material until he was happy with it. And then I came to this, to radio, which is a different medium altogether. I remember that at the beginning talking into a microphone was hard. You're not speaking as I am speaking to you — you are constantly aware that you are speaking to a lot more people, but each listener only becomes comfortable when they feel as if you are speaking just to them. The fact that you know you are speaking to another 550,000 or 600,000 people is part of the technique.

The medium is also very challenging because it's commercial radio; you know people don't particularly like commercials, but you still have to sell the product and make some money, and it's hard to do that in a way which doesn't detract from the value of the program. And the audience that I have are also very catholic in their interests — you might want me to talk about the Middle East, but another person might be worried about the funeral of Glenn McNally at Taree, another has just had their local bank branch at Gunning closed and is worried about that, and someone else is worried about the cricket in South Africa.

You have to be able, with your knowledge and your level of interest, to touch all those bases with enthusiasm. I am lucky that none of those things bothers me; I enjoy them all, but making the program intimate and warm and personal can be a challenge. People will be very critical, too. They will say, 'Oh, you don't sound too well', so eventually you learn to refine your presentation. I suppose it's as if you are giving a concert every day, you are on stage every day. One of the great mistakes that radio people make is to say, 'Oh God I'm tired. I was out last night, at bars and restaurants.' The people that I'm broadcasting to, 98 per cent of them will never be able to step inside these restaurants. I try constantly to identify more with their privation than with my 'excess'.

The listeners know whether it is synthetic or not. You can't be artificial. They're smart, they know whether it is contrived or not. That's why I answer all my letters, everything that comes to me, about 9000 a year.

You hope against hope that when you see the emails on the desk it's only a small pile, and when you see a huge pile you think, oh no! But every one of those people has sat down and typed away and it's the most important thing in their day. What a terrible thing it would be for me to be dismissive of them, so I answer them. Now everyone says to me, 'Oh mate, the emails, they don't write those to be answered', but I don't know anyone who would spend the kind of time in composition that they spend and then say, 'Well, I've sent this to Alan but I know he won't read it or won't see it.' They don't write that with that in mind; they expect a response.

You never know what an impact you can make. A while ago Nancy Gorton, John Gorton's wife, called me. John Gorton, the ex-Prime Minister, was 90 then, and I had spoken at the launch of his biography, because I thought he was a beautiful Australian. Being Prime Minister was the least important achievement of John Gorton's life: he was a magnificent soldier, he was a survivor of the war (he should have been killed five times) and he returned. He made a speech in Victoria when he returned to explain why Australians went to war, what that meant and what the legacy was. It was a beautiful speech, one of greatest speeches ever made, and whenever I have spoken in his presence I've embarrassed him by reminding him of it, but I know deep down he's pleased that anyone would even know that speech. So the book was launched by John Howard, John Howard and I spoke, and Gorton wrote this lovely note to thank me. He was 90, so I wrote back. I know that Nancy read him the letter, so he rang up. He was having a little lunch the next day — it was only him and Nancy and Ainsley Gotto, who had been his personal secretary — but he wanted me to come.

When a 90-year-old man asks you to lunch, whatever you have on has to stop, because it might be the last lunch you get to have with him, so you can't underestimate the impact you are having on his life. It's a privilege to have an impact, and it's a high responsibility to do justice to it.

It's very hard to balance work, family and other social commitments, but again I think I am lucky in my disposition. I'm not into being seen at parties, or dining in the flashiest restaurants. I'm not into all that. I'm a son of the farmer who had not much, I'm a lamb-chops-and-mashed-potato person. You can't live your life regretting what you are and what you might have been. Basically I find that the balance in my life derives from knowing that I have to be here now, that my work is honest work and has given me a propelling privilege. I try not to be selfish about it; I try to share it. Every Tom, Dick and Harry rings me wanting something, but I don't say, 'Why are you ringing me?', because it's a bit of a compliment. I'm out there as a sort of missionary, trying to solve problems, trying to help those stray dogs, and knowing that I'm doing that — succeeding in doing that — is very rewarding. So there could be someone ringing up tonight or knocking at the door, someone with a particular problem who has come to me because I'm unencumbered, they think — little do they know that I have work hanging around my head. I have to make them feel that what they are on about is the most important thing at this particular time, and I think I'm good at that.

I think obligation is very important. I mean, it would be easier to lie in bed — there'd be many mornings I can think of where I could say, 'I'm sick, I'm tired', but there's a whole heap of people out there and I am obligated to them. And it would be inconsistent with the ethic that I was brought up with. I am very — I hate this word — empowered by my parents, because they had none of what I have. My father never saw Sydney Harbour, for instance. I'm very mindful of the fact that they ploughed the field and I'm sort of reaping the harvest from it. So I have to keep my feet on the ground, and I always feel this sense of obligation. My father loved racing, and he could never afford to own a racehorse, but I can and I have horses: I had a horse running at Randwick last Saturday, I've had a horse in the Derby, in the Golden Slipper, in the Sydney Cup, I've had a horse in the Queen Elizabeth Stakes, and I think my father would have a smile on his face and would say, 'You've not done too badly, son.'

I really have no time for people who are embarrassed about their father or who want to cut themselves away from what they were or where they've come from. It's very sad, because we are what we began as. And as my father would say, it's not where you start but where you finish that counts; you have to make something of it. Whatever I am and whatever I've achieved it's because of my parents, no one else, and the little things they said, the things they did, the push they gave me and the opportunities they provided. When my parents had nothing, were desperate, they would still drive every Sunday to see me at school. It must have taken them three and a half hours to get there. They'd bring lunch and we'd have lunch in the park, and they'd give me a pound so I could get a few things from the tuckshop. Every week, unbelievable. Those are things you don't forget; they are powerful, motivating forces in your life which differentiate you from the next person.

Robert Browning said, 'A man's reach should exceed his grasp, Or what's a heaven for?' If you aim for the sky you'll at least get off the floor. I think people are frightened to aim too high, but I think your reach has to exceed your grasp — that's what I tell people.

Basically there are no shortcuts. I tell people what Formula 1 racing driver Stirling Moss said when they asked him how he won. He said, 'I'm competing against people who go through the corners a quarter of a second slower than the next person. They sit back and make a few bob every time but they're not racing, because if you're going to be a racing car driver you can't take your foot off the pedal. If you take your foot off the pedal people go past you; you have to accelerate when it's toughest.'

Strategies for living
YOUR DREAMS

Wealth creation = small but consistent gains Getting rich quickly simply does not happen. Anyone who promises that if you invest in this stock or that property you'll make a fortune in no time is being untruthful. Getting rich means small and consistent gains over a long period. Successful investments — and, therefore, financial gains — come with time, and with the understanding that you will not be risking significant capital that you cannot afford to lose.

Listen and learn, and follow the advice of those people who continually come out ahead. Most of them don't get emotionally involved in a specific investment; rather, they stay focused on a long-term goal, and are constantly re-evaluating their investments.

All of us know how hard it is to see the action speeding right past us. We want to be part of it. In this sort of situation we may purchase shares at a premium, generally just before they decline or stabilise. Then, if the share price drops we panic. We are often also reluctant to sell before a share has reached what we think will be its highest price: we might lose a part of the action! So we wait around until the price begins to fall — and then we've lost the gain we could have made. This is not a productive cycle! Remember, the key is small but consistent gains.

The common denominators are patience and action. As for all of our goals, we need to first take the plunge and then tread step by step, all the time staying focused on our goals and waiting for those small and consistent gains that build into success.

Keep focused on your long-term vision and goal and remember there are no short cuts!

Ian KIERNAN

Ian Kiernan was born in Sydney in 1940 and grew up learning to swim, fish and sail on the harbour, his favourite waterway. He became a builder, specialising in historic restorations. He also sailed competitively, and represented Australia at the Admiral's Cup, Southern Cross Cup and Trans Pacific yacht races. During the 1970s he took up solo yacht racing, and in 1986–87 he fulfilled a dream by representing Australia in the BOC Challenge, a solo around-the-world yacht race. During the BOC Challenge Ian began to notice the state of the world's oceans. When he returned to Australia he decided to do something about the problem of pollution. With the support of a committee of friends, he organised a community drive — Clean Up Sydney Harbour on Sunday, 8 January 1989. It attracted 40,000 volunteers, and was the start of something very big. In 1990 Ian then established Clean Up Australia, a national non-profit organisation which co-ordinates Clean Up Australia Day and conducts year-round community education programs and environmental 'fix up' projects. For the first four years he worked as a volunteer, but since 1993 — by which time Clean Up the World was also operating — he has worked full-time as Executive Chairman at Clean Up Australia.

In recognition of his leadership in the environment and the community, both at home and internationally, Ian Kiernan was named 1994 Australian of the Year, and was made an Officer of the Order of Australia (AO) in 1995. In 1993, he was made a United Nations

Environment Programme (UNEP) Global 500 Laureate for his work and leadership in the local and global environment. He has since won numerous other awards. He continues to sail competitively aboard his 37 ft Tasman Seabird Yawl, 'Canon Maris'. He has sailed in twelve Sydney–Hobart races.

I have always been magnetically drawn to the harbour and the ocean, ever since I was a small child, and I had the good fortune to grow up on the shores of Sydney Harbour, so I've always been familiar with it. I progressed from swimming to surfing to sailing. I felt a very strong connection with Sydney Harbour, but when I was younger I also felt great sadness seeing the continuing degradation of it. In some instances it was being corrected, but in others it was actually getting worse.

Sailing boats connects you very much with nature, and with the beauty and the fragility of it. In fact when I am on the ocean I feel as if I belong to it. I am part of it, just another creature out there, and I really like that feeling — I like to be associating with the marine and bird life as another species. I think humanity has a very poor attitude, thinking that just because we have title deeds we own the land.

The BOC single-handed around-the-world race motivated me to do something about Sydney Harbour. I had been concerned for a long time about the state of Sydney Harbour: I was seeing plastic, I was seeing a tide line of glass on the beach where I learned to swim. Any time I have been successful with a challenge I have always felt strengthened in myself, and then wanted to go on and look for the next challenge. So when I came back from the race we organised the first clean up of Sydney Harbour, with the simple goal of motivating the owners of Sydney Harbour, if you like, to look after their asset. It was so successful that it just expanded from there – it soon became Clean Up Australia and then Clean Up the World.

We did it as a one-off event, but the event was grasped by the community, and they just wanted to drive it further and further, so that's why it continued to evolve. It has changed in its character over the years — it is owned by the community now, and it has great strength.

First we had to get some money. I had friends around me that were prepared to help me, and they came from a variety of occupations — there were lawyers, there were advertising people, there were accountants, there were people from the construction industry, all sorts of different people, but we had to get money in order to oil the wheels so that it would move forward.

The next problem was logistics, because Sydney Harbour, we soon discovered, had 270 km of foreshore. It was a huge challenge. Where were we going to put the bins? Where would we put the muster points? Where would we have pick-ups? Where would we have places where you could hand out clean-up bags? There were all these challenges, but we were able to meet them. Then I guess the next challenge was to communicate our message to the community.

And we did a very strange thing. When we drew up the budget, we applied 85 per cent of our entire resources to communication. It would be very unusual in a business plan to get that accepted, but that's what we did, and that was one of the great factors in the success of the day — we communicated really effectively through community service announcements on television and radio.

I went to John Singleton — he was on our board at that time, and he is a very effective communicator — and he put me in touch with Peter Ritchie from McDonald's. Peter Ritchie agreed to give us the base funding so we had enough money to get us by. Also, we had been lent some space in an office building and we were able to use their switchboard. The fact that we jammed their switchboard for three days was a bit embarrassing, because they had something like 42 incoming lines, but the phone was just ringing off the hook.

As for the 270 km of foreshore, it was just a matter of getting out and surveying that and saying, 'This location is only accessible by water so we will have to bring in a barge with rubbish containers in it. This beach we can do with a small boat going in and bringing out the rubbish bags ...' and so on. We also forged a very strong relationship with local government, because they know what is going on in their own precincts and they knew where the rubbish hot spots were.

So we were able to establish the sites. Then we had to look at waste containers — we got those from the waste companies. Then we had to look at the disposal of the waste — we came to an arrangement with the waste services group. They gave us free tip delivery.

We became quite adept at asking people for goods and services, which in the long run allowed us to avoid writing out cheques and so preserve our capital.

I am very lucky that I have a very considerate and long-suffering family, because the travel is very difficult. I travel a lot, both in Australia and overseas. My wife really hates it when I go overseas, it depresses her, so I try to keep in contact as well as I can and I try to make it up to the family when I am here, but it's always one of the major challenges. It's difficult having to get to that airport again.

Having a considerate partner and a considerate family really helps, but it is difficult. I see plenty of my friends in important jobs that have the same problem, and their wives are always saying, 'You're never here, you're always travelling.' That's what I have to do — that's what's provided the where-withal and the lifestyle.

There are a few ingredients to my success: preparation,

determination and enthusiasm, I would say. I find enthusiasm is an incredibly infectious thing. If you are enthusiastic and positive it rubs off on your work mates and your team members, and it can run like wildfire. Determination is a very strong factor in achieving solutions to problems. In single-handed sailing you get complex problems — it's a bit like the building trade — and if you get one problem, another one develops over it, and then another one develops over that. Then you really have a problem, because you have to sort out each secondary problem until you get to the base problem.

I keep a personal log book that isn't for anyone else's eyes apart from my own, and in that log book I record the absolute truth about everything. It's not there to impress anyone or influence anyone, it's just there to record the absolute truth. I can remember very clearly in the lead-up to the round-the-world race writing in my book, 'Be careful, don't be cocky, be professional, use everything that you have learned and look after you boat and your neck because you have only got one of each.'

I have had some tough times in my life, some really tough times, and I have always just gritted my teeth and said, 'I will not be beaten, I will not beaten, I will not beaten.' And that little mantra tends to get me through. As I wrote in my personal log book, don't be cocky, be professional, be careful, use every bit of knowledge that you have and hold your head up high. If you do all those things you are off to a pretty good start. I believe that you can achieve anything that you wish to in this life — if you don't achieve it you didn't want it enough.

Everyone gets knocks, but I think that sometimes a hard knock or fear of failure, fear of the event, can be a great catalyst in motivating you. A good fright is sometimes good for you.

Michael
KLIM

Michael Klim was born in Poland and came to Australia as a child. He and his family have also lived in India, Canada and Germany. While the family home is in Victoria, Klim is a scholarship holder at the Australian Institute of Sport and lives in Canberra. After failing to live out his dreams in Atlanta at the Olympic Games, he came home and trained harder in his quest to be the best in the world. Today Michael is considered one of the most popular of Australian swimmers. He has a very impressive record, including titles at: the 2001 World Championships in Fukuoka in the 4 x 100 metres freestyle relay; the 2001 Goodwill Games, Brisbane, in the 100 metres butterfly; the 2000 Olympic Trials 100 metres freestyle; the 2000 Olympic Games, Sydney, in the 4 x 100 metres freestyle and the 4 x 200 metres freestyle (in a world record); the1999 Australian Championships, Melbourne, in the 100 metres butterfly; the 1998 World Championships, Perth, in the 200 metres freestyle and butterfly; and the 1998 Commonwealth Games, Kuala Lumpur, in the 100 metres freestyle. He was the star of the 1998 World Swimming Championships in Perth, where he picked up seven medals including a remarkable four golds and was named Male Swimmer of the Meet.

We lived in Bombay for four years, when I was between the ages of one and five, and because of the climate we went to the pool every day. That's how I became familiar with the water. Because of my dad's work commitments we travelled around the world a lot. We ended up coming to Australia in 1989 from Canada — before that we were in Germany, and Poland, where I was born.

The thing that stayed constant throughout all these different moves, travels, was my swimming and my interest in sport. Even though I was changing languages, schools, friends, what I could always be comfortable with was swimming. I guess as a kid you know what elite professional sport is but you don't really comprehend it — up until the age of 14, maybe 13, I'd say I was just doing it because I loved it.

I went to practice and training and I was competing, but I wasn't like kids are today, saying, 'I want to be the greatest swimmer of all time.' I just enjoyed myself, and I think that's the key. As a kid I used to knock on Mum and Dad's door to come and take me to training, not the other way around.

My parents gave me the opportunity to do a lot of different things and I was always very sport-orientated. As a youngster I played a lot of sports, from tennis to basketball to surf life-saving. That's where my talent lies, but then I even streamlined that. I basically found that my talent, my inspiration, was in swimming.

My parents never really pushed me; they just saw the joy I was getting out of it. I finished training at 9.30 this morning after starting at 7, and I was thinking how nice is it that I can do something that's a healthy lifestyle, in various climates, and still be a professional as well. I consider myself very lucky.

It's hard to go back to what you were thinking as a teenager. It's really clear for me now where I am going and the steps I want to take, but back then … you are so keen on racing the next weekend and trying to improve, it's great being able to challenge yourself all the time. And training … I would get up and always try to do my personal best times at training just because it was fun and challenging and I could do it. At 14, 15 I was probably one of the most successful juniors in the country, with six or seven gold medals in the national titles. That's when some of the coaches started taking notice of me, and I was invited to join the elite squad in Canberra at the age of 16. So I moved away from Melbourne and from my parents. That was a really big move in my life. I had just finished school and I was blasted into this professional environment where I was training with Alexander Popov and Gennadi Touretski. I was just a junior swimmer. That was an eye-opener, but I knew that this was what I had to do. It was the turning point in my career, being in that environment. It was hard, but I was very keen to go to Canberra and I was very keen to learn. The hardest part was leaving my parents, my family.

My first three years in Canberra, from the end of 1993 to my first Olympics, were a very hard time. I was trying to make the transition from junior athlete to professional and it took me quite some time to learn how to train and how to get the right mental approach to world sport.

I was very privileged to work with a very intelligent and knowledgeable man, Gennadi Touretski. I would say he is the most gifted coach I have ever worked with. Basically, what he taught me was that I got my confidence from training and the pool — the things I learned in the pool made me confident and made me believe in myself. I never really relied on the psychologists or people like that. He was my mentor and he guided me through those tough times. I guess I was also fortunate to be able to swim alongside Alex Popov, who was a great example.

So for the first three years I was just trying to build an image of myself that I was happy with. I knew that I couldn't be the same as Alex Popov — obviously everyone's different, with a different personality — but I was trying to shape myself. I had a vision of the guy that I wanted to be. I guess I was trying to make sure that what people perceive of me is how I see myself as well. You know, a lot of the time it's the complete opposite, but I think in sport you have to keep yourself within those boundaries.

By 1996 I had developed a mentality that worked for me for the next few years — every time I got on the block I tried to break the world record, even though sometimes I was a long way off. And I was very aggressive. I raced over 150 times a year for about three years. I put myself through this regime, making it second nature and having that sort of aggression all the time.

In 1997 I broke my first world record. 1998 was my breakthrough year but it had taken me until 1997 to be really successful. Even though I was practising all that time, I wasn't always very successful until then.

I enjoyed the whole process. Getting up in the morning for training was not a big issue for me, and I enjoyed doing the work. Gennadi used to say 'you have to listen to your muscles', and I enjoyed listening to my muscles — that was something that always kept me mentally stimulated.

People who are passionate about what they do and love what they do seem to get better results. This is a fundamental that we, as athletes, have in sport and carry over to life in general. Once I started realising I had the potential to be one of the best, obviously I tried to become the best, tried to make it a reality. I guess we are very privileged to be living at a time — and in a country — where swimming has reached the same sort of level that we had back in 1956, and where swimmers are placed on a pedestal compared with other big athletes.

I am very privileged to be swimming at the same time as Ian Thorpe, because we probably won't see a swimmer like him for a long time. These things are working in my favour. I have followed Kieren Perkins and Susie O'Neill, and broken some of the boundaries in endorsements. Endorsements took the burden off me psychologically. Once the results came, the security came as well. I knew that financially I could get on and enjoy it. As a junior, I never expected that to happen. People are starting to really regard us as professional athletes. It's a great time to be involved in elite sport.

Most of my challenges have been recent ones. At the start of 2001 my coach was suspended from the Institute of Sport because of drug allegations, so I could no longer be coached by him. That was the first obstacle. A couple of months later I broke my ankle. I went to the World Championships, swam with a broken ankle, came back and had an operation in September 2001. My back was also progressively getting worse, and by the end of January 2002 I had a back operation.

I missed out on the Commonwealth Games, the Pan-Pacific Games, and swimming freestyle at the World Championships. Those challenges have been both mental and physical. People say, 'Find something positive out of it.' So I did. I have been on the swim team since 1995 and I hadn't had a break, a competitive break, since then. I used the time as both a physical and mental break, a chance to rebuild my body — shoulders, back, ankles, everything. The year's schedule for swimmers has been very intense. People don't realise that that takes a lot out of you. I have been quite lucky that I have not had to endure that and I can go into next year with full gusto. So that's my positive side.

On the other hand, though, you know there are always times when you ask yourself whether or not, with all these injuries, you will be able to get back to where you were — or even better. Sometimes you see athletes who have been injured come back better than they were before; you also see some who never come back. The ones that do are a great example — Petria Thomas, for instance, has had two shoulder reconstructions; she is 27 or 28, and she is swimming faster than she ever has before. Sometimes you doubt your passion, but through this injury my passion has been greater than it was before. The results are not evident at the moment, but I hope they will show later.

This year I've been slowly climbing back up. I had my first race recently in Melbourne and I was quite successful — two wins out of two swims. It's good to come back on a winning note. I think things have turned around.

My vision is to see if I can get a personal best again. I think if I can achieve that, the results will follow in terms of Olympic golds and world records. The worst thing is that my personal best *is* a world record, so it's not hard to work out that if I can get to that level and a little bit better I will be very competitive.

I have recently taken a bit more initiative with my training and approach. Not having Gennadi on the side of the pool every day has been challenging, but I still keep in contact with him on the phone. I have a new coach and I have been working with him, but I have taken more initiative in guiding myself.

I want to have a good balance: be married with kids, be financially secure and be healthy and not have to worry about injuries. I just want to enjoy life. Balance is something that Gennadi was very strong on; I started university but I dropped out. I was constantly being educated by him — he would give me things to read and he would question me on them. We would regularly go to the National Gallery of Australia in Canberra and walk through it; he was my tutor in life.

He would make sure that we had a really good balance and an understanding of different aspects of life; we wouldn't just stay inside the boundaries of swimming. He opened my eyes. I like art, I like architecture and things like that, and basically

I consider myself in many aspects a normal person; I just have a very big interest in a certain area. I still enjoy dining out, going to the beach, just the normal things.

My first coach said to me when I was 13 — I still remember it to this day — that I would be a world record holder, an Olympic gold medallist. I was saying, 'Yes, yes, I will be.' Then he also said, 'Remember, it's nice to be important, but it's more important to be nice.' I was 13, so I said, 'I am probably not going to remember that', but I do.

It helps to smile. I am very happy. I am very privileged to have a very supportive family and crew to work with, and I always feel that if things aren't going my way there are people I can talk to who will support me no matter what — if I don't win or if my swimming career finishes today because I am injured, or whatever. If I don't feel the passion or the love isn't there any more, I will always have that support.

I think that's a big thing in life. If you have an environment that is supportive and conducive to a healthy and beneficial lifestyle, the only thing limiting you is your personal ambition, your drive. If you have ambition and drive and ability, and you enjoy what you're doing, there is nothing stopping you.

Early in my career I put a lot of pressure on myself. I still do that, but I don't feel there is pressure from any external source now. Susie O'Neill says something pretty interesting, that 'success doesn't make me full, it makes me hungry for more'.

Getting to the top has required knowledge and experience, and I have had to gain those step by step. Knowledge, experience and confidence are all part of the bridge, but really knowledge. You have to learn. Anyone can create that bridge if they learn. Experience just means you have to try time and time again. And how do you build confidence? By trying, over and over again.

Strategies for living
YOUR DREAMS

Starting your day with thanks Do we truly matter? Would the world be any different if any one of us had not been born? But we were born. Think of it: an amazing miracle of birth occurred just so that each one of us could be here right now. The very fact that you are here, in this place, at this time, and with these opportunities available to you, means that there is something to be done. Something that only you can do.

So each morning, as soon as you wake up, take a moment — the first moment of your new day — to acknowledge and give thanks for another day. Say, 'Thank you, God, for giving me life. Thank you for making my existence significant. Thank you for putting me on Earth with a distinct and unique mission: to make a difference.'

Try to make this your first conscious thought of the day, and these the first words you speak. Train yourself to do this every morning, and your entire life will gain a new, sharper focus.

By acknowledging, as soon as you wake up, that today is another day and that yesterday is gone, and that you are unable to change or alter what might have occurred, you start with a clean slate and with another chance to move up the ladder of life.

Beginning your day with such thoughts will make you handle life differently. You will find that things are put into perspective as you begin your day by acknowledging the deeper meaning and purpose of your presence in this world. This new approach will create a more meaningful life for you and your family.

Strategies for living
YOUR DREAMS

'I made a mistake' — say it. It's liberating When it comes to mistakes, the first thing is admit you made a mistake. It takes guts to say, 'I made a mistake', but say it. It's liberating.

We all make mistakes. That's a part of life. But like a child who touches a fire after being told not to go near it, we learn better when we make mistakes. We have to experience the mistakes.

Experience is the best teacher you can ever have. Books just tell you what is. Experience tells you how things really are.

Expect to make mistakes. No one is perfect, and no one can do everything perfectly all the time. If you expect yourself to do everything perfectly you put unnecessary pressure on yourself and cause yourself needless stress. Take the pressure off yourself and begin viewing your mistakes as opportunities you can learn from.

ROSS
LANE

At the age of 37, Ross Lane is the Managing Director of the OrotonGroup. Oroton International was founded in 1937 by Ross's grandfather. Ross, who has an entrepreneurial flair and style of his own, is highly driven and passionate and knew from an early age that his goal was to run Oroton. This may be attributed to the endless weekends and holidays Ross spent at Oroton unpacking boxes or observing meetings. With no tertiary qualification, Ross has worked in all facets of OrotonGroup's business since 1988. He was appointed MD in November 1996 and Chairman in 2001.

My grandfather started the business in 1937, and it was incorporated in 1938. He started it as a trading company. He would go to Japan and buy fabric, bring it home and sell it here — he was buying mill fabric and selling it to makers here. At one point I know he was selling the fabric to companies who were making clothing for the army. The information that was passed down was sketchy, because my grandfather died when I was 12.

There are some interesting things about the way he did business versus the way we do business now. My grandfather's secretary started working for us when my father was 18 months old, and she only left here about eight or ten years ago now. She was with the company for 52 years, and I learned more from her over the years than I might have, because my father wasn't there. For one thing, a business trip back then took three months. It used to take three weeks on a boat to sail to Japan, there would be a week of celebrations because he had arrived, a week of business, a week of celebrations because he was leaving and then three weeks back on a boat. So a buying trip took the best part of three months — today, a junior can order bulk fabric over the Internet or by email and it happens instantaneously.

It would have been a very different style of business and life back then, obviously. I know that when my father received a letter, the whole management team would get involved in the response, to make sure all the t's were crossed and the i's were dotted, and the communication was absolutely 100 per cent correct. I just wonder what went on for a lot of the time between the business trip and receiving the fabric and then selling it. A different pace!

I was given the opportunity to enter this company by my father. It was an opportunity that was made clear to me over the years as I grew up, and it was something that I always wanted to do — well, except for the time when I wanted to be a tractor driver or train driver — I wanted to run Oroton. I am not sure if I really contemplated what that meant until I was actually running Oroton but it was always a goal: 'I want to run Oroton.'

I do remember at one point during school — and this might not be the most potent point but it is a point — when I looked at all the colleagues in my year, I knew there wasn't one person who wanted to get involved in the handbag industry. So I figured that if there was not one person in the whole year getting involved in the handbag industry, and every woman has handbags, I had a pretty good chance of doing well, there was not a lot of competition out there. Mind you, there were a lot of people wanting to be doctors and lawyers and I could see that they were up for competition. So I suppose that was a bit of practical observation, and a sense that I could make my life a little easier by choosing this occupation. But it was also about controlling my own destiny.

There is something else that I did realise. I was in New York doing business with a guy who owns — or did own — 50 per cent of DKNY and 50 per cent of Anne Klein. This was my first meeting with the company, and he looked at me and he said, 'You look pretty young — how long have you been in the business?' My instant answer was, 'Thirty years.' I was thirty years old at the time. He looked at me as if to say, What do you mean? I said, 'Well, the business is in my blood.' I have always felt that. I suppose it comes from being a family business, and going into the warehouse in school holidays and weekends to unload stock as it came off the boat. I always thought that running the business would be good. My father had encouraged me to be involved in the business and I don't think I ever looked elsewhere. Why would I?

It was a public company when I joined — it had just gone public, and the obligations of a public company were very different from what I had seen as a child watching my father. In a public company everything becomes very professional, and a lot of the advantages of being private were no longer there. So I grew up in the environment of a public company, whereas my father had not. And that meant that more professionalism was required.

The biggest challenge was having people within the business see me for who I am and what I do, rather than just as my father's son. That was always, constantly, the biggest challenge. I am glad to say I am over that now, but it was certainly a challenge knowing that I could walk into a meeting and because I was my father's son I would be treated differently than if I was the product manager for XYZ. I think there was also an expectation from some people in the family that I knew what I was doing because I was my father's son. But really I needed to go through a significant learning curve.

I am not tertiary qualified. I flunked school — I had no interest in it. I was the only person in my year not to apply for university. The headmaster came to ask me, 'Why didn't you? You are the only one who hasn't applied. Let's put your name down.' I said, 'I have no interest in going to university — I know exactly what I am going to do.' The school tried to talk me out of that.

I felt quite sorry for my colleagues at school, because they didn't know what they wanted to do. They were going to university because they had nothing better to do. I knew exactly what I wanted to do, and university, whether I did or did not get in was not going to change what I wanted to do. I felt relatively driven, and I think that tenacity was always there. I was always going to run this company. If there was a hurdle in my way I needed first to understand what the hurdle was and then try to get over it, get round it, break through it, whatever the case was, because I was going to get over it — there was no doubt about that.

I believed then that university would not help me get to the position of running the company. Now perhaps that was naïve, I don't know, but again, I am my father's son and my father failed school. He left school when he was 13 or 14, and he has openly not had a lot of time for academia when it comes to running a business. I did finally go and study a tertiary course — I did an accounting course to understand the basic principles of accounting, which helped me, but I must admit, I learned much more on the job then I ever could have at university.

I spent a lot of time talking to people in the business, trying to understand exactly what they were doing. I also realised that having a goal of running the business is one thing, but I wasn't going to get to the position of, say, managing director and then automatically be successful. Running the business entails running the business successfully, and to do that you need to be doing certain things. I needed to understand how business worked and I needed to understand how to read the business. You can read a business from balance sheets and profit and loss statements, but you can also read a business by smell. How you come to get that, I don't know, but there were a number of people in the business at various times whose gut instinct I respected, and I would often spend a lot of time with them, trying to understand that if they thought there was a problem under a particular rock, why they thought that. So a lot of it is gut feel.

If you have the opportunity to get somewhere, the first question that has to be asked is: Do you want to get there? And do you want to take all the benefits that will result *and* all the negatives — because everything has pros and cons. Then if the goal is where you want to be, you need to decide what you need to get there. If tertiary requirements are mandatory, then you need to have tertiary education — if you want to be a doctor or a lawyer you can't do it without going to school — but if you want to be in business, you don't have to go to school. As we know, there are probably more people who do have an education than not, but I don't see tertiary education as a prerequisite to being successful. If it makes you more comfortable in getting to your goal, or if it is the ultimate thing in getting to your goal, then go and do it, but I don't think it is mandatory.

A guy giving a lecture in the States said that if you look at the top 20 richest people in America, 14 of them are self-made — they worked for themselves, didn't go to university.

The six of them who aren't self-made worked for one of the other 14.

I balance work and family very well, I think. First, I live up the road from work, and second, I have a very understanding family. There are certain times when I am at work at 4.30 in the morning but there are other times where I will knock off at midday. Thirdly, we have a very good team here now. We have been able to delegate responsibility and let people be responsible for their actions, which means that my position is not so much a hands-on position any more, it is more of a strategic position. It is a coaching position, a relationship position with certain key customers and the investment community. If you understand that, then you know I don't need to be here at 9 a.m. every Tuesday morning. So I take the kids to school once a week and I am often home. I go home for lunch, I see the kids, I am often home at 5.30 in the afternoon so I get some good time with them before they go to bed.

This changes, too — at reporting time, half year and full year, my job gets a lot busier because the numbers are coming out and there are institutions and stockbrokers to talk to and things like that. But there are other times of the year where things slow down a bit and I take advantage of those times.

I had the tenacity to want to take an opportunity and deal with the positives and the negatives, but I was also very lucky to have the father that I had, because when he gave me the opportunity, when I became managing director, I *was* the managing director, he wasn't.

As MD it was my decision whether the company was going to turn left or right or go up or down, whatever it might be. And my father let me run the business; he wasn't all over me. We talk — we have a very good relationship — and he has a different perspective to me and adds a lot, but at the end of the day it is my decision. I look around and I don't see a lot of father—son relationships where the father actually goes and hands it over. I think my father was 59 or 60 at the time, when he said, 'OK, you're MD' — and this company had been his life since he was 17.

That was something I do not take for granted; it was something I was given that was quite extraordinary. I think that has rubbed off on me in the way that I manage people: I don't sit over them. I expect that we will talk, discuss, and eventually get to where we think they need to go, and then it is up to them to get there.

I don't think we follow any rules or formulas from a book. I think what we do is pretty basic. I try to encourage a culture of co-operation within the management team. I also say to the guys who report directly to me, that at the end of the day their decision is their decision. I am happy to talk to them about it — I like to do that, I like to debate things with them — but they make the decisions. If you look at a decision made in the business, I often say the management team are 70 per cent of it and I am 30 per cent. If there is a problem I expect them to come to me with, 'OK, here is the problem, and here are three or four solutions that I have thought of', and we can go from there. In my mind it is more to do with culture than anything else. I think we remunerate our top people well, but I don't think we are absurd either. I don't think our shareholders would have a problem with the way we are remunerating them.

I think the success comes from the culture and the way that our business is set up. We have four distinct businesses. Each reports to me but there is a central one of the four, what we call operations, and operations provides services to the other three, so there is a lot of commonality between each of the other three businesses — what we call the front end. Our front ends are Polo, Oroton, Morrisey and Marcs.

It is a bit like sailing a boat. If you are going from here to a lighthouse, if that's the idea, so long as you get to the lighthouse — and I don't care if you have to tack four times, 400 times, or once on the way — if you get to the lighthouse that's all you have to do. I think that culture was born very much from my father. It's something I respect, and I think it is worth a lot. You never see it written down.

I like the idea that a rolling stone gathering no moss, of keeping the ball continuously moving forward, not becoming stagnant. I believe the world changes like that — what we know today is what we know today, but it is not what we are going to know tomorrow. We have to be open to change. That goes hand in hand with a saying: 'You know what you know.' This is quite profound, but it needs to go beside, 'But tomorrow you have the opportunity to know a lot more.'

That's always been important to me. Education is how you know what you know, but education is not just tertiary education. You can go out on the street and learn something. I have learned so much being on the street, travelling around the world, looking at cultures, being interested in people, because business is all about people, all about people's behaviour. So it's what you know and what you are prepared to know that is important.

Sophie
LEE

Well-known Australian-born actor Sophie Lee has graced our screens since the early 1990s, appearing in movies, television and on stage. She made her debut as the presenter of The Bugs Bunny Show in 1990. Most recently she performed the title role of Mim in The Virgin Mim for the Sydney Theatre Company. Previously she starred as Nina in the film He Died With a Felafel in His Hand and featured alongside Kate Winslet in Jane Campion's Holy Smoke. Other film credits include Muriel's Wedding, in which she played Muriel's arch-nemesis; The Castle, for which she was nominated Best Actress in a Supporting Role at the 1997 Australian Film Institute Awards; and the award-winning short film Titsiana Booberini.

I grew up in a suburb of Newcastle called Dudley — an idyllic suburb, with bushland and the beach. It remains to this day the most special place for me on Earth. My parents are academics. We grew up without a television, which meant that in our spare time my brothers and I would find other ways to occupy our time. I used to read a lot and write short stories. When I was about 11 there was a camp organised at my primary school for children who were interested in creative writing and drama. It involved going away for a long weekend to the Hawkesbury River and meeting with other children from the Hunter region and beyond. A local poet came to instruct and enlighten, and we dramatised one of his poems.

Anyway, that weekend was a mini-epiphany for me in terms of what I wanted to do with my life, which was acting. Even though I went to the camp for the creative writing side of things, in dramatising the poem I just felt this overwhelming kind of revelation.

So I went back to my parents and said, 'I know what I want to do with my life. I want to be an actress', and they said, 'Oh, you'll change your mind by next year', but I didn't. Every year my resolve strengthened and, from that age on, I pursued drama-related activities. There were really good drama groups in Newcastle, Young People's Theatre, repertory theatre companies, so I got involved with those after school a couple of days a week and Saturdays.

An actor's profession by and large is a very difficult road; it's almost like taking a vow of poverty. But if you have a real passion for it and it is all you want to do, you are willing to overcome the obstacles and you are willing to suffer — and you do. You really do suffer for your passion.

My parents are wonderfully loving and supportive, but were understandably concerned by my choice of profession, as it has little to offer by way of job security.

I suppose if a child came to me and said that they wanted to be an actor … well, you can tell if somebody really wants to do something. You know you can't dissuade them, but you encourage them to get advice from people all along the way. Like 'Have another trick up your sleeve, learn another trade, don't put all your eggs into that basket.' It's all great advice, but if you are really single-minded about what you want to do you don't want to give up because somebody has warned you against it. If you really love something and you get a lot out of it, then go for it.

Many of the greatest moments of my life have been on

stage or in front of a camera. Then I just feel completely and utterly content, fulfilled, elevated — but I am talking about a couple of moments a year! That is not a lot compared with the lows I have felt, which have been horrendous. Living in squalid flats, unemployed and asking, 'What am I doing? Is it worth it?'

A very frustrating part of being an actor is that you are at the whim of an indifferent machine unless you are writing your own pieces and performing them in the theatre — and even that is difficult. Actors feel frustrated creatively and financially. You can try to do other things; if you have another way to channel your creativity that is always a good thing. Over the years I did things like formed clubs with other out-of-work actors where we would write and try to keep our spirits up.

So if there is some way you can channel your creativity in your down time I would advise that. If there is a way that you can keep yourself afloat financially so that you don't end up taking jobs that are soul-destroying, you should do that too.

At 12 years old I told my parents, 'I want to be an actor and I want to do it now.' I didn't want to make a living out of it, but I wanted to get involved in a theatre group or something. We lived in Dudley and one of my teachers in Year 6 lived all the way across town in Lambton, where there was a drama group called '2 til 5'; I used to make him drive me there on Tuesday afternoons. You have to pester people to get them to facilitate you doing what you want, so joining repertory theatre was my first step.

I completed my HSC and then I wanted to jump straight into acting, so I left home. I got myself an agent and I did classes at the Australian Theatre for Young People and Playbox. I just did classes and went for auditions. I got my first acting job when I was 19 playing a corpse. I think I was alive for a couple of scenes and then I was a corpse for most of the rest of the telemovie. If you get one foot in the door then you can continue. When my agent said there was an audition for a job hosting a cartoon show for kids at 5.30 on weekday afternoons, I thought initially '$800 a week — or whatever it was — sounds good. $800 a week would fund acting classes and maybe I could save some as well.'

So I went for that audition with hundreds of people and I got the job. That show for Channel 9 became a huge success, a ratings winner, and I ended up having a huge media profile, which was something I had completely not expected. I was about 22 and I honestly thought, 'Who would watch a cartoon show for kids?' But it became very successful.

At school I was always really good at public speaking and won competitions. I like to be in front of the camera and I love to act most of all, but I also like public speaking, and although hosting something is a difficult job, I enjoyed it. So I did that show and I kind of got caught up in being very famous.

Then I auditioned for a show called *The Flying Doctors*, which was shot on film. And that was really my first big acting job. The day I got that I thanked God. I couldn't believe it. I was so grateful when I got that job. My cartoon show hosting was recorded all day Saturday, and then for the rest of the week I would work on *The Flying Doctors* from 5 a.m. until whatever time we wrapped. I really got to learn the ropes on that show, because they had brilliant actors and it was shot on film, as I said, which is unusual — a lot of TV shows are shot on video — so it was a quality show and I learned on my feet.

I also played in a band. I've always played musical instruments, from when I was little, and some my best friends wanted to be in a band ... so I had three jobs going. When I was little I played clarinet and euphonium, which is like a tuba but smaller — that was all they had in the school music cupboard the day they were handing out the instruments. I played with a brass band until I was 16. Then I worked in a milkbar, saved up my money and bought myself a saxophone, so I played saxophone from the age of 16 until I was 22, 23, when I was doing the cartoon show, *The Flying Doctors* and playing in a band.

The gigs were quite late at night, so it was a very big workload, including doing publicity for Channel 9. I was contractually obliged to do publicity for them and I was young and I wanted to do the right thing by them, but in retrospect, you really have to be careful with the publicity that you do. Sometimes you have to say no, but at that age I just wanted to do the right thing.

I became so swamped by the workload that I didn't realise I didn't have any perspective on my life. What I had always wanted to do was acting. I wanted to work in Australian theatre and film. All of a sudden my face was on the front page of *TV Week* and it wasn't about the work, and it had really kind of got out of my control. So after about three years when my contract was up for renewal with Channel 9 I walked away from it. It was a lot of money to walk away from, into the unknown, so it was scary saying, 'No, I am just going to focus on my acting and that's all I am going to do.' I had an introductory period where I had a retainer in the bank to look after me, and I was able to do what I loved, but I didn't have a clear picture of the true life of an actor. I quickly became aware of it.

The huge obstacle I had to overcome was finding really well-written Australian films and credible projects. I had this massive media profile but not much credibility. I had *The Flying Doctors*, but people didn't really take notice of that. It was more that I was famous for hosting a children's cartoon show. Journalists thought I was just a Channel 9 puppet, so I had a lot to prove to the press — and, I suppose, to myself. In interviews people would say, 'What are you trying to prove?' and I would reply, 'Look, I'm just trying to do good work'. I lived in a one-bedroom flat in St Kilda. Then I got a job in New Zealand, a mini-series, and worked over there for three or four months. When I came back it was welcome to real life.

That was a very confronting period for me because I had a lot of time to think about the whirlwind that I had just stepped out of — What did it all mean? What is life without working 15–18 hours a day? It really takes your mind off any problems you might have with yourself; there is no time to be introspective, which I hunger for sometimes. I didn't have loads of money any more but I would go down to buy milk and there I would still be on the front page of newspapers like the *Truth*, with articles saying horrible things about me. I ended up suing a newspaper, even though I didn't have any money to do it.

All this was like residue from a car accident, that I had to pick up the pieces of. I asked myself, 'Why did I do that cartoon show?' In retrospect, it was part of my journey. I was a young girl and it was a job opportunity, but at that time I was really self-critical: 'You shouldn't have done it, you should have focused on the acting.' So for the next couple of years I just did classes and fringe theatre.

I felt really depressed, felt that I had gone so far away from my goals. When I was really at my wits' end I went for an audition for *Muriel's Wedding*. When I read the script I thought, 'I would so love to be in this movie, it's so wonderful!' It was such a great part so I just went all out. I worked and worked on that audition, and I got dressed up in the costume and I went in really just thinking I was absolutely going to go for it and do it exactly the way I wanted to do it. If it didn't turn out, maybe it would be a sign that I should be doing something else.

Anyway, I got that part. The film was a joyous experience. It was a great success and it was good for me, because it meant I got a better class of auditions. I got to see directors who wouldn't normally see me.

Soon after that I auditioned for Robyn Nevin for the Melbourne Theatre Company's fortieth anniversary production of the classic Australian play *Summer of the Seventeenth Doll*. I got the part of Bubba, and that was wonderful too. When I was a 12-year-old girl I would say, 'I would like to work for the MTC or STC or to do a great Australian film', so that was really my goal. It wasn't to be on the cover of magazines or to be a movie star or anything; it was to be an actor. I guess that sounds like a simple goal.

I got very defensive about auditioning for parts in films that were the decorative female — the girlfriend or the girl in the red dress. I was quite bolshie and militant about it: 'No, I am not going for that, I want to go for parts that have nothing to do with what I look like. It's not about what I look like.' I did this to the point where I was almost cutting off my nose to spite my face.

I love doing comedy and I don't think there is any future in playing a decorative female. What's going to happen to you when you are 35? You can't be decorative all your life and there is always somebody younger and prettier. My career has to be more than that, but … life for an actress often ends around 40 anyway, so my advice would be that if there is a job that is not offensive and you can find a way of bringing something great to it, then do it. It's just that I really had something to prove, so I went out of my way to go to the other extreme.

There are daily challenges, and there are people who are

suffering to a far greater extent than an out-of-work actor in Australia. There are people in war-torn countries and children who do not have enough to eat. I can only talk about my own experience. After jumping over that hurdle, from about the age of 26 to 31 I had a steady stream of work in theatre and film and interesting, colourful kinds of support roles.

When I was 29 I was very excited to audition for Jane Campion, who is a hero to most actors, and got the part in her film *Holy Smoke*. That was a really big deal for me. Obviously, as Kate Winslet was the lead, it was going to have a worldwide release. At that point I thought, 'Maybe I'll go to Los Angeles and see what it is all about over there.' It wasn't as if I had always wanted to work in Los Angeles; it was just that you get to a point as an Australian actor where you have worked in Australian stage, television and film and you have to go somewhere else. But then I did another couple of films here after that. I think if you constantly compare yourself with others, that way happiness doesn't lie. You can only do your own career, your own way, I suppose.

I went to LA to follow up *Holy Smoke*. I didn't really like it that much, and I started thinking about the rest of my life and what sort of a person I wanted to be. I suppose if I had to evaluate it, I think I had a problem because I was equating happiness only with work. If you are working all the time and your life is consumed with work, maybe you can get away with it for a while, until — God forbid — something happens to you, like you break a leg, but then you have to face yourself.

I went through another huge kind of upheaval: acting made me happy but it didn't feed everything I needed in my life. I started wondering what I might be thinking on my death bed — what would be important to me and what things would I like to have achieved? Would it be just doing another film and another film? There is so much more to life that I wanted to be able to embrace, and I suppose I wanted to come down to earth a bit.

During this time I became really quite deeply unhappy. I suppose you have to … it's like a snake shedding its skin or something, a transformation. It was the bleakest period of my life. It was really very difficult. From a career perspective it was as if I was looking for more harmony and a more complete picture, sort of being able to look outward instead of inward. As an actor you are always looking inward; it's quite a selfish existence in some ways. 'If I just do this role then I will show them.' It becomes very insular. There is always going to be someone with a better career than you and there is always going to be someone richer, prettier, younger. You have to make the most of what you have and not focus on what you don't have. I think that is a key to happiness.

I just started slowly rebuilding my life, piece by piece, block by block. Searching your soul and asking yourself what sort of a person you want to be, what sort of people inspire you. And it's not gorgeous models in magazines; to me it's people with humility and with families and with a sense of humour, people who do good work for the community and are passionate about what they do and are hardworking. In a way I suppose it is people who have a balance in their life. Also, I read some Aristotelian philosophy: *Nicomachean Ethics* is about having a balance, which is something that I realised I had never had. I think that if the going gets tough, if you don't have the foundations, the philosophical foundations to cope, you wobble and fall over.

You have to keep going, but realise that it's all by increments; you have to take small steps. If you want to achieve something great, you have to start by doing it small. You have to start by going to the '2 til 5' theatre on Tuesday afternoons.

Or if you want to write the great Australian novel, set up your office first and write for one hour every day — you're not just going to sit down and arrive at something great without struggle. I think you have to try to be humble and think of grace. Be determined. You can't give up.

You should love the steps along the way; you should love the rehearsal period or really enjoy your auditions or enjoy drama school. I think in our generation we are always thinking 'when I get to this point I will be happy', but really it's just doing the work along the way that makes you happy.

I wrote down the different areas of life, my career goals and ambitions, family, and let's say community — what you can give back or do to help the society that you live in. I imagined myself on my death bed, as I said before, and asked what I would like to look back and say I achieved, what was really important to me. That would include things like a happy marriage, plus fulfilling career goals, and something a bit selfless for others who are in need.

If you look at things in the long term, you have to start with, 'What can I do today towards that?' It might be that you're busy and your husband is busy, so maybe making time to have dinner together would be a good step towards building a happy marriage, which would involve communication, and making time for each other.

But like everything, I guess the message is that if you start small, eventually you will find that you have achieved a great deal.

Strategies for living
YOUR DREAMS

It's OK to pat yourself on the back You've achieved the goal you have set for yourself. Well done, you did it, wow! It's OK to tell yourself that. There is a time to feel satisfaction with what you have accomplished.

But if you want to continue to grow and reach new heights, you have to keep on 'lifting the bar'.

By taking on additional challenges, and by 'lifting the bar', you continue to expand your comfort zone and then break through your comfort zone. By doing this you will be able to face and overcome new challenges, or set and reach new goals, which will give you additional personal fulfilment and confidence, and propel you to new heights.

So accomplish, pat yourself on the back, treat yourself, reward yourself — and move right on. Take action! Lift the bar and continue up to the next stage.

Quang Luu

In 1975 Quang Luu escaped from Vietnam in fear of his life. After drifting around the Gulf of Thailand on a bamboo raft only 1.5 metres wide he got to a place of safety, and was fortunate enough to join his family in Australia. Quang set out to make the most of this second chance and his career has been wide ranging: he has worked as a lawyer, academic and was State Director of the Department of Immigration and Multicultural Affairs, the first refugee to occupy such a position. Quang has dedicated part of his life to helping people make a new home in Australia. This resulted in him becoming the Head of SBS Radio in 1989. Under his leadership, SBS Radio has grown into a national network on-air and online, bringing Australians of all backgrounds together to build a harmonious society. Broadcasting in 68 languages including English, SBS is the world's most linguistically diverse radio network.

Quang was named 'Australian Achiever of the Year 2002' by the Prime Minister, John Howard, and was appointed an Officer of the Order of Australia (AO) in June 2002. As Head of SBS Radio, Quang has worked to encourage a harmonious and cohesive society for all Australians.

As a person I would like to have a more peaceful world, a world without conflict, a world where human dignity is respected, and a world where children have every opportunity to reach their potential, a world where everyone lives in harmony. As Head of SBS Radio, my job is to make sure that our programs on air provide a link for Australians of all backgrounds, whether they are Jewish Australians, Asian Australians, European Australians or American Australians. Regardless of their heritage, they can understand one another and as a result of that understanding can live in a very harmonious and cohesive society.

I grew up in a country at war, like most other Vietnam-born Australians, and because of that experience it's very important for me to be able to see that the way ahead is open to all of us as human beings, without hatred, without conflict. I started my career in South Vietnam in the foreign service, where, admittedly, a diplomat is looking after the interests of his or her own country, but to do that is not inconsistent with creating an atmosphere where people can work together.

I work with people, going forward, and I think perhaps the first step is to try to convince other people around you to share your vision and together take the same steps towards a common objective. That is certainly important. The second step is to see the opportunity, and if the opportunity is not there you have to create the opportunity and then convince your people to go with you towards that common objective. In a very modest way I think that where I used to work, and certainly where I work now, at SBS, I have had a fantastic team of people who are creative, who are professional, who share the vision of Australia as a multicultural nation. We share core values, but at the same time we are proud of our traditions and retain what is good for ourselves in terms of our beliefs, but also what is good for the wider community in terms of our membership of that community.

In any environment, the art of being able to achieve is to have a good mix, a good balance of things that are achievable and that are consistent with one's principles. You can't have everything to your liking, but you also can't have everything fit your own goal without sharing that goal with other people, and sometimes you may have to share goals with other people, to ensure that whatever is ahead of you, you can achieve through teamwork.

There is one saying in Asia, and it's said so many times that it is very common knowledge: that the journey of 10,000 miles starts with one step. That one step is important, because it starts a process through which one can be successful, or less successful, or even fail. And that first step is having confidence: confidence in yourself, confidence in the good nature of your fellow human beings, and confidence that your vision can be achieved.

I think for me the first step is internal: you convince yourself, you think that you can do it, you think you can do it even without people to go with you towards a common objective. To me that first and most difficult step is to prepare yourself mentally.

You can't inspire other people unless you inspire yourself, unless you convince yourself absolutely that your vision is a correct one and that your goals are worth pursuing. Once you convince yourself, you can convince other people more easily. And in order to convince other people you have to be open-minded. You have to be receptive to good ideas from other people and you have to acknowledge that people are different. What we are looking for is the common, overlapping, shared values, but we also must allow people to have differences and we must respect that.

I go out a lot; I meet a lot with people of different faiths and different backgrounds. I feel very at home when I visit a synagogue. I feel very at home when I visit a mosque. I feel very at home when I visit a church, even though basically my religion is Buddhist. I am at home everywhere because I have convinced myself that every faith, from its own point of view, is advocating good deeds and good people. I think basically people are good, and what we need to do is unlock that good nature in people and convince them that we can work together and go forward.

And that's the first step, because it is always important to have action, to convince others. Even though once you take that action you know that you may not be 100 per cent successful. Taking action to achieve something is much, much better than not taking action. To use an analogy, when you try to cross from one side of a river to the other the current may be strong. The bridge — the vision — to the other side, the implementation of an idea, may not at the time be able to span the space, though the mental bridge can perhaps go from one side to the other side, or go to an island. We must not be afraid of taking the action even though we know the difficulties ahead.

Before I was appointed Head of Radio I had been working in the Human Resettlement Program area. I was the state director for the federal Department of Immigration and Multicultural Affairs (DIMA — then known as DIEA) in Sydney; I was responsible for the New South Wales office. Most people see the immigration department as something that controls the borders, which is fair enough because that is in the news all the time, but a very important part of DIMA is to resettle people, to give them assistance when they come, to give those people connection to the world, connection to Australian society. Having worked in that situation, I feel that I understand perhaps the fabric or at least part of the components of the essential society.

SBS Radio stands within the wider community as an

organisation, an instrument that helps provide necessary

information so that people will feel at home in Australia, to make their new life successful. That made me confident that I could do the job, I took the job and I pushed forward on what I believed was the correct path towards transforming SBS Radio into a multilingual, multicultural, Australian broadcaster.

I was a diplomat in South Vietnam, and after the fall of Saigon in April 1975 I became a marked person. I had to flee because of the threat of execution. Escape was on a very small bamboo raft in the Gulf of Siam. There were three of us in the middle of nowhere, with strong gales and heavy rain, and I was the youngest so I had to bail out the water, because physically I was the strongest of the three. We did not see anything but the sky and the water. I was in complete isolation, mentally speaking, even though I was in the company of two other people.

Then I decided there must be something that would show me that I was still part of the world, so I used the shortwave radio to try to capture some programs, and by chance I was able to tune in to the BBC and the Voice of America. And then I felt that I was part of the living world again, listening to people talk; I felt that they were talking to me.

That experience is something that remains in my mind all the time, it showed me the strength of radio. Wherever you are, if you can connect with a radio program you are part of the whole living world. So because of that experience I always wished that I could have the opportunity to be involved in what I think is a very important part of connecting people together.

I started my life in Australia as a researcher at the Australian National University. Because of my background I worked on the perceptions of players in a crisis. Let's use the Berlin crisis in 1948, when the Communists blockaded West Berlin, as an example. During the crisis there were various people acting in particular ways, using the perceptions and information available to them at the time. Then you look back, after the passage of time, with hindsight, and examine how people reacted and how they might have reacted given more or different information.

By doing that you learn a lot about history, about how leaders formulate policy or reformulate policy, follow one line of action or another line of action. The good leaders are always the ones with vision, the ones with the confidence in themselves to make the right decision, the ones who have good advisers around to make sure everything is looked at and examined before they make a decision.

So from that point of view I think teamwork is very important, but leadership is also important and vision is also important. When all those factors are put together, we have a good chance of achieving our goal.

I was fortunate that I was picked up by a trawler, a fishing boat, which brought me to Thailand and eventually I flew to Australia. Once I was here, I knew that myself and my family were OK, I could lead a normal life easily. I didn't need to be rich. I could have a good job and make a living, but is that meant to be life? Is it meant to be like that? I thought that I had an opportunity to give back, to return the hospitality, to return the kindness, to return the assistance that Australia had given me as a refugee when I came.

So I got involved in community work. I was involved in forming community groups, community associations, particularly for those communities that were not well organised, that did not have a voice, that did not have structure, that didn't know who or where to turn to. And that is how I got involved in work with the wider community, in the resettlement of the refugees from Indochina who were very much in the minds of people in the 1970s.

I have continued my voluntary work from then until now — I am still a board member of the Refugee Council of Australia — and in the process I came across so many good friends. So that enriched my life, and taught me many things, and that's the best reward that you can get as a human being.

To keep focused for a long period of time is difficult. You need to manage your expectations, and at work as well as home you have to be realistic. You have to be able to detach yourself sometimes, just to make sure that you are not tired, you are not burnt out, because the worst thing that can happen to you is that you have something in mind, you try to achieve something and you are burnt out and can't do it. That's a question of management: management of your expectations, management of your plan and working with other people.

I work very hard, focus on something I am trying to achieve and at some stage in the process I step back and look at it to see if in fact I am on the right track or not — because sometimes you are too close to it and you can't see it. So I overcome challenges and failures by taking one step back-wards, to look at how far I have gone and what we can do better.

I have a very understanding family. I am fortunate to have children who are now grown up and are professional people — they understand my desires, my aspirations, and most of the time they respect what I am doing and share my views on things. I think that's good and great encouragement so far as family is concerned. I don't think it is too difficult to balance work, community work and family obligations if you know how to use your time effectively.

I believe I use my time effectively. I won't sit in a room to be idle for three hours, for instance; I like to do something. Doing something could be playing with the children, playing with my grandchildren or talking to the neighbours. That is something that you need to do to make sure you are not too focused on something all the time, or becoming burnt out.

Don't be afraid to take that first step, even though that first step may not be successful. That's important — we can learn from our failure as well as from our success, so take the first step and make sure that if it fails, you learn from the mistake and take another step. The worst thing that could happen is not do anything, or to take the first step and then, when it fails, stop and not do anything — because then I think most of the strength, most of the vision, will be wasted.

A vision has to be realised, a vision has to be pursued; you can't have a vision and do nothing.

In life I have failed many times as well as succeeded many times. And I think the point is don't be disappointed, don't be discouraged, learn from the mistakes and move forward.

We live in a very good democracy, Australia. I believe it is a very good democracy. But a great democracy can be even better if the majority doesn't ignore the needs of the minority. Australia as a democracy can be an even better one if the majority is caring, gives assistance to the socially disadvantaged, like the indigenous people, and the majority should have a caring, giving approach to those who are in need of a home because they are victims of human rights violations.

John
McGRATH

Having grown up living above his dad's pub in Bexley, John McGrath started his career at 17 as a trainee car salesman, earning $59 a week. Not satisfied, he moved into real estate two years later. Founder and chief executive officer of McGrath Estate Agents, the largest privately owned residential real estate agency in Australia, John McGrath is today considered one of the most influential figures in the Australian property industry.

John has become a well-respected spokesperson for the industry, both in Australia and internationally. He has also published two bestselling books. McGrath Estate Agents has received the NSW Real Estate Institute's Best Overall Marketing Campaign Award twice, and in 1994 and 1995 also won the award for Best Corporate Image. In 2003, it won the best website for the year at the awards. Channel Nine's 60 Minutes featured John as one of Australia's three most successful young entrepreneurs. In 2003 John McGrath was listed eighteenth in BRW's list of richest young Australians.

The thing that got me into real estate was that I wanted to get into a business that I thought was important in the community. Property, whether you're renting or buying, is your home, your base — it's where you start and where you finish. I originally started selling cars. I found that I could sell and I learned how to sell better but I wasn't passionate about it, so I transferred into property. Then I thought, if I'm going to be in property, I'd like to work for myself and take control of my own destiny, and if I'm going to work for myself I want to have the best company on the planet.

So I guess the vision was to create the world's best real estate company. I wanted to create a total solution focused on the customers: working out what their needs were and how we could support them. I wanted to change the way real estate is bought and sold — to put control in the hands of the consumer, not the agent. That's the path we continue on to this day — at management meetings we ask, 'Is it world's best?'

Why do we want to be the best? Because I think the best lead change, create a revolution; employees love being part of the best. They love being part of something different — customers benefit, clients benefit, shareholders ultimately benefit, and it's also a pretty cool place to be. I say to people, have fun — you're going to be here a third of your life! I say this to my office juniors: if you're photocopying paper be the best photocopier in the world, and if you're going to go up the street and get lunch or coffee for clients, do it fast, do it efficiently and add value — give a smile to the person who's serving you. We see ourselves as a learning organisation and a teaching organisation; we recognise that we have an influence in the community, because we get people coming here from everywhere — students for work experience, junior staff, customers, first home buyers. It's wonderful being able to inspire those people.

I gave a talk last night to a small business group and I gave another one this morning; two different groups, probably a total of about 600 people. I know that if you drop a pebble, there's a ripple effect — someone might walk away with a new idea. They talk to their kids, they talk to their boss, they talk to their staff, they talk to their boyfriend or girlfriend ... That can have a positive impact, so we embrace that within the business. We want to have an impact, so if we go out there, give great service and inspire someone to buy a good home from us while feeling good about it and enjoying the process, that's going to have other ramifications. Pay it forward!

I didn't do well in school, so I ended up with a lousy mark — which is what I deserved — and didn't get into university or any further education. I was 16, 17, staring at a fairly bleak future. I guess I made a decision then that I had to dramatically change what I was doing with my life; I had to stop blaming teachers, peer groups and my parents. I knew that if my life was going to change, I had to change.

So I started reading. Books were important to me — they were inspiration, they were access to new information, they were a vision of what other people had been through. I read about the Grafs, the Lowys — people who made the challenges I felt I had seem totally insignificant. Here was I complaining about X, Y and Z while reading about people who were lucky to get out of prison camps with their lives; they came to Australia with five dollars, nothing else, and they've created empires and changed their lives. I think reading a story about someone who had initial challenges and overcame them — not only overcame them, but went to the whole next level and changed their life — can be a life-changing catalyst.

That's why I tell it warts and all when I give speeches. I tell them about the mistakes I've made, the stupid things I've done, the failures I've had, because you relate to that better. If people think, 'Hang on, you were at a point where you had to worry about if you could pay next week's rent?' and you say, 'Yes, I was there not that long ago', and tell them the whole story, then they really start paying attention and listening to you.

Going back to my late teens, I'd been successful in the

sporting arena at school. I'd been a very good footballer, on the way to being a professional footballer, and I wanted to leave school but my mother encouraged me to stay on. That was a real crossroads of my life, because I thought, well, I'm only good at sport, I'm not really good at things to do with the mind. But then I thought, 'Well, hang on, why am I good at sport?' I was good because I was disciplined, I was focused, I watched what other good sportspeople did and I'd go and practise that by myself. I started thinking that if I could do all those things on the sporting oval, I could do them in the world of business, too.

I figured I had to have good people skills. I had to be intuitive, I had to have common sense, I had to be hungry and I had to be persistent. I figured I had all those traits anyway through sport — it was as if a light globe went on, as if someone had said, 'You know you can do all of this'. That's where I started. Then I realised that all the things I was learning at tech, or in the book I read at night before I fell asleep, or at a seminar during the day, I could put into practice in my workplace. And it worked! If the book said write goals, I wrote goals, and all of a sudden I started reaching them. If someone said, 'Product knowledge is critical, so you have to study it as you would for a test,' I would go and read contracts and leases and attend auctions and find out what properties were selling and leasing for. I built up this bank of knowledge and it worked. I'd give a presentation and someone would say 'What did this sell for?' or 'What's that worth?' and I would know. It gave me self confidence.

So I started realising that all this stuff really works. It's not just theoretical, it's real. That's when I changed, and to this day it's just a constant process, like going to the gym — you've just got to keep doing it. I read every night, I listen to tapes every day, I try to meet as many inspirational people as I can,

I try to teach as often as I can — speaking, lecturing, whatever — because I am learning when I am doing that. It's all a lot of fun.

I started getting really clear about what I wanted in my life. Until then I was just living day by day, which a lot of people do. I went to a seminar and the guy on the stage said, 'Write down everything you want your life to look like for the rest of your life.' I had never done that. It was actually quite intimidating — it was hard trying to design on paper a life that bore no resemblance to the life I was actually living. But I took a leap of faith and said, 'I'll just pretend it will happen — I'll pretend I can drive this car and have this company.' And then it just started happening. The first thing is getting really clear what it is you want.

The second thing was creating lots of small wins. Every day I wrote down what worked and what didn't work and what I learned — little wins. Just getting a little piece of business that was really important for me, or getting a compliment from a customer built my confidence (I did not have a lot of confidence then).

Another thing I worked on was relationship building — looking after people I came in contact with, whether they were suppliers or customers or staff. Just looking after them, treating them with common courtesy — even just saying please and thank you — is incredible. Be a mensch! It's such a great thing, and so few people do it. It costs you nothing, but it gives the other person a great gift. When you say, 'Thanks very much, I really appreciate you doing X, Y and Z', you give that person a little confidence boost, and it doesn't cost you anything.

When I was young I had to take a jump in my life, because I was not on the right track. I was travelling down the absolute wrong track and instead of just trying to incrementally improve that — it might have worked — I decided it would be better to say, 'Hang on, I'm probably on the wrong road here. I have to really reassess what I want. Who's achieving what I would like to achieve and how do they do it? Let me speak to them, let me read about them, let me listen to them.'

I sat down with a lot of my friends and told them that I was choosing a new direction. I wanted them to know, and I said, 'I'd love you to support it, but if you don't agree with it, that's fine too. It's your choice.' It's funny how that polarised people; I would say about half my friends said, 'Good on you. I'll support you,' and they cheered me on from the sidelines. The other half said, 'I don't want to know about you if you don't want to cut school, if you don't want to go here, if you don't want to do this — you must be crazy.' I had to accept that; it's part of the painful process of growing. I guess I had to break away from some of my peer group — those who wanted to head in a different direction.

I think that's one of the challenges for young people today — not enough people have the guts to actually create their own path. They think it's easier to just say yes to things, whether it's drugs or drink or cutting school or goofing off at work or complaining or whatever.

Changing my habits was another challenge. I think habits are either great things or terrible things — exercise is a wonderful habit, and giving people positive strokes and recognition is a wonderful habit, but there are so many negative habits too. Changing habits, changing your environment, is difficult — there are many nights you lie awake and hope you're on the right track, because you are fracturing yourself from your past.

Also, I was going into the unknown. I had done no business courses and I didn't have any capital. I didn't have any family history in the world of business, so it was really new stuff for me. That was a challenge. I just had to take the leap of faith and say, 'Well I'm just going to believe I can do it even if I have no basis for that belief.'

There's loneliness going that way, when everyone else is out in the pub drowning their sorrows and you're at home sweating for an exam at tech or getting a good night's sleep so you can start work early the next day. There's a degree of solitude and isolation that's not bad for a period of time — it's quite a nice thing to do and it gives you some clarity, some time to think. A lot of people don't give themselves time to think; they surround themselves with clatter and noise and chaos. I learnt meditation at a fairly early age, and that was a great thing, because it taught me how to go into a quiet space.

Another challenge for me was that my father passed away when I was 19. He died as an alcoholic. I think that's one of the reasons I've never drunk. It was his disease, something he was never able to get on top of. Then my mother moved to Melbourne when she remarried. A journalist interviewed me about two months ago and said it sounded as if I was abandoned. I said it certainly wasn't like that to me. When my mother remarried, she went to Melbourne with her new husband, as you would expect her to; I had to decide whether to follow her or stay and really consolidate my life in Sydney. I decided to do that. I was still playing sport up here, my social group was up here, my new place of work was up here — I didn't want to move.

People tell me it sounds as if my family was dysfunctional. Yes, my mother and father got divorced, my father died from alcoholism, my mother remarried and moved to Melbourne, but they were all opportunities for me — they weren't calamities. They were really opportunities for me to stand on my own two feet. Whatever these circumstances might look like to an outsider, to me they are things that made me independent and resilient and focused, and I don't see any of those things as bad.

One of my philosophies is that everything that happens to you happens for a reason that serves you. There's a purpose and a reward in everything, whether it is the company having financial troubles in the early days or a problem in your family life. All these 'challenges' have helped make me the person I am today. A lot of people look at challenges as excuses; I look at them as opportunities. We all have stuff that doesn't go right — diseases, relationship fallouts, economic cycles, all sorts of things that are not exactly as we want them. If we focus on the negative we will find negatives for ourselves, and if we focus on the positive we will see incredible opportunities.

A lot of people who have had an alcoholic father have become heavy drinkers themselves. They say, 'Well, with a father like mine, what would you expect?' I had an alcoholic father and became a teetotaller. That was a role model I didn't want to follow, because it led to his demise. The same set of circumstances or similar circumstances can lead different people in very different directions, depending on whether they see the glass as half full or half empty. This applies to every situation — so many great learning opportunities go by because people never see them. They're not looking for them. They say, 'Oh what a disaster! I can't believe this, I'm getting divorced (… or I am going bankrupt, or my business is challenged)' instead of saying, 'Where is the gift?' The gift in terms of divorce might be understanding that you were infatuated with your business instead of your partner. Maybe you learn a lesson going forward — make sure you don't take the same mistakes into the next relationship. A lot of people blame their partner — she was this and she didn't do that — rather than understanding the lesson: for the next one, I'm going try a whole lot harder. Those people really have lost everything.

I read a book called *Think and Grow Rich* by Napoleon

Hill (Fawcett Books, reissued 1990). It recommended living your life in day-tight compartments, so that when you are faced with the possibility of being overwhelmed, you just say, 'I only have to get to the end of this day; everything will be OK tomorrow.' It is a belief structure, where you always say, 'Whatever this is, it won't kill me; it will pass. There might be a bit of pain in the process but I can get through it.' I believe that I'll get through everything, that everything that happens to me has a purpose and that anything that doesn't destroy me makes me stronger. So I say, 'OK, I can get through this. There will be some pain — I'll mitigate that pain and I'll control any damage that I possibly can — but at the end of the day I'll be OK, and the focus bit is just focus till tonight.' That's how I stay focused.

I don't go out and socialise much. One, I don't like meeting lots and lots of people I don't know; I like coming across interesting people in my adventures. And, two, the real reason I don't go out is because I need that space at the end of the day to relax, restore my energy, get ready mentally and physically for the next day. For me it's been an important strategy — I need to give myself a break at the end of each day to recover from whatever challenges I've had.

The other thing I do is what I call a morning ritual. This is a set of questions I ask myself — they're actually laminated and on my shower wall — such as, 'What things are going right in my life right now?' Because people can have 150 things going right and one thing going wrong and where do you think their focus is? On the one thing that's going wrong. Rather than thinking about their kids and family — all the things that are going right — they think about the fact that their commission structure changed and they lost $50 on this month's pay cheque. Hello! There are more important things in life that you can focus on. I think asking myself these positive questions — 'What makes me happy? Who do I love and how can I show them?' — each morning works. It's like putting the right code in every morning. If I wake up feeling a little bit negative about this or that, I immediately go into the shower, look at the questions, and all of a sudden, bang! On the other side of the shower I'm focused and I'm excited, no matter what happened yesterday.

I used a metaphor in this morning's speech: it's like going to the gym — you can't not go to the gym for ten years and then go to the gym one day and expect to have physical fitness immediately. You have to keep going. There's some pain up front, but that gets better; you get stronger and you get used to it. It's the same with your mental gym, your attitude — you have to keep working on it. Even though I have some degree of ongoing momentum, I still have to keep working at it, so I keep reading the books, hanging out with the positive people. It's like compound interest — if you put a little bit more in every day, keep adding, it builds and builds. Definitely one can balance work and family. I don't think people need to compromise any more. In this place and in this time, with all our technology and with new views on life, you can have a brilliant business and a brilliant home life, and keep yourself physically fit.

You can keep your relationship very fresh, you just need to have an awareness and a focus on it. You can also run a great business, eight or ten hours a day, and have a lot of fun. I know I'm as balanced as I've ever been now — business has never been better, my physical life has never been better, my health and my relationships have never been better. I guess that's what balance is, but you have to have a belief structure around it. Some people say, 'I can't build a business any more because it will damage my relationships.' I'm saying, 'Hang on! Why don't you build a business and repair and enhance your relationships simultaneously? Why do you think you have to do one or the other?' Some people exhaust themselves — they say yes to too many things.

The main ingredient is belief in yourself, the second is attitude.

The other important thing is intention: you have to have a positive intention. I don't do business to make more money; that's a by-product. I do business to make a difference — I want people to learn and grow and become brilliant at what they do, and for customers to have wonderful experience, so my intention is very positive. I think a lot of people have goals, but their intention is questionable. This is where the integrity factor comes in. Back in the 1980s, many people made money short-term. Where did they end up? Many of them are dead, many of them are in jail, many of them have lost their money; very few have not had catastrophe fall upon them. I think this is because their intention was incorrect. The great lesson from the 1980s for all of us is that you can't build a business out of greed and self-interest; you have to have the community at heart. You can't rip people off. So even though it was a fairly distasteful decade in a lot of ways, there was a lot of great learning through all of it.

To someone from a similar background to mine I'd say take responsibility for your life. Don't blame anything or anyone, see everything that has happened to you as an opportunity to grow and enjoy the adventure. A lot of people think that they have to wait till they get 'there' to enjoy it; what I've learnt over the last 20 years is that there is no there, there is only here. I guess we've all heard that it's the journey, not the destination, that's important and that's very true. I heard that when I was young, but I didn't relate to it as much then as I do now.

I read an incredible book called *No Ordinary Moments* by

Dan Millman (Starseed Press, 1992). It talks about how every single moment in every single day is precious. There's a lot of people who are always waiting for the weekend, waiting for their holidays, waiting till they get a raise or a bonus — I'm saying don't wait for anything. Just go out there and do it today and enjoy it!

Someone gave me this quote by Robert Kennedy: 'Some men see things the way they are and say why? I dream things that never were and say why not?' I think that's it. Don't accept the status quo — yours or the planet's. Just say, 'Well, why couldn't there be world peace? Why couldn't I have a great company, and a great personal life, great physical balance and great spirituality?' If you look at things in a positive manner you just never know, you might get it all.

Strategies for living YOUR DREAMS

Love what you do! Did you ever notice that some people in extremely difficult, physically laborious jobs seem to be having a grand time? Or a postman delivering your mail with a smile, seeming to enjoy a very difficult occupation?

It's essential to love what you do, to really enjoy it. If you care about something you do it with a full heart, you give it your whole self. If you don't have a job that's giving you that feeling of fulfilment or excitement, change jobs or change your attitude — you spend half of your life in your workplace, so you'd better be having a good time there!

Find something you truly love, something that's going to get you out of bed in the morning, something you can do that will fulfil and inspire you.

Harry M. MILLER

Harry M. Miller moved to Australia from New Zealand in 1963 and has been part of Australian entertainment history. He introduced stars such as Judy Garland, Sammy Davis Jnr, Ella Fitzgerald, Chubby Checker, Louis Armstrong, Shirley Bassey, Tom Jones and the Rolling Stones to Australian audiences. In 1969, Harry launched a new phenomenon to Australia, the rock opera Hair, changing the face of live theatrical shows. In 1972, Miller produced the extremely successful production of The Rocky Horror Show.

In addition, Harry has made a contribution to both the arts and promotion of Australia internationally, serving as Marketing and Promotions Consultant to the Australian Opera, the Australian Ballet and the Melbourne Theatre Company, and pioneering Australia's first subscription schemes under which all Australian flagship companies now operate.

In 1992, Harry produced the first arena version of a stage musical. This production was seen by a million people and grossed $40 million in just 16 weeks. Harry also produced the New York play Madam Butterfly and the off-Broadway musical Pageant, to high acclaim. Harry continues to manage the careers of the country's top media, sporting and entertainment figures. And, in addition to running a successful management and marketing company, Harry is an active member of the Salvation Army Media Advisory Committee.

I don't suppose I ever really had a vision. I never wanted to be a doctor or a vet or a rabbi. I enjoyed the entertainment business; I was always interested in music, I suppose, and in some form or other of putting on shows. As a little kid we used to have something called a peep show, where you get a shoebox, put some cellophane at one end, wind a comic strip through it and charge the kids a marble to watch. I always did better than the other kids because I had the best show — I had little things in the foreground. However, all the extra marbles that I made on the shows I lost in the playground playing marbles, because I never learned how to flick them up properly. So that evened it up at the end of the day. I put on good shows, but I was never the school marble champion.

I never had a vision as such, and the older I get, the more I think that anybody who makes long-term plans now — in terms of business — is a fool, because everything changes so dramatically. I don't believe that anybody should have a business plan that goes past three years, because in terms of strategies, you have to do it now! You have to train yourself to react instantly and respond to the situation, because if you don't you'll end up sailing down the river.

The other thing I know that is very important is this: you have to base everything on the truth. There is just no way around that. I look at people, I talk to young people, I talk to journalists' classes at Canberra, and I tell them all, 'Just base everything on the truth.' When we do a business deal — when we do anything — the last question is, 'Is this the truth?', and if it doesn't qualify, we chuck it out. The world has changed: people are generally more concerned now with their fellow man. Our business philosophy is that we won't do anything that isn't beyond self-interest. Yes, we want to do things for the company, but we want it to have a flow-on effect, to do something else for other people. I think that is very important.

I don't know that things 'evolved' for me. I believe that there is no such thing as luck. Luck is when preparation meets opportunity. So you have to prepare yourself or your company — particularly yourself — so that you are ready to seize something as it comes past. But a lot of people don't do this. The same opportunity goes past 50 people and they are blind, they don't see it, but when it goes past someone who is ready, they just grab it. I've seen that happen a lot and it has happened a lot in my life.

I take action every day. I don't wake up in the morning and say, 'I must take action today.' I am automatically geared, spiritually and mentally, to take action when I should. It's sort of a 'do it now' philosophy. I've always done that. It's something you can refine and practise.

I started to read a book on speed reading, because I know that the amount of stuff we all have to read is a nightmare. I discovered in the first chapter that I am an average reader, which means I read about 210 words a minute. What I became convinced of at the end of the chapter was that I could get up to 1000 words a minute, easily. Early in the book they test your comprehension. My comprehension was high. When you increase your reading speed, you retain everything you read but you read four times as fast. These are skills that are available to the ordinary man.

What inspires me to do anything at all is the pursuit of excellence. I like to do things well — it doesn't matter what it is. If it is some little job I still like it to be done properly. It's about executing things properly and having pride in that.

When I first started in the theatre business in Australia they tried everything to crush me. All the established theatre managements blocked me out of everything, but there was one guy, a brash young New Zealander, who owned a theatre in Melbourne called the Princess Theatre. He took me to lunch and said, 'I reckon you will succeed, and when you succeed I want you to rent my theatres.' So he made a friend of me. Everybody else was terrible, but I've never beaten myself up about people being terrible. I suppose in a way I take a Buddhist or Hindu sort of philosophy of not allowing those sorts of people or circumstances to possess me. I am a detached observer — not unconcerned, but detached.

I think a lot of people come unstuck because they don't understand what happens if somebody is angry with you or mean to you. If you allow those people to attach their anger or their meanness to you, you just empower them more. You have to look at them and say, 'I am not going here.' I have dealt with some serious troublemakers in my time but I don't allow them to come near me. I hear their anger and I just stand there and look at them and think, 'I'm not getting involved in this. I'm not becoming a party to it.'

I practise focus and not getting distracted. I'm sitting here talking to you and I have no other thoughts in my mind whatsoever except you and what you are asking me, and when you leave I could describe you absolutely, visually. Tie matches your shirt, wide collar and wide knot! What I am saying is that you have to learn to do that, and you can practise it. One of the things that help you practise it, I believe, is meditation. Not going into a corner with your backside up in the air, but just shutting your mind down.

You don't have to do it for an hour; you can do it for ten seconds. I remember once when I was in India, a few years ago, trying to sneak in a few extra meditation sessions. One of the instructors told me one morning, 'You know you can meditate while you are talking to people.' He said, 'I bet you go to lots of boring meetings where you don't have to listen to the whole thing.' That's the moment you pull out your little meditation vision, he explained. You're listening to a guy speaking but you are actually thinking of something else, and it shuts you down. So I practise meditation, even in the office, about six or eight times a day. I just shut down, maybe for one minute, and create a vision of something else that has nothing to do with this office.

I went to a place in India once where they have a thing that is magic. It's called traffic control: on the hour, every hour, they play some music for one minute and everybody stops and shuts down. Puts life on hold. That's a very good thing to do with your life — just shut down for a minute, go for a walk, stand out on the balcony and sniff the breeze and feel the sun on your face. Not enough people do that. That helps me focus.

I'm hopeless at balancing work, family and commitments. Mark me one out of ten there. Of course it can be balanced, but I think it's much easier to do that if you actually don't like the work. If you love your work, whatever it is, it is a pleasure to do it, so it does melt into your leisure time. What I do is work very hard for probably 12 to 14 hours per day, but then I drive to my farm on Fridays and switch off for two days. If there is an important phone call they have to leave a message, because I don't pick up the phone.

It is very important to spend time with your family. My oldest daughter said last week we must have a weekend at the farm for everybody from Friday till Sunday night — set in stone, so that everyone knows we're together then. It is a very good idea, because when we are all together we have a lot of fun.

One of the things that I try to encourage people to do is listen carefully to what other people say — *really* listen. A lot of our business is negotiating, and I keep saying to our people, 'Listen to what they're saying. Not just the words — everything.' And when you tell someone the truth, you can't always just blurt it out. You have to do it with great stealth so that you don't hurt people. You have to be cautious with the way you tell the truth; sandwich it, make it last a bit longer.

Asking, 'Is it true?' can save you so much trouble in this office. If there were 988 petals on the flowers in that vase, nobody in this building would say there were 1000. Nobody. Because we know that the truth has a special power. I often send people a quotation that I keep on a wall here. It says: 'The truth will always reveal itself at the right moment and in the right place.' And 'Karma means you can't get away with anything.'

I am an enthusiast about everything I do. I've got that energy. It comes from just doing it. I don't sit in a pub and wait for things to happen. That would be the worst thing for me. Also, I find people want to work with me because they enjoy the momentum. You have to have that in yourself, and it's catchy. And you have to be generous with yourself and help people. There wouldn't be a month go past where somebody doesn't say, 'You don't remember me, but I asked you for something 20 years ago or 30 years ago, and you …' I find it happens a lot.

The most recent example was when we were handling a story. Why did the guy call us? Because 22 years ago, when he was a porter on CountryLink, I took some people to the station and he said, 'You were very polite and very respectful, asking me to look after them and get them to their destination.' That's why he phoned us, because he knows that sort of stuff and he remembered me being nice. And that's about having some non-self-interest.

So just do it. This is what people don't do; many give all the reasons why this won't work, when they should just do it.

I have to tell you, people don't need a kick in the pants to just do it; they need somebody to remind them. I remember years ago talking to a fantastic woman — she's about 85 now. Her name is Braddy Jankins, and she worked with the United Nations. She was an expert at yoga, and I had an opportunity to talk to her. I was giving her the third degree — as only I can! — on exactly how to meditate, because I was trying to learn. I kept on asking her things, and I watched a smile creep across her face. She leaned forward and said, 'Harry, just do it!'

We see it in the Bible: Joshua — Just blow the horn; Lot's wife — Don't look back!

It's all about just doing it!

Kieren PERKINS

Born in Brisbane, Kieren Perkins is an Australian swimming legend, being Olympic Gold medallist in the 1500 metres freestyle in 1992 and 1996. He has broken 11 world records and is the first person in history to hold Olympic, World, Commonwealth and Pan Pacific titles simultaneously for the same event. Winning the world record for the 400, 800 and 1500 metres freestyle, Kieren revolutionised swimming in Australia, entered his nation's psyche and became the stuff of legend. Since his retirement from competition Kieren has been appointed to the board of the Australian Sports Commission and has moved into the roles of corporate ambassador and media personality. Kieren has completed a series as a reporter for the Sydney-based program Weekend and was seen across the nation on A Current Affair reporting from the World Swimming Championships in Fukuoka, Japan.

When I was young — I'm talking 15 here — I made the Queensland state target team. That was the first representative team that I had been selected for, and at the very first meeting I went to we were given a task. A Rugby League coach came in, a motivational speaker, and he asked us to write down our short-, medium- and long-term goals. At that stage, I was just enjoying the ride. I wasn't one of those people who had a vision of being an Olympic champion, being the greatest swimmer ever. I was still loving it, having a good time and moving along, but this task really made me stop and think. I took it seriously, because I knew I had to do the right thing, being in the team, so I sat down and I wrote down a short-, a medium- and a long-term goal.

At that time Dawn Fraser was the only swimmer who had ever competed and won at three consecutive Olympic Games, and when the coach said 'long-term goal, eight to 10 years down the track', that seemed like an impossibility — that I would still be alive in 10 years! — but I thought, 'Well, Dawn Fraser did that, she is the greatest swimmer of all time, so I'd like to become the first man to win three consecutive Olympic gold medals in the same event.'

And, really, from that moment, my swimming career was set. That was basically the overwhelming force in everything I did for the rest of my career — I was pushing forward to try to get to that third Olympic Games and win. There wasn't an age limit on it, but I knew I would be 27 for my third Olympics — I knew that the chances of going to four were basically non-existent. I was 15, it was 1989, and we had the Barcelona Olympics in 1992. That was going to be my first opportunity to compete at the Olympic Games and I would be 19 then.

So it started with the idea — with the goal. The long-term goal was the first step. But I had short-term goals along the way, and for me at that stage the first step was the Commonwealth Games that were coming up. It was a journey that required a lot of little steps along the way. The first step was making the Australian team. Once I had made the Australian team it was competing internationally, learning about what it takes to cope with the pressure of international competition, learning to travel … for instance, going to Europe a lot — believe me, we weren't ever on the direct flights! There was a lot of toing and froing just to get from here to Europe.

Coping with obstacles and setbacks along the way was one of the biggest lessons. I learned early on that you can't really control much in life other than yourself, and that if you can't adapt to a situation and allow yourself to move forward, you will never go anywhere. Really, I've always treated life as a journey; I treat every little step along the way as another inch forward in my progress towards that end goal.

You hear people talk about the discipline that's required and the motivation that you need to commit yourself to the type of program that I needed to do to get to the Olympic Games. But at the end of the day, for me the simple answer was always about making a decision to do it. Once I decided I was going to do something it was a case of getting on with the job and doing it. Not spending too much time thinking about how or why or what — just getting on with it. That is one of the great, simple joys of sport, I suppose. It is not something where (from the individual's point of view) you need to sit down and put together huge long plans about exactly how you are going to get from point A to point B. You have a coach who takes care of your swimming program, you have physios, dietitians, nutritionists, strength coaches, all these experts around you, and you use their expertise and their knowledge to help you along the way. Really your own focus is internalised — 'What do I need to do right now to make sure that I am doing the best thing for my swimming career and to help me get to that end goal?'

For me, when I am doing something I am doing it, and that is it, and when it is done I go to the next thing, but I can cut backwards and forwards. I am not very good at doing five things at once, but I can do five things in succession very well. I believe this is one of the things that really helped me in my swimming career. Once I made a decision to do something I would move forward, and if something happened that was a setback or a problem, I would work out why it happened and then just keep going and forget it. I wouldn't even think about it again.

My parents had said right from when I was young that my brother and I had to do sport. They weren't particularly worried about what sport it was, but we had to be involved in a physical activity. I tried a lot of different things which I didn't really like, but I liked swimming. When I think about it, probably the thing that I liked about it most was that I was responsible for myself and nobody else. Team sports never appealed to me; I think for two reasons, first, because I have absolutely no co-ordination whatsoever, so I was always the worst member of the team, and second, because you are not solely responsible for the outcome of the game, and the way you play or the way other people play has a direct effect on the team's results, which I think I had trouble dealing with. Perhaps because it was always my fault that something went wrong!

So I started swimming and I loved it. I learned to swim when I was five, but it wasn't until I was nine that I did much. When I was nine I ran through a plate glass door at our house in Brisbane and completely severed my left calf muscle. After the doctor stitched me back up again, he told me I had to do kicking in the water to strengthen the muscle without actually re-tearing the injury. The closest heated pool to where we lived in Brisbane was a swim school, so I started going down there three afternoons a week, doing my 20 minutes of kicking in the water. I loved it so much I kept going back, and that was really what got me going. It was enjoyment, nothing more.

I enjoyed going to training, I enjoyed challenging myself

to get better, and that still holds true today. If you wanted to compare me personally with another individual, I would say that I am not that great. I don't have good hand–eye co-ordination and I don't have great balance, and for that reason I am not overly competitive in anything except swimming. But I am constantly challenging myself, because I want to do better, because I want to improve my own personal results; I really do enjoy doing that.

So at the age of nine I started training, and from that moment on it was a bit of a roller-coaster, up until I reached 15 years old. I did it because I loved it. I trained, I got better, I trained, I got better, and I developed my competition technique, dealing with nerves and the adrenalin that comes from competing against other people. Slowly but surely I improved, and that was always the main motivation for me — just getting better. And then I woke up one morning and I was almost the best.

The setting of the goals, I think, was what gave me the end point. But probably what gave me that first step, what really made me believe that I could do it, was seeing a young Australian by the name of Glen Houseman. Glen was the second person in history — and the first Australian — to break 15 minutes in the 1500 metres freestyle. At the selection trials for the 1990 Commonwealth Games in Adelaide in 1989, in the heats of the 1500 freestyle, Glen actually swam under the world record time. I stood in the stands and I watched this guy break 15 minutes — that was the first world record I ever saw. He was well under. He touched the wall. Everyone in the stands turned around and looked at the clock and even then, when we had done that, he was still under. Of course all the coaches in the stands had their handheld timers. It was stunning; it was an incredibly euphoric moment. But he didn't touch the pads or the touch pads didn't activate.

Whether it was his fault or the timing equipment no one will ever know, but the timing equipment did not activate, and because of that he was never credited with that swim, because the rules state that it must be electronically recorded. So it was followed up by a great tragedy, really, because he never really recovered. He went on to win at the Commonwealth Games, but he just missed the world record.

Seeing Glen do that, seeing this guy — I didn't know him, but I had seen him on the pool deck, I had swum in lanes with him and beside him, and I had seen him around, so he was somebody that I was aware of — actually break that world record was probably the moment when I realised that if I wanted to, I could. Because I didn't see anything special about him; to me he was just another swimmer, and when I looked at him I thought, 'Well, if he can, why can't I?'

That swim in Adelaide, I will never forget it. It was incredible. It was probably not until the Sydney 2000 Olympics that I actually, as a spectator, saw a swim that lifted me as much, and that was the men winning the 4 x 100 metres freestyle relay. So if we're talking about a bridge or a kick, for me it was that, Glen Houseman's swim, because at that moment I realised that anybody could do it; it was just a matter of how much you wanted it.

Mr Carew — he was the guy that I went to as a nine-year-old, and he was my coach for the rest of my career — always loved reminding me about how when I was 12, 13, 14, there were two girls who I trained with, both a year younger than me, who routinely beat me in training and competition. That was a very big challenge, as a male — coping with being beaten by girls on a regular basis. I was never a sprinter, and when you are young you start competing at 25 metres, then you go to 50 to 100 to 200, so I didn't actually swim my first 1500 until I was 14, going on 15 … and that was the time when I started to impress people, because the races got longer and I could keep going when everybody else would start to drop off. But for all-out speed I was never great, and that is why the competition with these girls was always so strong, because they were sprinters: they were better over the 50 and 100 metres races. That was certainly a challenge. Right up through the junior age group ranks I never won anything — I was never club champion, I wasn't state champion. I won my first state title at 14.

I think the challenge was finding a reason to keep going back, because society is very geared towards success. Everything is about the medal you won or the ribbon you received, and when you are continually competing and butting your head against a brick wall, never actually coming home with the goods, it can be very demoralising.

I learned to focus back on my own personal result and work out whether or not I had done my best. I have to credit my parents a little bit with this, because they always said that as long as you do your best that is all anybody can ask — as parents do. And I got to the point where I knew I wasn't going to win, so I had to focus on doing my best. It was about improving every time I got in the water, making sure that I did absolutely everything I could to swim my best race. As time went on, I got faster and faster, of course, and I built up my distances, and when I got to 400 metres and then the 1500 later, the success started to come, but the great thing about it was that the success that I attained was never enough.

I've often been asked, 'After you win an Olympic gold medal, what do you do?' and for me the answer was, 'Go faster, get better.' I never in my life swam a perfect race. I never got out the water and said to myself, 'Well, I can't do any better than that.' I always believed that I could improve — I could do better, whether it be in training or in the race itself. That is a direct result of having to overcome, as a young kid, the challenge of there not being any obvious success.

When I look back now, I feel that in a lot of ways I was just lucky, especially when I was a young child. Because I started so young — as most people in swimming do — a lot of things happened to me along the way that helped me develop which were really not my doing. They were situations I was put in or people around me who helped to guide me.

It is very easy for people to pass athletes off as being unintelligent: nine times out of ten it is not that they are unintelligent, but that they are not as well educated as other people, because they have devoted themselves to their sport and not to an academic career. But to be the very best at anything, you have to be incredibly intelligent. There is no getting around that.

I think at the end of the day a very large part of achieving success is self-belief — some people have the natural ability to never lose faith in themselves, no matter how bad a situation might seem. Sometimes we can get lost working out if success is the result of the chicken or the egg: is it innate self-belief that helps you reach your goal, or does having the goal and working towards it help create the self-belief? I think it is a bit of both. If you are a naturally positive person, and then add in all the work and the effort and the background that you have put into what you are doing, they are the things that can give you guaranteed self-belief.

In my career, let's take the race in Atlanta. I was world record holder and world champion in the 400 and 1500 metres freestyle going into the selection trials for the Olympic Games. I missed selection for the Australian team in the 400 metres, then picked up the last spot on the team for the 1500, coming second in the final. Then I got to Atlanta. The 1500 was my only race, and in the heats I swam quite badly — I took the last position in the final by two-tenths of a second — and then went on to win the race. Now I talk a lot about it, because Australians are fascinated about how I turned this seemingly impossible situation around.

What it comes down to at the end of the day is self-belief. For me the preparation was always where I drew my greatest strength: when I stood up for a race I knew that I had done all the work I needed to do — I had worked on my technique, my turns were good, my fitness, my dive. All the things that you do in your preparation cycle, I knew that I had given them 100 per cent. And when you get to the race itself you realise that you can't get fitter, can't get stronger, can't get faster, so therefore all you can do is get the very best out of what is already there. That realisation is what got me through Atlanta and created the opportunity for me to win. More than anything, it was about developing and maintaining my self-belief. It came from that strength of preparation — that is where I found it, that's the way I got that self-belief. Other people, I suppose, are very different, but at the end of the day, in just about everything in life, I have a belief that if I work at something I will be able to achieve it. That never seems to falter.

There have been two very specific phases in my life. In swimming, I started when was in school. I was a young kid, living at home, and it all came down to time management and balance, and recognising what was important and what was not. Throughout my adolescence, school was always more important than sport. I had to finish high school and I had to do well at high school. My coach, Mr Carew, always said that if I wanted to train with him, I had to concentrate on my schoolwork — if my grades dropped, I couldn't train to the level I wanted to. And my parents also always said that sport is not forever: 'One day you will retire, or you will get injured, or you just might not be successful, and you will need to have something to fall back on.' So I always focused on schoolwork first — but having said that, if I had applied myself as well to the schoolwork as I did to my swimming, I know I would have done a lot better.

It really comes down to time management — again, it's what I mean about focusing on doing something. I think it is very easy to get caught up in thinking, 'Well, I am going to do this, and I hope to do that, and then if that fits in I will try to do this …'. Instead I said, 'I will do this, then I will do this, then this, then this, and that is how my days will work.' When I was at school I would get up at five o'clock in the morning, go to the pool, train, eat breakfast in the car on the way to school, be at school all day, get out of school in the afternoon, eat more food in the car, go to the pool, train, come home, eat dinner, do homework, go to bed and start again. That was my life for probably the last seven or eight years of school.

As I got older, what became more obvious to me was that you need to have balance in your life. This is where marrying Sam and having the kids really helped me get going towards the Sydney Olympics. Because at that stage, by the time I got out of Atlanta, I was mentally pretty jaded — I had been working very hard for a very long time, and while the success was great and I was proud of what I achieved, swimming was not enough. Financially I was quite stable, with sponsors and a public profile and that sort of thing, but I did need something else in my life and that was where Sam and the kids came in.

Marrying Sam was about being able to step away from swimming every now and again, or every day, and having something in my life that wasn't dependent on or directly influenced by swimming. That really helped keep me sane. It helped me be as refreshed as possible every time I arrived at the pool to train in the morning — I wouldn't have spent the last 24 hours thinking about swimming and nothing else. I had time away from the sport. I was able to focus on Sam and the kids and what was happening in our lives. Obviously the extension of that was that as I got close to the end of my career, I was focusing more on life after sport — business, future opportunities, that sort of thing. The balance, especially over the last four years of my career, really saved me. I don't think I would have made it to Sydney if I'd had nothing but swimming to concentrate on; it would have driven me insane. I wouldn't have been able to cope with having that singular focus in life for over 18 years.

Now swimming has been replaced on a daily basis by work, but it's not your typical definition of work. I still have sponsors, so I do a lot of public promotion, public speaking. We also have some business opportunities that we are working on. I am on a couple of boards as well, so I have a mixed and varied work life, but for me the challenge is creating the future, creating a long-term future, because the sponsorships won't last for the rest of my life. The directorships don't pay enough to cover the mortgage and obviously having kids as well gives you a big financial burden, so I guess my work focus is creating a long-term future. But the life focus is maintaining a happy family life, and I am very heavily involved in my kids and their lives. When I am home, nine times out of ten I take them to school or pick them up in the afternoons, take them to soccer practice in the afternoons, tennis, karate. It is becoming very obvious to me that for Sam and me, our lives will stop for a while and the focus will all be on the kids and what they need to do and where they need to be. That is going to be an interesting challenge, for sure.

It is all about balance: if you don't have success in your personal life, you won't have success in your business or work life, because they directly influence each other. If you have somebody at home who is telling you constantly that you can't do it, when you get to work you will never do it, and vice versa, so home is a very important support system. Swimming is an individual sport, but it is a sport that no individual has ever been successful in without a team — without a strong, positive team of people around them, and probably the most integral part of that team is your family and home support network.

Success is all about making the decision. When I say 'making the decision' I don't mean, 'I think I will do this now', or 'It would be great to do that' — instead it is 'I *will*, I am *going to* … '. You can't kid yourself — you know if you have really made a decision to do something or not. Obviously the next decision, after you have made the first, major decision, is about creating a plan for your journey: how exactly you are going to get there. After that it is just doing it.

The one thing that never ceases to amaze me is how everybody already knows the answer. All of us, we all know how to do it; it is just that sometimes we forget how we did it. How hard we tried, the effort we put into it, how motivated we were, how desperate we were to get to that end goal. I think success sort of blurs your view in a positive way. It is like women having babies — they go through the most painful, terrible, traumatic moment of their lives, and six weeks later they want another one! They want to do it all again, and they don't remember the pain or the effort or the suffering or any of that.

At that base level, I think remembering is an issue for people who have been successful or who have achieved in the past, at whatever level. It is one of the reasons they find it so difficult to achieve their goal again. It is not so much that they don't know how to, but that they don't remember what it took or how difficult it was, and their vision of the path that they took the previous time has become a little rose-coloured.

My first message would be, if you don't enjoy it, don't bother. If we don't enjoy what we are striving for we will never actually achieve anything. No matter how motivated you are, no matter how positive you are, no matter how well organised and determined you are, if you don't enjoy what you are doing, it will eventually wear you down, so the first and most important thing is make sure you enjoy it.

The second thing is to find an end point, find something that you want to achieve long term, your long-term goal, because I think that in anything, if you just decide, 'I am going to swim (or run, or study), so let's see what happens', you will never reach your full potential. You will never get to the heights that you possibly could reach if you have a long-term, far-reaching, borderline-unrealistic kind of goal.

Once you have decided what that end vision is, reaching it is about coming up with the next step, on a daily basis, because — to use the old rungs-of-a-ladder analogy — if you want to get to the top, you have to stand on every rung along the way. Once you do have that long-term goal, it is then time to think, 'OK, today I am going to achieve this, next week I want to be here, this month I need to have done that, by the end of this year this is where I need to be'. And you have to constantly reassess those aims, because sometimes you won't get there, and other times you'll get there early — you need to continuously move the goal posts so that what you are aiming for next is just out of reach. That way, you are always going to move forward.

Probably the last thing I would say is that you shouldn't ever be bound by another person's perception of what you can or can't do. I am one of those people who if you tell me I can't do something, I will keep trying to do it until I succeed. In sport, as in life, if you want to become the very best, you have to believe you can do anything. You can do anything you set your mind to doing; don't be hemmed in by what other people believe. I guess an example of what I am trying to say is that people often ask me, 'Who was your hero when you were young, who did you want to be like?' The answer is that I didn't want to be like anybody. I wanted to be me — I didn't want to be as good as somebody else, because that might have limited me to the heights that person could achieve. Maybe I could do better, maybe I could go further, and maybe I couldn't. It works from both ends of the scale: I don't want to be disappointed if I can't become as good as another person, if it is just isn't possible, but I also don't want to be limited to their level of success because that is only as far as I ever try to reach.

I have a poem that sums up my beliefs, which I had on my wall when I was very young, although I don't remember it verbatim. It is called 'The Man Who Thinks He Can', by Walter D. Wintle:

> *If you think you are beaten, you are;*
> *If you think you dare not, you don't.*
> *If you'd like to win, but think you can't*
> *It's almost a cinch you won't.*
> *If you think you'll lose, you're lost,*
> *For out in the world we find*
> *Success begins with a fellow's will;*
> *It's all in the state of mind.*
> *If you think you're outclassed, you are.*
> *You've got to think high to rise.*
> *You've got to be sure of yourself before*
> *You can ever win a prize.*
> *Life's battles don't always go*
> *To the stronger or faster man;*
> *But sooner or later the man who wins*
> *Is the one who thinks he can.*

The poem is about how every individual has the opportunity to be exceptional at something and, at the end of the day, the one who reaches his goal is the one who believed that he could the most. I am a firm believer in that.

At the Olympic Games, in the final of any race you have eight people standing behind the box ready to swim. Now, when you consider the number of people worldwide who compete in that particular event, and break it down to the national champions, and then break it down to those who make it to the Olympics, and to all of those who are then culled to make the final, I don't believe that genetically there is that much difference between them. I also think that the innate talent, the amount of work we have put in, all the things we have sacrificed and done to get ourselves there, is similar. The question then is, what makes the difference? What enables one athlete to win by 10 seconds? I honestly believe it is mental state. It is how much you believe in yourself and how much you believe that you can win, that enables you to do it. This is basically what the idea behind the poem is.

I get asked all the time: 'In your opinion, what is the ratio between talent and hard work for someone to become successful?' And I answer every time, 'At best five per cent talent and 95 per cent hard work', but it is probably more like one per cent talent and 99 per cent hard work, because the most talented people in life ultimately often don't become successful. When they start a task it is easy, they do it very well. They are good because they are immensely talented, so success comes very easily. Then something goes wrong: there is a difficulty, or the competition catches up, or one of the hurdles that we all constantly face occurs. Sometimes the most talented people, who haven't had to fight to get their initial success, don't know how to cope; they don't know how to overcome adversity, they don't know how to turn around a difficult situation that looks as if it is going to destroy everything. More often than not, those talented people will just give up — they will go on to something else or they will be prepared to stay at a certain level of mediocrity because it is easy for them.

Those who ultimately make it to the very top will tell you — and I think if you talk to anybody who is the ultimate leader in their field they will probably agree — that to get where they are didn't take a lot of talent. Yes, it took some talent, but it didn't take a lot of talent; it took a lot of hard work and self-belief. At the Olympic Games you see people compete, but you don't get overawed by other athletes, you don't see them as being extraordinary. They are not extraordinary people; they are just people who have achieved extraordinary things. When you have that perspective and you stand in an Olympic Village and see 10,000 of the very best athletes from all over the world, all of those people together, it does become very plain, very quickly, that talent is such a minuscule part of what it took for those people to get there. It took everything else — hard work, determination, a bit of luck!

Strategies for living
YOUR DREAMS

Need any fixing? Schedule a check up! A teacher was with his students when they were disturbed by a knock on the shutter. A peasant, hauling a cart of tools, peered through the window. 'Need any fixing?' he cried. 'Do you have any shaky tables or any broken chairs? What about a leaky roof, perhaps?'

'No, no,' came the impatient reply from within. 'Everything is in perfect condition. There's no need for any repairs.'

'Indeed? Nothing to repair?' called the peasant. 'That simply cannot be. Look well, and you're sure to find something that needs fixing!'

The teacher subsequently addressed his students: 'Many times I have taught you that nothing is by chance in this world; that every event and experience is purposeful, that everything one sees or hears is a lesson. Think of the words we just heard from this simple peasant. How profoundly relevant they are to each and every one of us! Is everything really in perfect condition? At times it might seem so, but if one truly searches his heart and evaluates his life, is he not sure to find something that requires repair ...?'

We all have facets of our life that we can 'fix' — improve and grow — and take ourselves to a new level. As you would go to the doctor or dentist for an annual check-up, it makes sense to schedule an annual check-up to evaluate where you are in your life. Is there anything that needs 'fixing'? Can you improve in certain areas? You are the best judge of what has worked and what needs fixing.

So go ahead and schedule a check-up for yourself. Evaluate your life and start fixing anything that needs fixing!

Strategies for living
YOUR DREAMS

Never, ever give up! The common characteristic of all those featured in this book is that each and every one has faced numerous challenges in their career or journey. But they realise that these challenges are part of the ride — part of the process — and while they may get discouraged for a short while, they bounce back. They have conditioned themselves to shrug off the problems, bounce back and move on. They simply never give up. It is inevitable that you are going to face setbacks; it's dealing with the setbacks and challenges that will propel you to new heights and enable you to realise your dream and your vision.

When things go wrong, as they sometimes will,
When the road you're trudging seems all uphill,
When the funds are low and the debts are high,
And you want to smile but you have to sigh.

When care is pressing you down a bit,
Rest, if you must, but don't you quit.

Life is queer, with its twists and turns,
As every one of us sometimes learns,
And many a failure turns about
When he might have won had he stuck it out.

Don't give up though the pace seems slow
You may succeed with another blow.

Success is failure turned inside out,
The silver tint of the cloud of doubt,
And you never can tell how close you are,
It may be near when it seems so far.
So stick to the fight when you're hardest hit.
It's when things seem the worst you must not quit.

AUTHOR UNKNOWN

Richard
PRATT

Richard Pratt came to Australia in the late 1930s as a four-year-old when his parents decided to leave Poland. Richard inherited a small box-making business when his father died in 1969. Today, Visy Industries is a multi-billion-dollar packaging and recycling business empire on two continents.

Richard Pratt received the Companion of the Order of Australia (AC) in 1998, Australia's highest honour, and the Officer of the Order of Australia (AO) in 1985. He has been awarded honorary doctorates from Swinburne University of Technology and Monash University. Currently chairman of Visy Industries, Richard Pratt's public services include foundation chancellor, Swinburne University of Technology; chair of finance committee, US Coral Sea Commemorative Council; president, Victorian Arts Centre Trust; chairman, Australian Business Arts Foundation; and chairman, Mental Health Research Institute of Victoria.

In 1948, when I was 13 years old, my vision was to be as good as I could be, wherever I had the skills or talents. I found that I had talent for sports. I played a lot of sports and I was very competitive. I enjoy being in a competition as long as I have a chance of coming out successfully. I wasn't a very good scholar, but I worked hard. Naturally I had all the problems that 13-year-olds have — getting into trouble from time to time. But I had one other characteristic — I was very honest, very trustworthy. I can remember my father included me in all family discussions, and if there was anything private — family issues, etc. — I would be very careful not to talk about it.

My father was a European father who was brought up through the Depression. My mother was the businessman in the family. I learned a lot from my mother. She was concerned about other people but both my parents were very generous and made donations whenever they could afford to. People often ask me why I give so much money to charity. 'Where did you learn to behave like that?' I say, 'In the house of my mother and father, it was a tradition.' And the issue of generosity has been one of my problems — I can't say no to anybody.

My mother was a people person. Sometimes, I must say, I was amazed at her flamboyance, her extroversion, but it was all with an interest to embrace. My father was a very good chess player, a master chess player — he won the Baltic States championship in the 1930s.

My parents were farmers in Shepparton. I remember at 13 sitting at the table when my father made a deal with my uncle and a Mr Feldman. The three of them became partners in this very small company — with a capitalisation of two thousand pounds — and I was invited to sit at the table and listen to what they had to say. I had no interest in business whatsoever, I didn't know the difference between business and anything else. I was more interested in my friends, country friends, farming friends.

I was the only son. My mother loved me dearly, very dearly, and she encouraged me — she told me how competent I was, that I could do anything. She boosted my confidence, and she was my example; she showed me how to integrate, because I am probably not an integrated person by nature. I learned a lot from her. She would come and watch me at sport and do all the things good mothers do, and bad mothers don't do. So there was a sense of family and a sense of encouragement, a sense of love, which is a good thing to have, a good background.

My father left me in Shepparton for two years when he went to Melbourne to start Visy. I joined the company when I was 18. But I had been involved in all the meetings and all the chats that were had from time to time, so I knew a lot about the business when I joined. My only skills at the time were as a salesman, so I started selling the product. We grew quite quickly, and I continued to work in the company until 1957.

As well as working in the company full-time, I did a part-time course in economics at Melbourne University, I played football with Carlton, I took out girls, did some other extracurricular activities, went on holidays. There was plenty of time for everything, except maybe for sleep!

In 1955 I helped start the Ajax football club and I helped start a Jewish play group called Habimah Players. In 1957 I left the business because by then I was a professional actor and I had decided to spend two years on the stage. I was acting in *Summer of the Seventeenth Doll* and I went overseas with the play and performed in the West End and on Broadway. Naturally, that opened up my world.

I came back to Australia in 1958, rejoined the company, and decided that I'd better settle down, so I got married in 1959 to a lady I still love and cherish. It so happened that she had exactly the same background as me — she had come from Poland in 1939 when she was three years old and her family were Yiddish-speaking, which was my language at home. It was important to me that we had the same background, that I didn't marry someone who was culturally different, with different expectations.

We soon had three children. I was working for the company, I was involved with the Ajax football club and I did some acting. When I was 34 my father died. I was anxious to grow the business very quickly, so we opened a branch in Sydney. I travelled overseas a couple of times looking at the industry, and I very quickly identified quality people to complement my weaknesses. That was very important. Through all this I was not afraid to take risks, or to use my personality — I had a strong, persuasive manner. The important thing is to use the qualities that you have.

I'm very self-critical — I identify what I'm good at. I set the ducks up in a row so that I can knock them down in one shot. I'm not a politician, I never could be a politician. In terms of problem-solving, I'm not a chess player either. I'm quite good at attack, but I am hopeless at defence, which is why I surround myself with people who are very good at defence — accountants and lawyers — and I don't interfere with them. They just tell me what to do and what their objectives are.

My first challenge was how to secure myself against those people who could do me damage. There was an established company called Amcor, and I called them up and I said, 'Look, we do a lot of business with you and we owe you a lot of money at the end of every month. Would you mind if I asked you to send one of your top managers to my factory to work with me, to keep an eye on things?' And they did. For a couple of years I had their people in my company, not because we owed them a lot of money, not because we were going broke or we had receivers or anything like that — I invited them to help me and talk to me about what was going on in the world of packaging and boxes. I also spent a lot of time with the bankers.

When my father died, I said to myself, 'I can replace my

father, but who's going to replace me?' I was a successful salesman, but I stayed out of the sales part and let other people do
it — the general manager was actually selling full-time, the
chief executive and chairman of the company was selling all
the time, while my managers were running the company. And
they were doing a great job; they were inspired to turn this
company into a great company.

The most important part of my methodology is this: you
don't make money out of an idea; it is the implementation of
the idea that makes money. So I am an action-oriented go-
and-make-it-happen person.

I also say to myself, 'If you do everything that is common
sense and leave nothing that is common sense undone, then
you can do anything.' But you mustn't leave any of the common
sense things undone, so you surround yourself with people
that remind you that this is common sense, that is common
sense, so why are you not doing that? The other thing I found
is that if you ask academics what the issues are, they give you
a list of 30 or 40 issues. I know that I can't cope with more
than two or three issues, so I very quickly gravitate to the
main issues.

The economy is booming, according to the papers every
day. OK, what do I want? To get a big piece of that economic
activity. How is it possible? An inch at a time, always heading
in the same direction. The plan never changes, the strategy
changes from time to time, the tactics are always changing —
the tactics are jumping all over the place — but the plan never
changes.

I have found in my life that whenever I have a difficult
problem, I have to get fully involved in it, physically and
emotionally. Every time I have a big question to answer, I
always give myself overnight to sleep on it. I say, 'I'll let you
know tomorrow.' One of the best ways for me to solve problems

is to say to myself, 'Who are the six people I know who know about the realm of this problem?' I say to them, 'I've got a problem. I trust you. Please help me.' Those people might take two hours or three hours to tell me what I have to do — who I have to get to help me, when I have do it, the time-frame, how I should do it and where. This is all put together by people who are not as emotionally involved as I am.

Coming probably close to the end of the story, I'm 68 this year — you have to stop yourself from making any more big decisions and hand it over to the people who are now 42 or 43. That's the great moment in a man's life; he's young enough to still have that strength and stamina, and not so old that he can't carry things through.

I worked very long hours. I'm not sure if I worked very hard, but I worked very long. I'm physically very strong and I have a lot of stamina and can live with uncertainty — if you add those things together, they are probably the rules every business person should have: be strong, have stamina, be able to live with uncertainty, and have a very strong work ethic. I am a workaholic; as I said, not a hard worker but a long worker.

Siimon
REYNOLDS

Still in his thirties, Siimon Reynolds has already founded, built and successfully sold three advertising agencies. He has won almost every major advertising award for creative thinking, including the Golden Lion at Cannes and the Grand Prize at the London International Advertising Awards. He has won Advertising Agency of the Year three times and is the only Australian to have won Newspaper Ad of the Year, Magazine Ad of the Year and TV Commercial of the Year. Siimon has lectured nationally to over 30,000 business people and appeared on numerous television and radio shows. He is a successful author with books published in six countries.

When I first started out, my biggest fear was that I would be a failure. I did pretty averagely at school. I didn't know what I wanted to do, but I knew I didn't want to go to uni, because I couldn't stand school. So in my mind my options were stockbroking, real estate or advertising; all three enabled you to make a good income without going to uni. It was a close call between real estate and advertising, but eventually advertising won. When I began, my goal was to be a creative director of an advertising agency, but in my early years I read a book called *Think and Grow Rich* by Napoleon Hill and it changed my life.

My sister's boyfriend had these get-rich-quick books. I had

never seen them before. I bought him *Think and Grow Rich* for his birthday and before I gave it to him I started to read a few chapters. Of course when you are a young kid you look up to guys who are a few years older than you, and if I hadn't seen these books I wouldn't have even known that they existed.

Its whole concept was that life wasn't a lottery, that we are able, through our own efforts and belief systems and the power of visualisation and personal affirmation, to sculpt a life for ourselves as we dream it. This was an extraordinary thing, and even now the number of people I have seen who were influenced by this book and who are at the top of their professions is enormous.

So I read that book and — I was still a teenager — decided I wanted to be great at advertising. I started aiming for that, mimicking not only the techniques but also the ways of thinking of the top American and British advertising people. I got a fire in my belly about becoming great at it.

In contrast, at school I was concentrating on survival. I knew I was getting very low marks in maths and science but reasonable marks in English and subjects like history, so I thought, 'OK, there is some aptitude there.' I was also very lucky that my mum got me a few weeks' work experience in advertising when I was 15. So I was able to work in a creative department, and I kind of sensed that it was fun — everybody was wearing jeans and playing darts and going to lunch. This could be a career for me! I tried to do work experience in different places over my last few years at school and I decided in my final year that advertising was going to be it.

A friend of mine at school told me that his uncle was the editor of *B&T*, an advertising industry magazine, and he arranged a meeting. I said to the guy, 'I really need a job, can you give me some advice about how to get one?' He said he would not only do that, but he would also place an ad for me.

In it I talked about how I was going to be the new star in advertising, and that they better hire me now while I was cheap! As a result of that ad, I started working four days a week after school writing brochures in my HSC year. So school was when I rested before I went to work at 4 p.m. Then I accepted a fulltime job based on that ad two weeks after my HSC finished. People said, 'Don't you need a holiday?' I said to them, 'I have been on holiday for 12 years. It's time to do some work!' I started working for an agency in November 1982 for about $9750 a year. It was a little agency in Kings Cross called Stewart Roche Watson. That was the beginning.

I remember in those early days I and the other junior would go down to McDonald's, where we would get all the scratch'n'match cards, line them up and look for printing errors. When we detected a printing error we knew that there were burgers in particular places on those cards. So we managed to supplement our income by getting free burgers for some months.

We were having a lot of fun, but in those days I was very unsure whether I'd be successful. My biggest fear was that five years down the track I'd realise that I was mediocre at it. Advertising's a good career if you are at the top but a poor career if you are at the bottom. It's not like law or medicine, where you make a reasonable living no matter where you are on the scale. I was driven by that fear and it was a great propellant for me. So I began to work harder and harder, trying to be good at it.

I had learned about the concept of seeing a movie in your mind of how things are supposed to be and emotionally attaching to it, and I took that to heart to an incredible degree: I would literally spend sometimes hours a day playing music and visualising myself achieving enormous things. I know that a lot of Olympic athletes do this. I think there is something metaphysical about the process, and I have absolutely no doubt that I magnetised amazing, fortuitous events to me as a result of playing them over in my head, again and again. The intensity with which I did it was amazing.

I would imagine for hours that I was winning all these awards for advertising, and within two years I had won arguably the highest award in Australia for advertising. It looks like a tremendous degree of luck, but something happens when you do this, when you are so sure of your purpose. When you are as intense as that, many of the successful people in this book will agree that things happen; things move in your favour when you get very clear and passionate about your goals. I trusted in this book, *Think and Grow Rich*; it says that when you visualise something, it will happen.

I had two things powering me, one negative and one positive: one was fear of failure and the other was that belief in what I could become. Those two things together were pretty potent.

I remember seeing an advertising award that I wanted to win. Another advertising agency had won it, and people around me were holding the award and saying it was a great award, but I wouldn't touch it. I remember thinking that, 'The first time I touch this will be the time I win it.' And finally when I did win it, it was a very incredible experience.

During the first few years I moved to a different agency every year. The good thing about the advertising industry is that it's a meritocracy, and it doesn't always pay for you to stay in the same agency in your first few years. If you moved to another agency you could get, or were often given, a more senior job, so by moving you got better work and you also got more money. I became a creative director at 21, which was ten or 15 years earlier than the normal person. Basically that came down to ringing up companies and asking for the job. The first one turned me down but the second one didn't. I tried to get a headhunter to represent me but they said I was too young.

I have a good friend — Matthew Rockman, who is Irvin Rockman's son (head of Rockman's Regency Hotels in Melbourne). Matt is a very successful businessman and a co-founder of seek.com.au, the number one online job search site. He said his motto is simply 'Ask', and I think that is really powerful.

You can transform your life by just having that philosophy of asking. It was as a result of asking that I was able to get a job as creative director. I hadn't really defined that I would be a creative director when I started out; it just kind of came into my head after a while. I was sacked from that job a year later, and to this day I don't know why. I could be living in a complete illusion, or I could be just being naïve, but I seemed to have done a good job. And when I got sacked, I got sacked very publicly, just after I had written the AIDS commercial, which was also very, very public and on the front page of the papers. No one would offer me a job. No one rang, and I sat by my phone for two weeks. My only choices were to work overseas or start my own company; I started my own company with two partners at age 23. That was a great success. We opened in New York as well, also with good success.

I left four years later and opened another agency, which I sold to John Singleton, then I ended up opening Love three years ago. Love is part of a joint venture with Reg Grundy: we own twelve marketing companies, under the umbrella of the Photon Group — a photon is a particle of great energy and movement.

It is hard to look back with accuracy and report on your mental state, but what I became very excited about was human potential, the idea that there was a limitless future, and the concept that your future is only dictated by your own imagination. This is said so often, but you only appreciate it when you really think about it. It is perhaps the most profound idea of all leaving aside spiritual ideas. I fell in love with the idea that I could be great. I am not saying now that I have got anywhere near that, but it doesn't really matter; the point is that I became very future-focused rather than past-focused.

I think there are two types of people in the world. There are past-based people, people who have had a certain amount of success with something in their lives and try to replicate it — it may be success in a subject at school — so they do that forever in some form, or success socially, and they replicate that forever. Then there are future-based people, who are always three years or five years out of where they want to be, but who are moving towards something. They are not letting their past dictate what their future is going to be. This is not my concept, it is a concept developed by a great personal coach in Canada named Dan Sutherland.

So I moved from being 'I am no good at school' to 'What could I become?' Past-based to future-based.

First of all, I had no idea whether I was any good at this craft called advertising, so the first challenge was learning how to do it. And that took years. I couldn't understand why some ads were good and some ads were bad, and why my boss would turn ads down. I had to really learn about it. And so I had to sit down and study this. I became very well known in my office for never, for instance, going to the men's room without taking an annual of the best advertising work with me. I studied these annuals to the point where I could tell you, from an annual ten years ago, who wrote this major ad, what the last line in the copy was, who art directed it and sometimes who set the type in it, because I was relentlessly studying the great writers in advertising.

The first step was to learn how to do it; the second step was to get to an agency that was doing award-winning work, because if you get stuck in an agency that is doing poor work, then your teacher is probably not even skilled enough to teach you how to be great. You have to get out and get someone above you who can be your mentor.

What I realised was that I loved learning; what I didn't like was learning about things that I didn't enjoy. The truth was that I was quite an able student, it was just that no subjects inspired me at school. I sometimes think, 'Wow! If I was at school now I would have a fantastic time.' I probably have 600 books at home, but if you tried to make me read one at school I would be kicking and screaming all the way to the library. So I fell in love with learning, and of course it's like Einstein said, people love chopping wood because you can see immediate results. I would see an improvement month by month in my skill in advertising, and that would be exciting and would propel me and motivate me to move to the next stage.

There are two parts to advertising, which is why it is such a vibrant industry — it really is a collision between creativity and business. After a few years I had learned how to write ads, I had learned the creative side, but I had hair down to my shoulders and would dress in wacky outfits and was the complete creative cliché. What I had to learn about was business, so for the next few years I cut my hair shorter, I began to dress a little bit more responsibly and I tried to learn about business. I am now 39, and I still have an enormous amount to learn about business. About how to get the sales machine going, how to get the new business machine going, how to read balance sheets well, how to predict cash flow, how to do all these other things. They are not my core competencies yet, but at the end of the day I need to advise clients on enormous issues to do with brand strategy, so they have to become core competencies.

At a certain stage you no longer go from junior to senior; the shift becomes from just doing ads to creating a strategy. People will spend $10–15 million on what you suggest, so you can't be cavalier about it. You often see, in our business, creative people reach a ceiling of complexity when it comes to understanding business growth — they can't rise above the ceiling, because all they are about is doing clever headlines. That's why I am now trying to finesse my understanding of profit creation.

A creative person has to be a great strategist, too, so that is another skill set that has to be learned if you are going to be at the top of your field. In many ways it is more important than the pure creativity — a lot of my business now is getting people underneath me to work to a high level, and part of that is being able to guide them to what the right strategy is. The world is full of funny ads or original ads, but original ads that can really improve sales are rooted in sound strategy rather than just originality. I now read books on business rather than on creativity.

I have a morning ritual which I got from an executive coach in New Zealand, Dr Fred Grosse: as soon as I get up in the morning, on most days, I go into the bathroom, open my goals book and read through the person I want to be and what my goals are. I usually spend a few minutes visualising that while I am waiting for the bath to fill, seeing my life unfolding in that way. You can go through a whole day without being focused if you don't start out right in the morning, so that's been a critical aid. The second thing — and this is no surprise — is the first thing that nine out of ten successful people do when they get up in the morning, which is write a 'to do' list for the day. I use a highlighter pen to outline the most important ones: I could have 12 things on my to do list today but only about four are absolutely vital, so I try to do those first.

I also have a personal philosophy which sounds incredibly simple, but took me 20 years to work out. I have stuck this on my desk so I can see it all the time: PD 20. PD 20 stands for what I think are the three most important ingredients of becoming successful.

P stands for positive thinking. If you achieve anything of note you are going to have to overcome enormous obstacles, so you need to be able to persist, and in order to persist you need sheer willpower. The only way you are going to do it is by believing that you can, and that creates the motivation to go forward, so it's P for positive thinking.

D is for definiteness of purpose. Very late in his life Napoleon Hill had a conversation with Clement Stone, who was a big supporter of his and also an extremely successful man. Hill had studied hundreds of the most successful people in the world and been introduced to presidents. They had an argument over which was more important — Clement Stone said positive thinking and Napoleon Hill said definiteness of purpose. I think in many ways they are both right: positive thinking and definiteness of purpose are both critical. I put definiteness of purpose equal with positive thinking because one of my flaws has been waiting, or going off and doing other things.

And the final 20 is just based on the 80/20 principle: just do the 20 per cent of things that matter. PD 20 — just do the things that matter. At the end of the day we have information overload, we have activity overload, and only a little amount of what we do is really going to make a difference. Focus on the 20 per cent that creates the 80 per cent.

Balance in my life? Well, first of all I don't generally work long hours. I work from 9 a.m. until 6.30 or 7, and I do a few hours on Sunday, but that's about it, so compared to many people who are senior in their profession I work shorter hours. I think limiting your hours forces urgency and effectiveness on you — if you can work until 10 p.m. on something, there is no impetus for you to do it quickly.

I used to work night and day, but I don't think it is particularly productive. Once, when I was working at an agency, my creative partner and I would work until every single other person in the agency had gone home. Didn't matter if they worked until 11 p.m., they would see us still at our desks. That was lunacy; that was trying to psyche everybody else out, to let them know that they could never work harder than us.

There are people in the world who do in two hours what other people do in a week. The thing is, you need to be only interested in output. You should be judged by your output. The world is full of people working 16 hours a day and not earning any money. Literally, what is the output? How many people have you helped? How have you leveraged your talents?

So number one, I limit the amount of time I spend, for balance. Two, I meditate. I try to meditate 20 minutes a day and on Thursday and Sunday I meditate for an hour or an hour and a half. Three, I have a girlfriend who always has social activities on and hates to be picked up late, so I have to finish work early to take care of her.

The hardest thing when you're young is deciding what you want to do. The way to decide is to begin doing something and stick with it for a while. You just have to begin. My suggestion, having looked at this issue a lot, is to give yourself a time limit. So you say, 'I will commit to this career for one year or two years and on this date I will re-evaluate it.' The biggest mistake that young people can make is to go half-heartedly into something and always be questioning whether

216

they are doing the right thing — a year or two soon goes by and they have achieved hardly anything. They still are in a state of uncertainty, and they have been passed by people in the same career stream who are committed to it.

So go full on, but give yourself a date when you will evaluate it. If worst comes to worst and one year on you decide that what you're doing is not what you want to do, then go full on into the next thing. Ultimately, you will probably decide that being totally committed to something is the right thing, because the truth is it doesn't matter what career you commit to — if you're committed you will do well. You will also have learned a lot in the meantime; you may have been in the wrong career, but you will have learned discipline and skills anyway.

Strategies for living
YOUR DREAMS

Nurture your interpersonal relationships Treat others as you wish to be treated, respect others as you like to be respected, listen to others as you wish to be listened to, speak to others as you like to be spoken to, share with others, give to others without wanting anything in return. Be a mensch!

The key to success in interpersonal relationships is to be able to give unconditionally, to love a person for who they are — not for what they can provide or for the entertainment of their company.

You never know the extent and the impact of a kind word or a smile. Countless tales have been told by those who have been on the brink of suicide and who have re-evaluated their lives after being assisted, even smiled at, by a complete stranger. These selfless acts of kindness and caring can change lives — if we all think for a moment, I'm sure each of us can recall a moment of pure kindness, kindness with absolutely no ulterior motive.

Giving a smile leaves you no weaker or poorer, takes less effort than frowning, and could light up your life and the lives of countless others.

Take action — smile and give unconditionally for a few days, treat others as you wish to be treated and you'll see, it will make your day.

Julia ROSS

Julia Ross was born and educated in the United Kingdom. In 1988 she formed what is now well known as Julia Ross Recruitment, which is the first female wholly-owned company to list on the Australian Stock Exchange. Since listing, the group has acquired several other companies including the Global Human Resources Division of PricewaterhouseCoopers, renamed Firstwater. The group's activities now include specialisation in office support, call centre and administration as well as providing executive and specialist recruitment in accounting, sales and marketing, IT, and banking and finance. As Managing Director, Julia Ross has almost 20 years' experience in the personnel and recruitment industry. Julia has been a finalist several times in the Telstra Businesswoman of the Year awards, has won the Chief Executive of the Year Award, and her business has been ranked as one of the Top 25 businesses in New South Wales.

My goal in starting my own company was to build something that had all the things that my competitors' companies had — all the processes and systems — but was a little different from a cultural perspective. I wanted to give the people inside the business more ownership of what they were doing. I'd worked for a very large multinational before and found that people really didn't share in the benefits, so my idea was very much about allowing the people in the organisation to share

219

in what we are doing. I also wanted to build something that was more innovative — younger, fresher, and with our people more involved.

I come from a family where my sisters and brothers were all similar. We always talked, as children, about what we were going to do, so I think that's where it started. I was also very lucky that early on in my career I had several mentors, who took my germ of an idea and helped me think that it was possible for a woman to do it. I was lucky to have those mentors or I might not have carried it through. It had really been in my head as a child that I would go into business for myself so it wasn't something that just happened. There was also a trigger — I disliked the person I was working for in the company I was in, and we parted ways. That was the catalyst, but the idea had always been there.

When I went out on my own, I originally had no grand vision. People talk about having an amazing vision from day one, wanting to conquer the world. I didn't have that sort of vision. I just wanted to create something here in Australia that was different, that was unique, that was a challenger to the internationals, but that was a different type of company culturally. So there wasn't a grand vision, but my personality is that enough is never enough. Each time I achieve something I find something else: I say I want to have a $10 million turnover this year, I want to achieve such-and-such things, I want to be dealing with these clients. Then I'd achieve that, and the next year I'd say let's do twenty, let's do fifty, let's do a hundred and let's go and win these clients or come out with this new service or this new division … whatever it would be sort of evolved. The company evolved over time.

I certainly didn't sit there 12 years ago and think we were going to be a publicly listed company now or how we were going to do it. It's just been a progression — and it still is. The plans I have now are way away from where we are, so there's still a lot more to do.

I think money is always the biggest challenge. Attention to cash flow in the early stages is crucial: this is a negative cash flow business, so whenever you grow you're eating up cash. Keeping firm control of the financial side of the business was perhaps the most worrying part, but it was not what I was doing most of the time — I was out selling, and employing people (as we started growing) to do the consulting.

I suppose the most challenging thing was learning. I had been part of a large group and was very fortunate that I was trained in a lot of things. But I had not been trained in how to do it with no cash or very little cash. That was the big difference. When you work for a big multinational company you just ask them to send over a few more millions because you have to do this or that, and they do, so you don't really think about these sorts of challenges. Being a female, the banks weren't interested in helping me and there was a lot of opposition — there was certainly no confidence that I was going to make it. A lot of people were very negative and really couldn't see why I should go out on my own. The most worrying part was the financial part, so that became the most challenging. For me hard work is hard work; that's not really challenging. The challenging things are the things you can't always fix, such as finding more money.

I control things very much myself. I did my own books, and therefore understood what was going to be needed from a cash perspective from early on in the piece, which has been very good as the company grew — I've always understood the company's financial dynamics. That was very important. I didn't employ an accountant in the business. Obviously I had my external accountant, but I did the books myself and really kept a very firm handle on what was going on.

I understood that if we had five more temps out next week, or ten or twenty, we were going to have to pay them, and it would take us four to six weeks to get the money back from the client. I understood the negative flow of that. If I were going to advertise, I knew when we had to pay for those ads and when I was likely to fill the job advertised. I am a very hands-on person. I have a very inquisitive mind and I don't like surprises, I don't like shifting sands. I like to know where things are, so in the early stages I did all of that myself. I think that was very important. Most people that I've seen in business startups fall over because of lack of control; I kept the controls very firm to begin with.

The company is my lifeblood. I can never be interested in another venture while I have this business. It is me, it is my people.

When we publicly listed on the stock exchange people invested a lot of money in the float and I made a commitment to what we were going to do over the next few years. I am certainly going to achieve that. I enjoy it. I love what I do. I can't imagine having as much fun doing many other things; this is what I know. I am sure people on the Internet have great fun with what they do but this is a real business, it's something that's very tangible. When you go into a company and put temporaries into their call centre, you fix the problem for them; you get their customer service the way they want it to be. Or you supply staff, you get a top executive a fabulous PA. It makes a real difference to the companies we deal with when we do that. It's a real business.

My life is very stable. My son, who is 14, always knows where I am. There's not a moment that he doesn't know what number to get me on, so he knows he's very cared for. We spend a lot of time together before I come to work. He probably knows how to put make-up on better than me! He stands alongside me and we talk. I ask him what he's going to be doing that day — if he's not at school, of course! The days he's home he comes in and we have a proper chat about what he's going to be doing. We talk about how he's going at school, what's happening, and when I get home we do the same again: we sit down at the table and have dinner together. He's 14, so he comes out for dinner with me and we do things. Kids are happy if you communicate with them, if they know where they are at.

I've always had a policy that weekends are free. I've virtually never accepted doing anything on the weekend. I do work long hours during the week but I won't work on weekends; it's just a thing that I have. So my son and I have a lot of time; his father died, so we have a lot of special time just the two of us. We have a special relationship. James's school asked me to speak to their school leavers recently and James was so proud that I was the only person invited to do a speech. He knows that I am off doing something that's important to me, and he wants me to be happy.

I think I am a better person for having that really good relationship. I think I've been a calmer person because of it. If I had been frustrated and not been able to do what I wanted to do, I don't think we would have discussed the things that we have. I don't think I would have been calm. There's never a time that I've shouted at him or hit him; we sit and have great conversations. If there's something that I think is not good for him or if there's something I want to explain, we talk about it. It's communication — we have a very calm relationship because we're both happy. I'm very happy with what I do and I am very happy that he allows me to do that.

The worst thing parents can do is beat themselves up about not being something that they can't be. You're either the sort of person who enjoys doing tuck shop or you're not, and maybe your child would prefer you to be who you are and do the best you can with yourself. Many women get so upset that they have to get up an hour earlier than their male counterparts because they have to dress the kids and get them off to school and then go to work — they have to be great mothers, great lovers, great workpeople. They have to fill all these roles that their male counterparts don't, and they're judged on many other things. For me, you have to accept that you can't please everyone; you have to be yourself and do the best that you can do and not beat yourself up over it. I am not a perfect person, but I do the best I can — that's all you can do — and James seems to be happy.

My people are great motivators to me, and that's a very big thing with me — when I come back and I've won a new client, my people feel so proud of the business. We've just delivered eucalyptus trees to all our clients, for example. We asked them to plant a tree for Australia Day and my people were just so proud that we'd done something like that, as opposed to other companies that might send something that's really not significant for Australia Day. We felt that was something we wanted to do. My people inspire me a lot — we also ordered meat pies for Australia Day, so all our people are having lunch internally and our branches are having a bit of fun today, too.

My son James, of course, also inspired me; when he was little I really wanted to provide for him, and that motivated me, because it was a basic necessity that I made enough money to be able to educate James well. Of course that stage of his life passed and I had to re-evaluate why I was doing things at a certain stage in my life — there really wasn't any need financially. I had to think about what my new values were, in a way, what my reasons were for doing it — it turned out to be a sense of achievement.

I am a person for whom, as I said, enough is never enough. I keep challenging myself all the time. I have fun with new challenges. I don't want to necessarily be the largest recruitment company but I want to be the best. I like to give my competitors a run. I find it fun that they gnash their teeth! They sit out there and they know we do different things, innovative things. We challenge who they are and what they're doing by some of the stuff we do. I know they're going to be very upset about things we do.

Enough is never enough — that's what they call me.

Brian
SHERMAN

Leading businessman Brian Sherman is President of the Australian
Museum Trust, a director of Channel Ten (Ten Network Holdings Limited
and The Ten Group Pty Limited), Chairman of Sonic Communications
Pty Limited and Pulse International Pty Limited, director of a number of
investment companies listed on the American, Canadian and Australian
stock exchanges and a member of IIBAB, which advises the New South
Wales Government on policies for IT companies. Brian was also
Chairman and Joint Managing Director of the EquitiLink Group from its
inception in 1981 until its sale to the Aberdeen Group in December 2000.
EquitiLink was one of the largest independent funds management groups
in Australia, managing some A$6 billion on behalf of international
investors in world share markets and fixed income markets. In 1996,
Brian was appointed to the main board of the Sydney Organising
Committee for the Olympic Games (SOCOG) as a director and also
chaired SOCOG's Finance Committee. He is involved in a number of
charitable projects and was Executive Producer of a documentary movie
that was nominated for two AFI (Australian Film Industry) Awards in 2000.

I was brought up in South Africa and I grew up in a rather
complex situation. It was during apartheid, which was a
corrupt regime morally and ethically. My short-term goal was
to gain an education and to move out from where I had been
brought up.

I think it was really a moral and ethical view that my family had, that apartheid was reprehensible, and as a Jew I was more acutely aware of injustices than most people. So given the situation in South Africa in 1976 we made a decision to move. Our immigration papers came through on the day of the Soweto riots, an important day in the history of South Africa. On that day I gave notice to the investment bank where I worked and shortly thereafter we came to Australia.

We looked at the US, because most of my family is in the US — I have first cousins in nine American cities — but my wife Gene's family had already migrated to Australia. She had emigrated there with her family in the early 1960s, but went back to South Africa after a year. For us it was a toss up between New York and Sydney. At the end of the day we came here because it's a beautiful city with lots of opportunity and people were extremely friendly; that's never changed for us.

On coming to Australia I joined one of the major banks on the investment management side. I really had to become a cadet again. I had to go backwards in order to learn about Australia, Australian stocks and regulations. Obviously I knew no one aside from a few members of my wife's family in Australia, so I had to retrain myself. I stayed within the ambience of a bank, and became one of the three senior fund managers at Westpac. Gene's cousin Laurence Freedman was in competition with me in the fund management area, with Bankers Trust; we used to see each other in the lobby of companies like Western Mining, both of us pitching for business for our respective firms.

We decided to get together and start a fund management company of our own. We started from scratch, with no clients and no funds, but we had experience and a track record, and over 19 years we built up a business with over $6 billion under management. We raised some $4 billion in America, listed five companies there, and made about 72 trips to the US on road shows from Australia. We really cracked the US market — we were the only Australian fund managers ever to crack the US market — and we were backed by Prudential, Merrill Lynch and Smith Barney.

As a migrant you're, first, looking to remake yourself. Second, the South African schooling system was very tough and formalised and organised, so I came from a very structured environment. Third, as a Jew I was always looking for better things — not necessarily materialistic things, but certainly mental things, and expanding one's vision and horizon. Maybe coming from a small town contributed as well, as did having a father who had migrated in 1910 from Lithuania and who went out to work at 14 — I continued that trend.

Starting anew in Australia was a humbling experience, but it had a positive impact. I knew that I could start from scratch — with a clean piece of paper — and remake myself in my own world. We never looked back on the emigration. When we came here, we said in two years we would sit down and discuss how we were going. We never did sit down after two years, though, and we never looked back.

I've been very successful. I sold EquitiLink and made a lot of money. I've done a huge number of things in the community, in a variety of situations. I did the memorial for the 11 Israeli athletes killed in Munich at the Olympics, which the IOC had blocked for 20 years, for example.

I still have that inner drive and force. I've now gone into a technology company. It was a one-man show originally, but we had 55 people working there in a year. I'm on the Channel Ten board, and I am President of the Australian Museum Trust, and a whole host of other things.

I'm a lateral thinker. I don't work logically: I don't go from A to B and from B to C. I try to get the whole picture and then I like filling in the missing pieces. I need to understand the vision and the core, and that's what becomes my driving force. I really enjoy the challenge of coming to grips conceptually with different things and that's why I've now gone into technology, the museum, the environment and animal rights — they're all new worlds for me, and I'm always struggling to try to come to grips with new worlds. Once I've done that I can start adding pieces and actually progressing things and pushing them along.

The Olympics is a good example. I was appointed to the SOCOG board in 1996, and was then appointed the chairman of finance. I knew nothing about the Olympics or about SOCOG when I joined. It would have taken me all the time between then and the Olympics to learn everything I needed to know if I'd used a logical approach, so I kind of tackled the whole thing simultaneously. Running the finances was a huge responsibility, but we did it successfully and we made a trading profit. It was a major challenge, though. I think it's the determination to understand that pushes me along.

To remain focused and not get distracted is something internal. I think what's important is the determination to understand — I don't let go until I accomplish that.

The family is absolutely number one for me. I have a very close relationship with my son and daughter. I'm working with both of them and doing things with both of them. My wife's also been extremely active running Sherman Galleries, on lots of cultural boards and having gained a PhD in French Literature and lectured at Sydney University. We've been in step together over 33 years. We've both gone forward, both accomplishing. It's not a smooth ride in terms of accomplishment, though — you go up and down. It's like a duck gliding on a lake: you have to be paddling underneath. It looks like plain sailing but it never is. Essentially it's striving. I think we both respect each other in the way we operate. The family side has worked extremely well.

Determination is one main ingredient, and maybe seeing oneself within the overall context of the community. At the end of the day, as an individual, you can either contribute to the community or you can just be passive, munch on the grass and depart peacefully.

There are always going to be ups and downs. I think one learns from the downs. I think my recommendation would be to not question continuously, but to push on — you only have one life, so make the best of it. It's crazy to make the worst of it!

I can take risks to an extent greater than many others I know because I see myself as a grain of sand within the cosmos — that means that at the end of the day, what I do is not all that serious. So on the one hand I take things seriously and I push forward, but on the other I know that I'm just here for a short while and that I'm just a fragment of the world, of the universe. I can take risks; I'm not scared to take risks.

I also like to beat the odds. I like to accomplish. I like to go forward. It's really like a psychotic game of chess. I'm playing the game, making the moves and I'm also part of it. I like to win the games. I like the challenge of understanding and that understanding comes for me through daily activity. I like to play different games of chess — technology chess, environment chess, a whole lot of different kinds. It's the reaching of understanding that drives me. At the end of the day I balance the accomplishment of understanding and the knowledge that I will never fully understand, that I am just one part of the cosmos.

Strategies for living
YOUR DREAMS

Overcome your fears There's absolutely nothing wrong with being afraid. It's simply part of being human. The difference between most people and successful people is that successful people take action and move forward despite the fact that they are terrified.

To achieve your goals and realise your potential you must be willing to be uncomfortable — to do things that you're afraid to do.

When you're gripped by fear and apprehension, it's usually because you're stepping out of your comfort zone. But by confronting your fears one by one and taking action, you expand your comfort zone and develop additional confidence. With practice, activities that previously may have terrified you become part of your routine.

So next time you are faced with a fearful task, remember that by taking action you are an instant champion!

Do the thing you fear and the death of fear is certain.

RALPH WALDO EMERSON

Juanita
STEIN

Singing sensation Juanita Stein, the lead singer and guitar player of the Sydney-based band Waikiki, is going for gold with their unique brand of melodic pop music. After only four years Waikiki is riding high, with a well-received string of singles and a debut album, I'm Already Home. With her creative energy and zest for life, Juanita has capitalised on a new-found writing partnership with her brother, producing 25 songs. Having completed a very successful tour on New Zealand and Australia earlier this year with the Big Day Out, Juanita hints at being more experimental as the band prepares for their next album. With their rave reviews, Waikiki will continue to produce music that their audience loves and appreciates.

You know I think it all began when I was in my mother's womb. My father (he is a musician) used to write songs, and every time he would write a new song he would play it to me in the womb, so it is an inherent gift — it is a thing my father pushed on to me before I was born. He was a huge fan of Bob Dylan and The Beatles and he used to play all their songs. I think I was getting those vibes, because it is inherent in me now. It is just something that's in me.

I remember that at a pretty young age I kind of knew that whatever I did in life I would be successful at it. I knew I was interested in entertaining, so at that point I either wanted to be in film or music. I wasn't sure which way it was going to go, because I loved movies and I still love movies — and I still hope that I will be involved in that at some point.

It all fell into place when I picked up a guitar for the first time. I was probably 12 or 13, and that was it. It was so simple. You know when something is right — it just feels right and it is easy; it isn't a struggle. Within 20 minutes I had written my first song — I had never had a lesson but taught myself how to play chords. It was not that I knew immediately what to do, but I knew intuitively that I had to keep going and that I had no choice — I just had to keep going and it would all fall into place. The further you go, the clearer your vision becomes.

I recall at one point thinking, 'I don't want to play other people's music — I don't want to be just another band. I write songs that are interesting enough for people to hear, and Joel's a guitarist so I'll ask him.' Joel, my brother, had just started guitar — he was obsessed. I am talking about locking himself up in his bedroom for eight hours a day, playing guitar. I knocked on his door, asked 'Do you want to start a band?' and he said, 'Yeah' and that was it. I kind of knew.

I feel it is some people's fate to struggle with whatever field they choose to be in. There may be some areas of my life that are a struggle, but I always felt my career would not be a struggle. Although there are definite goals you have to achieve — I don't want to say it's easy, because it has been hard work — it has been fairly obvious what has to be done to make the band work.

When I got together with Joel, I knew that the formula was right, and as obsessed with music as we were, we had the elements that could come together. Our ambition is phenomenal, and what we want to achieve is phenomenal, and I don't see any reason why we can't achieve it. To start my band Waikiki was the first step. I had been in one other band before and it didn't feel right. I also sang a lot in duos and had done a few shows by myself and it just wasn't the thing either.

Now I want us to establish ourselves as respected, successful musicians and as people who are respected and recognised. I want that to be long term, but I also want to be recognised on a greater scale, and I want to influence other people the way that great musicians influenced me. I am so unbelievably determined to make it happen. I have so much to give and so much to prove. It's that perpetual kind of desire that pushes you.

The arts is an impossible and crazy industry — all the arts. To be a successful musician — or actor, fashion designer, artist — is not based purely on talent. So the initial challenge is to get heard among all the others. I believe it is a combination of talent and luck.

We were a little lucky because when we first started we recorded our own demo. We didn't have any help or any management, instinctively I knew what to do. And then Daniel, who was a really good friend and had been involved in the music industry, took eight or nine copies of the demos and gave out a few and we got some really strong responses almost instantly. That was the first step to getting heard.

A major challenge is to keep being successful. You can make an impact, but I don't want that impact to be for a few seconds. We had a little bit of a reaction when we started and it was all really positive. We got good reviews and it was like … hey, we're here! But staying there is hard — you've got to be consistently good. You can't just put out one good single; you have to keep impressing all the time. It is a challenge to make yourself known. Writing good music, evolving and pushing yourself and being competitive and, as cheesy as this sounds, keeping the dream alive …

Touring has probably been one of the hardest things. I consider myself a fairly balanced human being, and to spend

80 per cent of your time in a car or on a plane — it does really strange things to your head. People talk about it all the time, but until you start doing it you can't really understand. It's like: get out of a car, into a car, get on a plane, get on a bus — and all for the 45 minutes that you are on stage. You give every bit of energy that you have, and then you get off and that's it, but you have do the whole thing again the next day. Touring really does get to the point where you wake up and you forget what city you are in, and that can mess with you — in terms of keeping balance.

Occasionally Joel, or Brendan or Glen, the other guys in the band, will look at me and say, 'We're doing well. It's worth it!' This is why we do it — the response, the reaction, the appreciation. When you have fans who come up to you after the show and get you to sign autographs and tell you that a particular song really moves them — that's worth it, that is what you do it for.

The first ingredient is that you have to believe in yourself. If you don't have that initial belief success is not going to happen. Why would I sell something to the public that I didn't believe in? So you have to believe in yourself beyond all means — that is the most important thing to me. And two, you have to be persistent, and persistent means not giving up, no matter what. I can't say that I have had all the triumphs and tragedies yet that I know a lot of artists have experienced, but you have to have belief and persistence, a combination of the two.

I would love to confidently say that gender wasn't at all an issue in the music industry, but it is because they do treat you differently and you do meet fairly different hurdles. But if I had to advise another girl — a guy or a girl, either one — I would say exactly the same thing: you just need belief and persistence. Then I believe that if it is your path you will get there. Amelia Earhart was a huge hero of mine growing up —

she was the first female record-setting pilot. I am not particularly interested in aviation or planes; it was more her struggle and the fact that she succeeded. Another hero was Josephine Baker, a black female performer in the 1920s who pushed through all the boundaries, and John Lennon and Bob Dylan and Arthur Rimbaud, a nineteenth-century poet. They were all fiercely independent, creative individuals who marched to the beat of their own drum, didn't subscribe to convention and kept going no matter what hurdles were thrown in their way. They made their mark. In the end that is what I want to do: I want to make a mark, I want people to remember me, so they are my heroes.

My parents have been a huge influence. They are extremely inspirational and supportive. My dad is a musician and I think he has taught me more about music than anyone has. My mother, who was an actress, is also very artistic.

We grew up in a very, very tight, artistic, bohemian kind of family — anything goes and whatever you want to do just do it, as long as you love it. So if we stumbled along the way and hit a few walls, our parents watched and helped and guided. And ever since I was a child my mother has told me that if you want something badly enough you will get it. As simple as that. So I have taken her advice. She might regret it sometimes! My brother Ari has been a great inspiration too.

We've been a band now for four years, and the process is slow. You record an album or you record one song and it's only played on the radio maybe a year later, and then it might be 18 months later before commercial radio picks up it. One territory starts becoming familiar with you and then you start another territory — we might not get to America for another five years, and we'll have to start all over again there. In terms of determination it helps to be patient, not to have a particular timeframe.

When we first started the band I was so shy, and in fact throughout my high school years I was shy. I was not the most obvious entertainer. I did school concerts and stuff but I was very nervous. With performing it is time that counts — confidence is something that grows. It's not like determination, which I had from the very beginning: my confidence has propelled beyond what I had imagined, and it's all to do with life experience and how you choose to grow.

When I began I didn't know if anybody would like what I did. You need a bit of a pat on the back, and once you get that — just a few people to say, 'Well done, we really believe in what you do', and some really positive reviews from the media — it's easier.

I know that in ten years I am going to be successful at what I do. It is not easy. The general nature of an artist is a very sensitive one. We give our hearts and souls. It's not like I am writing an essay on the life of Albert Einstein and someone is going to critique it. I am giving my *everything*. For someone to then turn around and say, 'You know what? I give that five out of ten', it's like, 'Wow, you are rating my soul here!' Rejection is something I am particularly sensitive to. Joel, on the other hand, is a lot better with it. But I have learned to follow what Joel says: I do what I do and if they don't like it, that's their stuff. I am getting more of that attitude. The more confident I get the better I deal with rejection.

The Lord makes roads and we just drive — that was a phrase I heard once. I really like that idea. Your path is made and you have a general sense of what you need to do in life and you just do it. You push through and you are confident and you are proud. You are most definitely going to be rejected and knocked around, and if you give up, then it's not meant to be, so stay positive and fiercely determined.

Amanda
STEVENS

In 1995, at the age of 21, Amanda Stevens founded Splash Group, a specialist communications consultancy based in North Sydney. Since then she has doubled the size of the business every year and has grown the company to a multi-million-dollar business. In 2002 Amanda won the Young Australian of the Year Award for Career Achievement in NSW and in 2000 she was named Young Business Woman of the Year by the Sydney Business Review. In 2003 she was awarded the Centenary Medal for Career Achievement and her work for charities such as the Make-A-Wish Foundation. Amanda is also the author of High Heeled Steps to Success, a collection of inspiring stories of 22 successful young Australian women under the age of 33.

In 1994 I was freelancing and I came to Sydney for a contract. I had built up some freelance work around about the same time and when my contract finished I had a lot of freelance projects to complete. My plan was to finish those and then get a proper job again. What happened was that I was getting a lot of work doing brochures and direct mail and realised that there was a gap in the market, and that I was really enjoying working for myself. I always wanted to have my own company but I never saw myself doing it at the age of 21. It was just about being flexible enough to realise that the opportunity was there.

I think I've always been really ambitious and I've always questioned things. I've asked why? Why does it need to be like this? I've always questioned people's standard vision of life. People tell you that you should go to school and then to university and then work for a really good, big company and earn a good salary, then buy a house. I wanted something a little bit different for my life. I just wanted to be a little bit more in control of my own destiny.

I was raised by my mum and we didn't have a lot of money. I think seeing her face such adversity — a divorce and then having to raise me on her own — inspired me. She was an alcoholic and seeing how unhappy she was drove me to create something better.

When I get really excited about something I will show that, and when I get really down about things I will show that as well. There is a perception that in business you should be a little bit more neutral about things, and it seems to be unprofessional if you show too much of your personality. But I have realised lately that this kind of suppression of feelings is not me. It's probably the one thing that I would say to people, particularly women, because a lot of women think that in order to be successful they have to act like a man. I think that women bring a lot of unique things to the table in a business situation and taking things personally is one of them. I see that as a positive now, rather than a negative.

There were a lot of challenges at first, a lot of near-death experiences — for the business, not for me! Anyone who starts a business from scratch knows how hard it is to get from point A to point B. At the moment, we have pretty much doubled in size each year. No one who grows a business at that rate over six or seven years will tell you that it's smooth sailing, because it never is. Unexpected things always happen. For instance, I took on a business partner in 1995–96, someone I really trusted and looked up to, and he did the wrong thing by me. I ended up responsible for about $60,000 in debt that he had accrued in my name. It's funny ... I was near bankruptcy, and it's something I highly recommend, because it's really at that point that you find out what you're made of. I look back on that time now and I'm really glad that it happened. Going through that probably saved me from something worse down the track.

I have a long way to go in business still, and I know I have a lot to learn, but when I think about what I know now compared with what I knew six or seven years ago, it's all been learned through trial and error. The only way you learn in business — at any age, whether you are 21 or 50 — is by making mistakes and learning from them. I like to fast-track everything and cram in many mistakes at once, early.

It is very difficult to start a business when you are both very young and female because people don't feel that you have any credibility. You have to work twice as hard to get the same level of respect as other people, but the outcome is the same. I was fighting the perception that you can't start a business when you're 21. My reaction to that is, why not? There are a lot of 21-year-olds I know who have far greater skills to start a business than a lot of 50-year-olds I know, yet it's far more socially acceptable to start a business when you're 50. What it comes down to is that a long time ago I just stopped caring what people think. At the end of the day, if you're doing your job, age shouldn't come into it.

I think it's always been part of my vision to be in control of my own life and not be running someone else's. My old boss actually said to me one day, 'You're really great at what you do, Amanda, but you know what your problem is? You just want to be the boss.' That's when I thought, 'What's wrong with that? Maybe I should be the boss.'

I have my own opinions on balance. Again, it's society's perception that you should have a life that looks balanced. If you read a book or listen to a seminar on the subject, or have a life coach tell you what your life should look like from a balanced perspective, you are told you should have equal quadrants of career, health — physical and spiritual — and family. Now that's not my idea of a balanced life; that is some-one else's idea of balanced. My idea of balance is with a work component that's far greater than the other areas. At the moment I choose to spend a huge proportion of my time on work and my physical health, and a smaller amount on family and spiritual wellbeing or whatever. Now someone could look at that and say, 'You're out of balance,' but to me my life is in perfect balance. I know people who work so hard trying to achieve someone else's notion of balance that it actually causes them stress.

Each to their own, I guess; it's just what feels comfortable. I have friends who are really focused on spiritual and health issues. They might focus probably 50 per cent on those issues and 20 per cent on their careers, because they're not as ambi-tious in that area.

To be honest, the other thing about balance is that it changes all the time. Family is not a huge priority for me at the moment, but in a few years' time when I want to have a baby it is going to be a much greater proportion of my balance equation. So my philosophy is to make sure that what you're striving for from a balance perspective is aligned to your goals, not aligned to what someone else thinks your balance should be.

I prioritise, and I have really good people around me. I'm working with a time management coach at the moment, because I know that I'm not working at an effective produc-tivity level. I'm creative and my mind races so quickly that while I'm doing something I will start thinking about something else, and I'll start working on the second idea … and soon I have five tasks happening at once and often not finishing two of them! I'm working with the coach on getting one thing finished before moving on to the next, rather than trying to race ahead.

For me, one of the hardest things about business is managing people. I don't think I'm a natural leader, I don't think I'm a natural manager. I'm more interested in being in control of my life. I think the whole concept of managing people is an oxymoron, because people are such an unquantifiable, unpredictable variable that trying to manage people doesn't make sense for me. I don't know that you can manage people; you can manage systems and then get people to follow those systems.

I motivate my team by being honest with them. Again, a lot of people say I'm too close to my team, I shouldn't show them so much of myself. Maybe that's true, but what I say is, 'That may work for you, but it doesn't work for me.' I don't want to wear a different persona when I walk into the office. I socialise with my team. The culture that I try to create here is one of a family, because I don't think it's fair for me to expect my team to spend eight, nine or ten hours here, five days a week, and not feel that they can share their personality and be themselves. And if that's what I want for my team, that is what I have to be too. We are like a family here, we know about each other's personal lives and we socialise together.

From the company's perspective, if things aren't going well — or if things are going really well — I'm honest about it with my team, because I'd rather they hear about it from me and get the full details than pick up a bit of it and not really understand the full story. I try to create an organisation that's very transparent, and to communicate and share my vision for the company with the team so that they are on board and feel that they're helping to achieve that vision. I don't know if it would work for everyone, and I'm not saying it's a break-through management technique, because it has its problems — you certainly expose yourself as a leader when you take on this style. I just decided that that's how I'd prefer to be. I prefer to run the risk of exposing myself for the up-side of having an environment like that.

Another challenge is growing the company at the rate that we've grown. There are standard issues of cash flow. I don't have a business partner and haven't had huge capital injections, so it's really been about growing it step by step. When you are growing a business rapidly, your cash flow has to stay ahead of the rate that you are expanding the business, and that can often be a bit of a juggle. But we're getting there.

The other part of our culture I really try to instil in the team is that if something is worth doing it is worth doing properly. If we can't walk into a pitch and say to ourselves, 'This is the very best we could have done', then there is no point in walking in that door. So when we know that we've produced our best work and we still don't win, it's soul destroying. I do take things really personally and when we lose some business or lose a pitch we really feel it. I don't know whether we feel it more than other companies, but we do feel it.

In fact we lost a piece of business this week. It was nothing to do with our work; it was a political decision and that's out of our control. I took the team out for drinks last night and we basically said, 'What can we learn from this?' The result is that we haven't really lost, as the situation has been a valuable learning experience. It's about trying to take something away from a negative outcome. Running a business is all about atti-tude. Things that disappoint you are always going to happen.

Things that are out of your control, that seem to be negative, are always going to happen too. You have to acknowledge that something has happened, the reality of it, and then ask, 'What is the up-side? What can I learn from this so I can move forward?'

You know something I've realised? I lost both my parents this year, and I think what I've taken away from that is understanding that if you don't experience the negative — the sadness and loss in life — there is no contrast; it's only because you've had sadness and negativity in your life that you can have really high highs.

I've had times where I've just thought, 'How the hell am I going to get out of this? You just have to push through. You get up in the morning and you just do it! And you NEVER, EVER GIVE UP!

One saying that really inspires me is from Eleanor Roosevelt. She said, 'The future belongs to those who believe in the future of their dreams.' That probably sums it up. Another one is a quote from Jim Rohn: 'You can live your life as either a warning or an example.'

Strategies for living
YOUR DREAMS

Overcoming challenges There is no one method of dealing with challenges. Some panic and give up right away; others try a little longer and then give up; others grit their teeth and say, 'I'll get through this, and I'll move on to the next step.' Although each person handles challenges and adversity differently, truly successful individuals proceed in similar ways. First, they don't panic. Second, they look at the challenge as an opportunity. Third, they never give up.

When you panic, you lose the ability to think rationally or focus on the issues at hand. You try to find the quickest, least painful way out — this is usually the wrong one, and is often one that drags you deeper into the whirlpool. Taking a deep breath and going for a walk to clear your mind is a good first step to defuse panic. It gives you an opportunity to get back your sense and tackle the challenge with clarity.

Assess what has happened. Gather all the information and material you need, and ask questions. What happened? Why did it happen? What are your options? What lessons can you learn from this? It's a whole lot easier to pick yourself up and brush off the dirt from a fall if you view these stumbling blocks as steps on the ladder of life, tests to be passed before you can graduate to the next level, the next stage in your life.

And finally, never give up! Each and every one of the people interviewed said that the ability to keep on trying and never give up, no matter how challenging or hopeless a situation may seem, is one of the key ingredients — if not the main ingredient — in the recipe for success.

John SYMOND

Aussie Home Loans is the brainchild of John Symond. John Symond grew up in New South Wales where he studied one year of dentistry, two years of Arts and then Law. He went on to establish one of Sydney's biggest suburban legal practices. In 1984 he set up his own financial services group which collapsed, leaving a three million dollar debt which John vowed to repay rather than be bankrupted. Financially broken, he determined to put up a fight against the unfair domination of banks. In 1992 John established Aussie Home Loans, which has grown to be Australia's sixth-largest home lender and the largest non-bank lender. Aussie Home Loan's loan portfolio is now worth more than $12 billion, with 170,000 customers.

I had a successful stint originally — 15 years in law — and then set up my own financial services group, and that was going very well. My first mistake was partnering with a State Government owned bank. I went into a joint venture with them and they ended up going broke. This joint venture included other people, and the bank dragged everybody down. That was in the late 1980s, when interest rates were 20 per cent. Over a two-year period I was forced to sell all my assets, and at the worst possible time, really. I lost everything, and still I had a shortfall; instead of going bankrupt I agreed with creditors to pay some millions over three years. I didn't know how I was going to do it. I didn't have a job, and I didn't have a marriage. I had two young kids at the time and no business, so I really had to work out a way to make sure my children — they were four and eight at the time — were going to get an education and survive. Plus I didn't want them growing up thinking their old man was a loser. So I thought, 'Well, what do I know?'

I knew I couldn't go and get a job with a normal salary — how was I going to pay back millions of dollars that way? My family and friends and advisers told me I was crazy to have taken on that amount, and they were probably right in the sense that it's impossible to pay millions back when you don't have a job. They thought I was just putting off the inevitable — I would go bankrupt anyway, so why put myself through the extra trauma? But giving up was never an option for me. I never ever considered it; I felt that if I did that I would be saying I was washed up for life, and I always felt I was going to do something big.

When you fall on hard times yourself, and you don't have $10 in your pocket, you realise how many other people are doing it tough, particularly people with kids — and I have always had a soft spot for kids, particularly my two kids. These people's kids may not get an education. My hard times made me a lot more sensitive to other people's worries and concerns.

I knew that the banking system in this country was just terrible — no service, no dignity, no choice. It was a cartel, really. I'd picked up a few ideas over the years from the US in terms of raising money, but I knew it was going to be difficult for me — I had no money, no reputation, a failed business, was bordering on bankruptcy and still owed millions. So I decided to try to put together an alternative. I developed a very strong, passionate vision to get out there and try to do something for both the community and myself, to help make sure my kids were looked after. That was my main reason for starting something that hadn't been done before.

Even though I'd always helped charities, it's the old story: when you hear these tragic stories about mishaps with kids or abuse it doesn't sink in as deep unless you have children yourself — then you think, if they were my kids how would I feel? I guess it's like being used to watching free-to-air TV, with three or four stations, and all of a sudden having someone come in and plug in cable, so that now there are 100 stations. It just widens your horizons. I became a lot more compassionate and sensitive to what people were going through, and I promised myself that if ever I got out of the mess I was in I would set up a children's charity, which is why I established the John Symond Foundation.

My main inspiration, without any doubt, was responsibility and concern for my kids. In fact that also gave me strength, because when I was upset emotionally, feeling that no one could help me, the best remedy was to ask myself what would my kids, if they were old enough, advise me to do — and they would say, 'Dad, don't give up, go for it.' Every time I'd do that, it was like recharging my batteries. I would just rise up again, strong and powerful. So every time I would get down — and this was a very regular thing, being down in the dumps to the point where I questioned myself — I would do that, and it worked every time. That feeling of responsibility gave me strength, and the more I met people in terrible circumstances, the more I felt that if what I was doing was successful, not only would my kids be looked after, but I could help these other people and show them the way too.

I knew that I had something like a 100-piece jigsaw puzzle, and that every piece had to be addressed separately before the picture could be formed. So I worked, and made sure that despite all the dramas I was encountering personally — plus holding off bankruptcy and putting out the fires from before — I was still putting Aussie together. And I learned that you have to separate the issues you are experiencing. People get engulfed by their problems and become totally focused on the negatives, and they forget about going forward. So I would go three steps back in some areas, but I would make sure that I was still moving forward in other areas. I found that that worked. I would say, 'Look, I know this is killing me, but hang on, I have to concentrate for the next three hours on this, I am not going to walk away from it.' And I would make sure I worked on that thing for those three hours. I had to concentrate on the 100 pieces of the jigsaw puzzle: Where do you get the money to lend to people if you're broke? How do you operate out of an office when you can't pay rent? How do you hire staff if you don't have wages for them? How do you do this, how do you do that? Every issue was a piece of the jigsaw puzzle.

You have to have something to hang on to when you're sinking. I had my two kids, who needed me. I am a very responsible person, so every time I was slipping, that anchor was there and I held on to it and climbed up again.

I had no social life for probably eight years. I was in a cocoon, I was totally focused. I used to hear people say, 'How hopeless is that guy — he has no life?' When I was still in chaos I had no balance, no relationships; I was alone. I wouldn't go out with girlfriends. I just said, 'I cannot do that, I cannot be distracted.' I just had to keep my hands firmly on the wheel.

Everything was an adventure. We re-created the rules every week, if not every day, and things were happening that had never happened before in business; it kept me alert, because I didn't know where the next missile was going to hit. And then when we were finally getting somewhere, the banks would do terrible things behind the scenes to try to smash us. The tougher it got, the more passionate and determined I became; the dirty acts that were happening just made me even stronger and more determined. I said, 'These bastards are not going to beat me,' and I could see even then that this thing was far bigger than I had ever envisaged. We were the only ones at that stage, there was no RAMS or Wizard — they came three or four years later.

There was no securitisation of home loans, which meant that I had to find a way to tap into capital markets so that Mum and Dad in suburban Blacktown could afford a house and get the same finance deal that BHP would get. That was a momentous thing, and after the jigsaw was complete, a whole host of new players came in — the blueprints were done, and other non-bank players entered the market copying what we had created. Now you have hundreds of players out there, which is great; it's a whole new industry employing tens of thousands of people.

I kept focused because it was very exciting. It was as if my adrenalin was pumping all the time, and eventually I felt that we were getting somewhere, that I had a chance of this business actually keeping its doors open. For the first three years I couldn't borrow money from anyone, so it was all done by juggling.

I found that I had strengths I never dreamed I had. When I was in high school I played rugby, but I could never go on the debating team. I would be great talking to three or four of my mates, but in front of people, no. What I learned during this process was that I can do that, and I often go and give talks to people now — groups, schools, charities, whatever.

I look at what we created, and I say to people, 'Picture me, on the mat bleeding to death, and a personnel crowd looking for a CEO to head up an organisation called Aussie Home

Loans. They need someone who is going to turn banking on its head, and change the way things have been done for a hundred years. They are looking for someone who is going to end up employing thousands of people, creating jobs for tens of thousands, changing government perception, dealing with the media … in an era when banks are going broke and people are getting ripped off — they want someone who can handle that. Not someone who is broke and owes money, but someone who is strong enough to re-create rules and, above all, make a difference.'

With my limited experience and my lousy current predicament, would I have even applied for the job at Aussie Home Loans? I am the most optimistic person, but I would have said no way. Skills? None at all. Well now picture me, still on the mat dying, and the crystal ball says, 'Just to make it hard, you are not going to have any money from anywhere to help you, and you are going to have to come up with millions of dollars to pay your creditors, and you are going to have no money to advertise.' Would I have tried? I wouldn't.

Yet now I find myself having steered the ship without any of the skills I was presumed to have, so I say to people, 'We all go through tough times, some tougher than others. There is an old saying, "When God gives you a gift he wraps it in a problem", and He gave me a big one. But you'll never know what treasures lie ahead if you don't have the guts and the determination to unravel that problem.' We have skills that we don't know we have. We just don't put ourselves to the test.

Now we have a very successful, large business. I have a strong management team around the country, and they don't need me to do 18 hours a day seven days a week. I still work hard though, because I have always been that way. But I do save weekends for myself. Always, even during the tough time, I've spent time with my children.

So now I have much better balance. Two years ago I broke out of my cocoon, and started going out and having a bit of fun. I never realised how obvious it was to the rest of the world that I was in a cocoon, locked away.

What I was trying to achieve was sort of the impossible. It wasn't normal; it was creating a whole new industry under very adverse conditions — not just adverse financial conditions, but an adverse personal, emotional state. When your emotions are affected it's more damaging than financial loss, because you lose your self-esteem, your credibility.

I honestly believe that people can have a balance; it depends on how high up the mountain you want to climb. If you really want to create new records or a whole new industry, you have to risk a lot more. I guess in a lot of ways I still was taking a risk, but I wasn't risking what normal people were risking.

There has to be compromise in life, in relationships, whether it's in how you manage people or in the way you operate. You have to recognise that you must compromise. A lot of people won't compromise, so they don't really get too far, because life is all about perception as opposed to reality, and it's how you are perceived that matters in business and relationships. It's not so much how you feel, it's how others feel about you. You need to demonstrate integrity in everything you do.

Ever since I was a young kid, there was always something quietly speaking to me, saying that I had an important role to play. I never knew what it was, but as the days and weeks went on when I started Aussie Home Loans, I started to realise that this, what I was doing now, was what this feeling I had always had was about, and that what I was doing could make a humungous change for many people.

Today, governments admit — as do the media, banks, and every part of the housing industry — that people in every street, every suburb, and every state in this country are three or four hundred dollars (after tax) better off every month because of the competition which we started.

So knowing this could be fantastic gave me the determination not to let it go. I realised that this wasn't just 'Hey, it will help my kids, it will help me' — it was bigger than that; this was a real community thing, a real people thing. When I started recognising that people power was the thing that was going to create this, I hopped up on banana boxes and did what no one had ever done before. I was outspoken and controversial.

And people listened. I say to people, including my senior executives, 'You don't have to be liked, but you do have to be respected, and if you haven't got good people on side you have no hope.'

I talk to people about the movie *Gladiator*. Two gladiators fight in it and Russell Crowe, one of them, ends up holding a pitchfork to the other guy's throat and looking at Caesar to see whether or not he should kill the man. Caesar is saying to kill him, but he is looking around at the mob and they are all going, 'No!' Caesar had to change, even though he was head honcho, because the mob wasn't on his side. In life, whether it is in business or whatever, if you don't have the mob on your side you'll fail, so never forget the respect of the mob. You have to make sure that you respect the mob, and you have to make sure that the mob respects you. And you can't get respect unless you give respect. I get along very well with the public around the country. I can't walk in the street without people coming up to me or smiling or yelling at me or whatever. That's where politicians fall down — they forget about the mob, but the mob doesn't forget them.

If you really believe in something, you have to be prepared to make sacrifices, you have to have a plan. I had a plan, though it didn't much feel like it at the time. I look back and think, yes, I did have strategies — the idea of the 100-piece jigsaw, for one.

You have to understand the industry you are in, inside out. You have to understand where the industry is heading; it's no good just trying to adopt best practice so you're as good as everybody else. You have to see where the industry is going to go over the next two, three, four, five years. You have to be able to visualise that and then you have to picture where you want to be then. Once you have done that, you have to make the hard decisions about what you need to do today to get to that position. That means sacrifice, that means determination, that means being really focused, that means being really positive, because it is very easy to get knocked over in life. You will continually stumble — you have to expect that — but if you are doing something good, something will happen.

You have just got to make a promise to yourself that regardless of how tough it is going to be, you will make the sacrifices you have to make. You have to remain positive, and stick with positive people. Avoid negative people. You have to know that the glass is always half full, not half empty. You also have to know when to quit something and move on to the next thing. Often, people — particularly in this country — have too many escape routes. We sit on the fence and we wait to be pushed. I waited to be pushed. The sad thing is that 99.9 per cent of the time, when we do get pushed it's too late.

Make the move yourself, because you might find that you have wings to fly — the means to survive and grow. When you get pushed, you usually end up crashing.

Years ago I heard one quote that stuck in my mind: 'Your future will be exactly what you decide it to be.' You're going to have to make that decision; no one else can do that for you. That is a favourite saying of mine.

254

I have six brothers and sisters; Dad and Mum were hard workers seven days a week, running a greengrocer's shop. I used to come home from school with my older brother and sister and we would go out the back and pack potatoes or other jobs. On weekends we would take it in turns serving customers. My dad did well. I really admired him. He had no formal education, and I thought, 'Gosh, I have been given an education, so I am going to have to do better, but how?' I always used to wonder what I was going to do and how I was going to be successful, and I always had this feeling — just a funny feeling like a whisper — that I would do something important. I didn't know what it was, but I heard the whisper.

Strategies for living
YOUR DREAMS

Think positive! I know you've heard this so many times before, and you may be saying 'Yeah, right!' But I do it myself, and have heard from many successful people that this is what helps them achieve their successes: they fill their minds with positive (can do) thoughts. There is no question that what you are thinking has a direct impact on your performance. It's evident in conversation and in the way you conduct yourself.

The trick is to fill your mind with positive thoughts at the beginning of each day, so that you have a reservoir of positive thoughts. Stop every now and then during your busy day to reflect for a moment on the positive components of your life: the people who love you and care for you, the successes that you have experienced so far, and the things that are going well for you. It's these thoughts that will encourage you and enable you to make that call, ask that question, accept that challenge and do an all-round fantastic job — your positive thoughts will help you think and realise that yes, you can do it, you are able and competent to get through all the challenges and obstacles you face.

Strategies for living
YOUR DREAMS

Learn from a thief!
1. What a thief does, he keeps to himself — he doesn't brag or seek attention.
2. A thief is willing to take risks to attain his goal.
3. A thief does not distinguish between 'major' and 'minor' when taking into account what might be in store, but devotes equal care to each and every detail.
4. He invests great deal of effort in what he does.
5. He is swift.
6. He is always optimistic.
7. If at first he fails, he goes back time and again for another try.

Simon
TEDESCHI

Simon Tedeschi was born in Sydney in 1981 and studied piano with
Neta Maughan for 10 years. He was a child prodigy, performing a
Mozart Piano Concerto at the age of nine in the Sydney Opera House.
This brilliant young Australian pianist has won many international
awards and prizes, toured widely locally and overseas, and has given
numerous broadcasts and recitals. He was the Symphony Australia
'Young Performer of the Year' in 1998. He is perhaps best known to a
wide audience for playing the hands of young David Helfgott in the
acclaimed movie Shine. His debut CD was released in May 2000.
He now lives in London where he is studying with Noretta Conci.

When it all began I must admit that visions and goals were
pretty much beyond me. I basically felt that I had some
sort of calling but I had no idea what it was, and then I saw a
boy with cerebral palsy playing a piano and something just hit
me: I knew I must be a pianist.

I was five, and to this day I do not understand the meaning or the rationale of that event. All I can say is that had it
not happened I would definitely not be playing, because I am
not what one would call an extremely focused, goal-oriented
person, yet I must have been back then, so ...

It all began with piano lessons with a local teacher. By
divine providence — or by council planning — she was living

in the same street as me and I embarked on piano lessons with her. She initially said that she would not take very young students, and she would not take students as young as me — I looked about three when I was five. I was very underdeveloped. But she did take me, and before long I was her best pupil. I played in her classes and tutorials for three years. In fact I learned the cello with her as well, but that was a dismal failure. She was very anxious for me to develop a sound technique, to be able to play by memory from the very beginning. She was a great teacher, she instilled very good discipline in me. After that I went to Neta Maughan, whom I was with for ten years.

That was really something. Neta was an amazing teacher, and her teacher had been a student of a student of Rachmaninov, so I come from a very proud musical heritage. She was a very eccentric lady, but she really did teach me all I know. I can say that with some certainty.

After that, well, since I was about 13, it has just been constant touring and performing, which obviously precluded some things — such as schooling, the HSC, having a normal life … everything has been thrown out the window because of piano playing. In one sense tunnel vision can be good, but it can also have a very unhealthy side. I think I have experienced both sides. I have kind of made up for all that now.

My mother was a very, very strong influence in my life. She was a pianist herself, before she had children. I have no hesitation in saying she did push me, and she gave me lots of great opportunities. She was a very overpowering presence and my father was a very stabilising influence. He's not musical at all, he is a lawyer, but he always made sure I con-centrated on other things apart from piano. I was very lucky in that respect.

I'm not sure what inspired me to keep going. I don't know.

I think the applause, the sense that I have done a good job, nothing more complicated than that. Just the satisfaction of coming off the stage and knowing that I have done a marvellous job and conveyed the composer's intentions in my own particular way and made some people very happy.

There is a very weird disparity between being a normal young man yet also being a musician, which nowadays entails being a psychologist, a businessman, a lawyer — it has so many facets to it. Yet trying to being a normal person, just doing normal things like going to the movies, going fishing, going kayaking, playing piano, I absolutely adore. However, playing piano is my job, so if I am going to relax I am not going to sit there and say, 'I would love to play a concert.' This is the difficulty: people assume music is something I do to relax, but I have been doing it for so long that it is very much a profession, which means that I don't understand the concept of music being a relaxant. Normally when I am playing seriously I am quite nervous, and the adrenalin is coursing through my veins.

I have had to live the life of an adult from childhood, and that is no easy feat. School was an enormous challenge, making and keeping friends was an enormous challenge … basically everything. Just development was an enormous challenge, being a coherent family member. For instance, going on holidays with my family — often I couldn't, or if I did I would have to bring a keyboard. These are very big things. And of course something I have had to deal with since I was a young boy is the inevitable phenomenon of jealousy, and also the tall poppy syndrome.

And there are other negative traits of this profession, such as difficult conductors, difficult composers, difficult people I have to work with. When I was a young boy I had to work with a conductor for about five years who was the most fearsome man I have ever worked with, and I think I am still traumatised because it really affected my development and my psyche.

My entire life has been a challenge — signing contracts, having to drink champagne with the heavies from a very early age. But then I would have a group of friends over and I would wreak havoc in the neighbourhood I lived in. I love wrestling and this has provided an amazing escape. Also kayaking. These things really save me from insanity, because as a young child it does go against the grain to be living 24/7 in the guise of an adult.

It has been about having fun — some would say unhealthy escape, but I call it having fun and just allowing my childhood not to be too stultified. That has been a really big thing, because the whole notion of the prodigy is so damaging to many a young player. I was called a prodigy, a genius, you know, whatever, and while it of course appealed to my ego and my narcissism, it does have long-term effects. Some people let it go to their heads, which I never did, or they let it be the backdrop for expectation, and that is something I have been struggling with my entire life — the notion of expectation, audiences' expectations.

By making sure I have a balanced life, and also by not doing too much, I try to make sure the old adage of quality and not quantity always remains in my life.

It's very difficult to balance work, family and commitments and I still have not got it right. I still have not got there. I just try to balance by spending my free time with friends, plus doing basic day-to-day things like business things or errands you've got to run. And then there's practising — and it is very easy not to practise at all. It is extremely easy just to let that fall by the wayside.

But if I am playing these amazingly wonderful pieces to appreciative audiences, I owe it to everybody in this eternal triangle of music — which is, I suppose, the audience and myself and the composer — to do a damn good job.

Practising — that is work for me. It depends on the piece I am learning, it depends on how I feel, it depends on how committed I am to the piece I am learning. It depends on the difficulties, it depends on whether or not I am playing it through to my teacher, but normally it is just slow practice, and that means taking the whole piece down to a basic tempo and really trying to get all the muscle movements right, and that is something that a pianist can take a whole year to master.

It sounds awfully pretentious to say this, but I feel that in some ways I have an old head on my shoulders. I don't know quite what the meaning of that is, but I feel that it is extremely important. I can't give you any abstract nouns now, like determination, because sometimes I am determined and yet other times I fail dismally.

I would say that a sense of humour in the music business is invaluable and imperative. The ability to laugh at yourself, to laugh at this whole strange perverse job, because if you can't laugh you will pretty much find yourself in a psychiatric home.

Someone thinking of being a musician should ask themselves, number one, whether they really want to do it, that it is not just other people who want them to do it more than they want to do it. Then they should ask whether they love music enough, and how talented they feel. You have to be at a certain level, and you have to be prepared to put in the hard yards, put in the hours. There is no escaping that. You also have to be prepared to work with other people quite collaboratively — in a symphony orchestra you are working with 70 other people. They are behind you, but ultimately you are out there by yourself, so it's quite paradoxical — you're there by yourself and yet you are with other people. And you might often not get to know any of these people very well.

Another big challenge I face is spending most of my life travelling by myself, with a suitcase, and living in a hotel room. I go to a foreign city and everybody says, 'Simon, you are so lucky.' I say, 'I am not lucky — I go in and go out.' It's very lonely. I have done this for years on end sometimes, and I have no qualms in admitting that this is one part of the job I really hate — the loneliness, the solitude.

A quote that's really pervaded my sense of self is, 'Ships in harbour are safe, but that is not what ships are for.' I thought that was a good line. It means that if you are really going to achieve something, musically or otherwise, you have to be projected out of your comfort zone, and that is very difficult. It is especially difficult when you are a child, because you are meant to be in your comfort zone then — that is what being a child is — and I never was. But you have to be outside it if you are going to succeed professionally.

So I would say just take action, but make sure you are able to watch a good wrestling movie in between, or get some time to yourself, take time to stop and smell the roses. You need to have fun, and in the end, if you are involved in some sort of creative endeavour, that will help — if you go to the museum or the art gallery it will help your piano playing. I don't know what it is like with sport, but I know that with something like music you need your brain to have all kinds of external influences — that is very important.

Strategies for living
YOUR DREAMS

Share your dream Surround yourself with and confide in people who are likeminded and will be supportive of your goals, values and dreams.

When you've just decided to take that first step, it is very easy to be knocked down by a well-meaning friend or associate who tells you it's not possible — you're too young, no way, don't even try, you'll be made a fool of, you'll lose money, you'll never be able to keep it up. And so on. We've heard it all before.

However, it's imperative that at this early stage you do ask for direction and possible constructive criticism. Talk to people who — even if they're not likeminded — are experienced in what it is you want to do. You need to be prepared for at least some of the challenges you may face along the way!

So until you're ready to take action, don't discuss your goals or dreams with friends or colleagues who are not likeminded, no matter how tempting it is. Some of these people may have a history of knocking you back and mocking your efforts; others may genuinely care about you but not share your ambitions and values.

Dream, think big, but only share your goals and plans with people who will encourage and support you. Then take action!

Karin
UPTON BAKER

An award-winning writer and editor, Karin Upton Baker spent 20 years working in fashion journalism and publishing. Since January 2001 she has worked for the French luxury group, Hermès, as Managing Director of their Australian operations. Upton Baker began her career at Condé Nast in 1980 working for Vogue Australia, where she held numerous positions including Beauty Director, Style Director and Deputy Editor. In 1995 Australian Consolidated Press, the country's largest publishing house, actively pursued her for the editorship of MODE Australia. The next year she led the magazine to its first ASME (Australian Society of Magazine Editors) award. As Editor-in-Chief, she brought Harper's BAZAAR Australia local and international acclaim, exceeding readership and business expectations. In 1999, the Magazines Publishers Association (MPA) named Upton Baker Editor of the Year. Karin Upton Baker lives in Sydney with her husband and two sons.

My original goal was to be a newspaper journalist, which is something I never did. Not by design, necessarily — by chance. You talk about people having a vision and having a very definite goal, but I actually haven't worked that way very much in my career. I suppose I went with the ebb and flow of what became apparent to me at the time, when I was looking for a job and to start making a salary after studying. I think that sometimes finding what you want to do, or reaching your goal, has more to do with being open-minded than with being single-minded.

I was armed with some specific skills from my studies: being able to write — I am not going to say it was anything extraordinary — and a strong visual sense. Generally speaking I had communication skills, which is what I had studied.

Originally I went to work at Estée Lauder, in their advertising department as an assistant. This seems very different from being a journalist, but I could utilise some of the basic skills I had learned at university, and from there I went to *Vogue*, simply because there happened to be someone who worked at Lauder who had worked at *Vogue*. It was just that connection, really, that took me there. I never intended to work on a fashion magazine. *Ever*.

That said, I was interested in fashion like any girl my age. I suspect though what really drew me in was visual information and visual creation rather than fashion per se, but I never thought, 'Yes, I want to work on a fashion magazine'. When the opportunity at *Vogue* presented itself I went with it — not really knowing what you did if you worked on a magazine. The biggest challenge at first was simply learning. But I am a quick study, so it wasn't really a struggle for me to take in the information.

On the other hand, it was a complicated time for me — I was starting my career and I was very young. Certainly I was very insecure — just a girl from the suburbs and here I was working at *Vogue*. I felt I was stepping into a quite foreign world — but of course when you get down to it, lots of girls working on magazines are from the suburbs. I think the insecurity was because of my age, my lack of experience and some degree of personal shyness. And I found overcoming that insecurity was a bigger challenge in the long run than the learning curve.

I overcame it by talking myself through it. I had applied that technique against my shyness for quite some time, even as a teenager, and I have used it even as a much more experienced adult. You say to yourself, 'You can do this, it's fine, just take it step by step, you can handle it.' It sounds silly, simplistic, but it's about giving yourself a little bit of inner encouragement and not always relying on reinforcement from outside, from other people.

I had to use that a lot when I went to the US to edit American *Bazaar* for a while, because I knew I was stepping into probably the most difficult professional situation I have ever dealt with to date. I arrived a matter of weeks after Elizabeth Tilberis, the much-loved editor-in-chief of *Bazaar*, had passed away. She had been suffering from cancer over a long period.

I was brought in as a kind of caretaking role.

I remember thinking on the plane travelling to New York, 'Now it is 24 hours (or whatever) till I start', and building up an incredible fear about what I was about to do. I arrived in New York in the middle of the night with that anxiety building, and realised I was becoming overwhelmed by what I was about to do, so I used that inner encouragement again, saying, 'Well, you know you can't really change the situation, so just deal with it step by step. Be really sure of your plan about how you will tackle this difficult situation, and maybe also talk to the people you know are going to give you good advice.'

It was the discipline of saying, 'Take it step by step.' I had a game plan for how I was going to deal with working with people who (a) didn't know me, (b) didn't necessarily want me to be there, and (c) were grieving the death of Liz Tilberis.

It was a matter of me thinking through how I would want to be dealt with if I was in that situation, trying to sort of superimpose myself on it. Of course, I was dealing with people who worked on a magazine, and as I had worked in magazines for 15 or 20 years, even though I didn't know these particular people, I had some feeling about what sort of people they would be.

Also, I had spoken with somebody who deals a lot in human resources, a kind of adviser. I talked to him about my approach and asked him for his comments, and was able to take those on board. So I did prepare. I suppose I would sum all that up by saying, 'Be prepared for what you are about to do.' I always use it as my key when I am giving a speech. It is a very good thing to be prepared when you're giving a speech! You should prepare by asking others, and think the situation through, giving yourself time to work on it, even if you have to squeeze the time into a really busy day.

The third thing that helped me in New York came from my boss from Australian *Bazaar*. He was really looking after me. We were going to a function and I said, 'You know, George, I am really, really nervous about dealing with this situation.

And he looked at me and said, 'Karin, it is not as if you are someone we plucked off the street who doesn't know anything about magazines. You know about magazines. You will be fine, don't worry about it.'

It was the most simple reassurance really. He wasn't talking to me about how to handle this personality or that personality; he just reminded me that I actually was already well prepared, well equipped, and I only had to take it one step at a time. And that he had confidence in me.

You shouldn't let things get complicated, because everyone else will do that anyway. So if you can cut to the heart of the matter, cut to the chase, sometimes you can make it better.

Be prepared, seek advice and just reassure yourself that you are prepared for whatever the situation is.

I took a job in 2001 that was probably outside my realm of experience. Even though people would say I'd worked in the *fashion* business, I had actually been working in the *publishing* business, and now I was going to work in the retailing business. Of course, I also said — like everybody else — 'Oh, it's just the fashion business, it's fine', but I knew that in a way I was crossing over to the other side and it was both a challenge and a revealing experience.

I didn't seek this change — in fact I had just had a baby, so I wasn't really thinking about career changes — but it presented itself and I think it is important get outside your safety zone or your comfort zone. I must admit that I haven't had much skill transfer into this job, and that has made it possibly more challenging, but I learnt a lot of things in the first year. And I know I have more to learn.

It's important to work out where you need help. I mean, you can't do everything yourself. You can't have every possible skill. I felt that in publishing I had many skills; not all the skills required, but many of them. When I made the move to retailing, it was to very upscale luxury goods; the commonality was the prestige market. In that regard I feel very confident — I understand branding and what these companies are about, their positioning. But I did need some very strong support in areas where I was lacking and was fortunate to find that among my colleagues.

My style is more of a collegial style of management. That was how I worked on the magazine. I worked within a creative team and I think that style works.

I am inclusive. I give people I work with responsibility, I allow them to work solo. I also communicate with them very very strongly, about what I think. It might not be about their performance; it might be information about what we are doing, what are we planning, what our company is about.

And it's the same philosophy at Hermes. I suppose I am the boss, but I hate it when people call me the boss. I would rather be seen as just the team leader.

Balancing work, family and social commitments is a challenge every single day. It's a bit like choosing which school to send your child to — you want them to be an all-round person, not the type of person who only knows about one thing. I know that, and it's always stood me in good stead — when I go out and mix with people, and when I spend time with my family, I always find ideas that I can apply in my work.

I have always known that it is really important to me to try as much as possible to be a well-rounded woman. I make sure I am home before the children go to bed — that's a key thing. I think family comes first. But for other people 'family' may not be traditional; it might be their own definition of 'family', which might be a support network of friends. Balance is about juggling and I am very fortunate that I have so many supportive people in my life who help me out.

'Stick with people who wish you well in life.' That's a piece of advice from a late friend who really knew what she was talking about.

What makes you keep doing what you are doing? For me it is the reward. The reward could be monetary, or it could be emotional, or it could be intellectual. Because you can do different things with money, money *is* a motivating factor. On the other hand, I don't think it's by any means the only factor, certainly not for me. I mean I worked in publishing for a long, long time and I would say that financial reward was right down the bottom of the list for me in publishing.

Also, feedback from your colleagues is a great reward — people saying you did a great job. Being able to go to a board meeting and show them a positive result, it's all part of the motivation. And there is a little fear built in; the fear of not succeeding and that is just fine.

There are also elements of faith, luck, hard work, and application to success; I don't think there is a secret ingredient, to be honest.

A quotation to live by? 'Give me the luxuries of life and I will willingly do without the necessities' — Frank Lloyd Wright.

Guan WEI

Guan Wei, an acclaimed artist, was born in China, where in the mid-seventeenth century his ancestors were part of the Manchu nobility. He studied fine arts at Beijing Capital University, then emigrated to Australia in 1989. He has consolidated his national and international reputation with a survey exhibition at the Museum of Contemporary Art, Sydney, had a major work included in the Third Asia-Pacific Triennial in Brisbane in 1999 and he represented Australia at the 2000 Kwangju Biennial in Korea. His painting focuses on east/west interactions, often with humour and whimsy but also with political critique. Guan Wei was invited to La Salle College of the Arts, Singapore, to exhibit at their Earl Lu Gallery in February 2000 and Asialink's residency funding allowed him to extend his time there.

When I was a little child my father really wanted me to become an actor, or sing in the opera. But after I turned 14 my voice broke, which meant my career was broken too, because I couldn't sing very well. After that I moved more towards drawing. I think you know, yourself, if you can draw and make interesting pictures. Drawing can be a career for life.

My family is a very old family, going back to the Qing dynasty. The whole family are artistic. My father is an actor but he can also paint, and he can do calligraphy very well. I think I was very strongly influenced by my father. I remember that in the beginning I just put some colours on the covers of my books — my first drawings. Also, I made drawings of tigers and camels, things a child would do. But then I took on more difficult drawings and sketches.

I never thought I would come to Australia and become an international artist. When I was 15 the Cultural Revolution began. All the universities were closed. My father introduced me to his artist friends, so that they could teach me. I painted a lot of pictures at home. Every two weeks or month I would take 10 or more to my father's friends' homes. They would tell me which ones were good and guide me. And they would teach me in private.

At the time no university or art school was permitted. They were all closed. But I had six or seven very good friends; we were all interested in art, and every day we made art together. During the Cultural Revolution the authorities sent all the children to the country to work so when I finished high school I went to the country, to a farm. The farm was in the mountains and we were looking after sheep. It was a very romantic setting. I was with a good friend, who was an artist too. We worked very hard for the farmer but we still had time to paint landscapes and portraits.

I remember making portraits in the farmer's home at night. The light was very dim, so we brought the light bulb from another room in for one or two hours to give ourselves enough light to paint — then we put it back. We made some great portraits. There were even times when I would draw outlines on the ground when I didn't have materials or canvas. I never thought I would become an important artist. I was just doing what I liked.

After three years I came back to the city. I became a builder, making houses. I found that hard — I found it hard to build and draw pictures. Then, after the fall of the Gang of Four — in 1976 — China opened its doors to the West. Many Western ideas and books came to China at that time. In 1978 we young students were thirsty to learn about other ways and new things. All we knew of Western culture before that was Marxism and Communism; we never knew much about contemporary Western things. They opened the doors and we opened our eyes — we read everything we could find, every book on Western culture. We shared every book we found. It was very exciting; we were young, and we were learning, arguing, talking and creating pictures.

In 1979 or 1980 I started to take creative art seriously; before that it was just like being a student. In China the government controlled everything, including the galleries and the museums. If you wanted to show your work you had to take photos, apply, and then have meetings. I applied to have a public show but they always refused. They would say, 'We can't understand the meaning of this picture.' That's why my friends and I only showed our work in private, to our friends.

Later, in 1983 or 1984, another important thing happened: I got involved with a Western friend. Through that person I met a journalist working in Beijing and also some staff working in an embassy. So I had some Australian friends and some Spanish friends who were involved in art, and they gave me very great support. I first sold some of my work in 1986. One of the foreigners came to my home and finally bought one of my pictures. I remember they gave me 600 or 800 Chinese yuan. I was very happy; this money was very important at the time because it allowed me to buy more materials.

In 1988 Dr Nicholas Jose the Cultural Councillor at the Embassy of Australia got a group show going for us. Three friends and I put on the show together. This attaché had people visiting, including professors from an art school in Australia and a director from the National Gallery. They said my work was 'very fresh, very interesting'. Two months later we all got invitations to study at the art school in Tasmania.

In 1989 I came to Australia to do art training in Tasmania for two months. I did a lot in that time — I painted about 38 pictures, and then there was an exhibition. Just as I got back to China, the student democracy movement in Tiananmen Square happened. Professor Geoff Parr from the Tasmanian School of Art wrote a letter to invite me back to Australia — he was really worried about my safety.

I wasn't too keen to go then, because I had just come back home. I wanted to stay in China for a little while and work. The following year, 1990, Professor Parr, Bernice Murphy the Director of the Sydney Museum of Contemporary Art and Dr Nicholas Jose the Cultural Councillor at the Australian Embassy all wrote a letter to the Australia Council saying that I was a very good artist and should be brought back to Australia. So I was invited to come back. In August 1990 I came back to Tasmania and the Australia Council gave me a $10,000 grant. This was a grant they normally only gave to citizens of Australia, never to foreigners, so I was very surprised that they gave it to me.

I spent one and a half years in Tasmania, created hundreds of pieces of work and got a touring exhibition. I showed my work in Canberra, Melbourne, Tasmania and Sydney. Many of my friends were Chinese artists, but they were all living in Sydney, so it was lonely in Tasmania. But I think it was very good for me, because I could concentrate on my work. Also, feeling lonely brings out your emotions. The paintings reflect my emotions at the time: this one is more serious, this one is more relaxed and meditative. During the summer holidays all the students and teachers left the campus, and sometimes I had the big school all to myself. I remember just working and working, and even not talking for one week.

Finally I came to Sydney in 1992. I got a one-year artist-in-residence position at the Museum of Contemporary Art. All my artist friends were working in factories because they needed money. I asked one of my friends to come walking around Paddington with me, looking for a gallery where we could show our work. Each gallery liked the pictures but flatly refused to give us a show. Finally we found the Sherman Galleries and Gene Sherman said, 'This looks interesting.' Two days later she gave me a call and six months later we had a group show in her gallery in Hargrave Street, Paddington. The following year I had work in another show — of eight Australian contemporary artists. The following year I had a solo show.

When you become Australian you lose your Chinese citizenship. It was not easy to make the decision to do this, but eventually, in 1997, I became an Australian citizen. I think Australia has treated me very well. It has given me many chances, and I thought I should become a citizen.

My wife is very good; she understands what I am doing and gives me very great support. She used to help me make my colours, and sometimes she gives me ideas. Also, she is my critic — this one is good, this one is no good. After we had a child, everything came together.

Strategies for living
YOUR DREAMS

You can either contribute or just munch on the grass Some
people like to lie low, not make any waves, live their lives quietly and be
content with what they are doing; they don't want to take on anything
new or accept additional responsibility. They 'munch on the grass'.
They may even be critical of those who have taken action.

But by not seizing opportunities and by passing responsibilities to
others, you are forgoing the opportunity to live life to its full potential
and to receive the rewards you deserve.

To reach your full potential and reap the benefits, you must be
prepared to sweat a little, to step out of your comfort zone and get
involved. It may start with volunteering for a local cause or taking on
additional responsibilities in your workplace ... it may lead to your
eventually taking up a significant challenge which may change your
life forever. By taking action you will be able to savour the experience
of triumph and success. As Theodore Roosevelt, the twenty-sixth
President of the United States, once said:

It is not the critic who counts; not the man who points out how the strong man
stumbles, or where the doer of deeds could have done better. The credit belongs
to the man who is actually in the arena, whose face is marred by dust and sweat
and blood, who strives valiantly, who errs and comes up short again and again,
because there is no effort without error or shortcoming, but who knows the great
enthusiasms, the great devotions, who spends himself for a worthy cause; who,
at the best, knows, in the end, the triumph of high achievement and who, at the
worst, if he fails, at least he fails while daring greatly, so that his place shall never
be with those cold and timid souls who knew neither victory nor defeat.

277

Carla
ZAMPATTI

Born in Italy, Carla Zampatti, one of Australia's most creative, innovative and influential fashion designers, heads a retail network of 31 boutiques. She is one of Australia's most recognised women and has been honoured for her contributions to both fashion and business. Her awards include one of the country's top distinctions, a Member in the Order of Australia (AM) and she is also a former Businesswoman of the Year. Carla is the Chairman, SBS Corporation and serves on a number of other boards including Westfield Holdings, McDonald's Australia and several not-for-profit organisations. A unique achievement was her involvement with Ford Australia: she is believed to be the first woman designer asked to design a car for the women's market. She worked on the Ford Laser produced in 1985.

Fashion was my original vision — my goal — from a very early age. For me it was a fairly single-minded view that it was the area that I wanted to be in.

Being Italian, living in Italy, played a part — the way people dress there is a very big part of the culture. I visited dressmakers with my mother, and witnessed the creativity and excitement in the workroom, which was like a design house. That's how women had their clothes made. I just loved the atmosphere. I loved the process and I felt that it was what I wanted to do. But I always knew I didn't want to be a dressmaker. I wanted to have a business, because being a dressmaker would not have given me the satisfaction. I wanted to take it further than that, the creative process through to retailing.

No one in my family had anything to do with fashion so it was an innate thing. I guess you innately know what you're probably quite good at, or what you might be good at. To discover that early and to have the attitude that it's what I wanted to do helped me; by the age of 24 I had my own business. But it wasn't without difficulty getting there — working for other people, learning, experiencing different kind of areas, all helped in achieving my goal. It helped me in understanding business and what business required.

I worked as a public relations person and I also worked a little in retail. Each job gave me experience which was of enormous benefit when I actually started my own business. In business you have to have a very open mind and you have to keep on learning. I think that's most important. Fashion is a very good business to be in to keep your mind open, because you don't stay in the fashion business if you close your mind. You have to change your look every six months. With every collection you have to change your direction — not radically, but quite substantially, to stay fresh and exciting.

My first step was taking a job within the industry. Eventually I moved more into retail and public relations, because I knew that I needed that experience. Then I met someone who gave me the kind of work that enabled me to understand how the industry worked. Some time later I made the decision that I wanted to do it myself, I wanted to take the risk, to give up my job and put all my savings into a business. Creating my first retail store was very important, because at the beginning I used to design and wholesale only. So eventually I was able to go totally vertical and just have my own outlets.

Each of these steps represented a very important decision in terms of creating the business that I have today, which works really well.

I think the gradual development was very important. I have a strong belief that if people have a huge ambition, it's sometimes difficult for them to achieve it because they want to get there too quickly. My ambition was really much more limited — I imagined a smaller business, not the size my business is today. What I have achieved today is way past my ambition, which I think is very healthy, because it means I was focusing on each step and succeeding in that before I moved on to the next one, rather than being dissatisfied because I wasn't 'there' yet.

Growing is about having a focus on how you reach your goal, and when you are there, knowing that you want to reach the next step. I think some people get frustrated because they want to get there too quickly. If you can perfect whatever you are doing at any particular moment, you will be open for new ambitions, for growth. Today's young people are sometimes too ambitious in that they want to reach their enormous goal but they haven't really worked out how they're going to get there; then they become disappointed, lose focus and momentum.

When you are building up a brand, your initial challenge is developing a good product and becoming known as a brand, both in the media and with the public. It's easy to sell a product if you have a strong brand, but at the beginning it's really quite tough.

Along the way I learned that I could work much harder than I ever thought possible. I liked what I did and doing it well. But I found when I had created my own business and was running it single-handed at the beginning, that it wasn't an eight-hour-a-day job, it was really a day, night and weekend job. But you learn your strengths and your determination. It was a challenge, but it was a very exciting one.

My family were not in business and I wasn't familiar with how businesses worked. Business from a distance can look mysterious and perhaps difficult, but it is not. I think running a business needs logic and application. I have since learned that I knew more about business than I thought. That was very reassuring.

Eventually when you start employing people you realise the value of other people. Their contribution, how much people are prepared to give. I don't think you can be a good manager unless you have people skills, know how to inspire people, know how to make people want to follow you — I think that is very important. I think it's about getting them involved and giving them responsibility. People like to be involved, they like to feel that they are achieving something. The business now is being managed by a really wonderful young team. I learned to let go and allow them to grow, and they have proven that they can do it and are very dependable.

I don't know any successful person that has not worked very hard. Frank Lowy [of Westfield Holdings] is an example, he works harder than anyone I know. I really think it's just determination to win, absolutely knowing that you have to apply yourself and you're not going to win unless you do, there are no shortcuts.

When an opportunity comes your way, seize it but make sure it is going to work. The IT area, for instance, is an area which really captivated the imagination of a lot of people but it didn't work. So if something comes your way you have to analyse whether it is going to add value and if it makes sense.

For someone starting out in this business I would suggest study as far as you can go, because today it's more competitive. Study business as well as design. Fashion creativity cannot be achieved without business ability. Fashion is a business, it's not only about design. You have to also know about marketing, so you need to learn these skills. A young designer today needs to gain some experience in the industry by working for someone whom they think is running a good business. By keeping a very open mind and trying to learn as much as possible from that person they will be better prepared when they are ready start their own brand. It won't happen overnight and they will have to work very hard. There will be disappointments but they will just have to keep focused and they will gain knowledge from this experience.

If you can find work which is inspirational you will succeed, simply because you'll enjoy doing it. In my early days of work I knew I had to find something that I enjoyed. So work has to be something that you find stimulating.

Strategies for living
YOUR DREAMS

Working as part of a team No one can do everything on their own. Successful people see their task as a puzzle — and they know that they are just one piece of the puzzle. They delegate and share responsibility. They find advisers and professionals who have experience in specific areas, and they invite such people to step in and help.

It may be a humbling experience to give away some power and responsibility, but you'll soon find that when you work with likeminded and trustworthy people you can propel yourself — and them! — to tremendous heights.

To keep your team motivated, don't just think money. Involve your team in the whole process, make them feel that they are appreciated and valued and are indeed part of a vision. Treat your staff as you wish to be treated.

One Chief Executive invites one additional staff member to each management meeting (the staff rotate, so everyone gets a turn). He invites the person to contribute to the discussions and listens to their input. Imagine how that makes his employees feel! They know that they are part of a team and that their opinions and suggestions are valued. People who feel valued give more, and become more creative in their approach to work — everyone wins.

Nicky
ZIMMERMANN

As one of Australia's most successful fashion designers Nicky Zimmermann created the perfect recipe for success. In 1990 Nicky and her sister Simone launched their first collection out of their parents' garage and at street markets. Zimmermann has since made a name for itself, and its fashionable swimsuit designs have enabled the company to reach both local and international markets for some years. Today Nicky is part-owner of four stores in Australia and together the Zimmermanns continue to escalate their presence in international markets, with stockists including Victoria's Secret and major US department stores Saks Fifth Avenue and Bloomingdales.

My desire was that I wanted to be in charge of what I was doing myself, it was really a lifestyle thing. That was probably the first motivation. But once you get into something, it's a bit like a baby — it just keeps growing and you have to feed it, and teach it things and then it does the same back to you.

I grew up in a family where my father always had his own business and worked very, very hard. He was an immigrant and came here with absolutely nothing, with hardly any education, but he managed to give me a very comfortable life and the opportunities to do whatever I wanted. So I think probably my first inspiration would be my family, and what I was taught and saw as I was growing up.

After I finished design school I really only had a full-time job for about six months, and then I started my own business. I was in a position that most young students who had just left college would love to be in — directly designing for a company — and there were possibilities of going overseas and things like that, but it still wasn't something that really drew me in. My first step was leaving that job and saving a little bit of money to buy an overlocker. I already had a very good sewing machine but I needed more equipment, because I made everything when I first started.

I don't think it was quite as competitive then — around 14 years ago — as it is now. I was making garments in my parents' garage at home and selling them to local girls that knew me and knew what I had been doing. People in Cronulla, in Sydney's southern suburbs, knew I'd been to design school, so I had a bit of a clientele fairly early on. From there I went to Paddington markets and that was quite successful and I got a couple of pages in *Vogue* magazine within the first six months. Then shops started to call me, and it progressed fairly quickly from there. That was pretty much the base, the beginning.

There was a lot of physically hard work, especially in the beginning. I pattern made, printed, machined, sold, did everything. For the first six months we did it all and then probably for the next five years there was still quite a lot of physical work, even though I had moved on to using machinists and things like that. My sister and I remained cutting for probably the next two years. We just did everything.

Money wasn't all that difficult. Overheads were down to a minimum because Simone and I did everything. It was more the actual learning of business, like having your first employee and learning how to manage things like that. That was probably the first very challenging thing that came up, because we didn't have difficulties selling. Things happened really quite well for us. We got our first store, that worked well, we got our second store, that worked well, and then later we had an enormous amount of growth, both wholesale and in the retail outlets. Cash flow became difficult, in that we were totally financed by ourselves, my sister and I; we had no bank finance, no overdraft, no nothing.

The main challenge today is having a business that is still growing rapidly; I think we've had something like 70 per cent growth in our business since 1997. It's massive, and you can feel the momentum of it; that scares me a little bit, in that the growth needs to be harnessed and looked after. We are probably now at a point where we need more professional financial help. We almost need to get back to the basics of business again and redo a business plan, because we've outgrown our business plan. We need to harness the growth and take advantage of it, so that the growth allows more growth. Money begets money.

When we got our first shop, it was Simone and I and one employee, we would all work in the shop and do everything else as well. We have six shops now; we export, practically all around the world. We have about 40 employees.

We have a very successful product with our swimwear. We have opened two swimwear stores, and I want to open two more — but nationally and internationally, and that would be quite a big step. That is definitely where we are heading. And I want to consolidate what we do and make it solid and good for people that work here, and good for Simone and me, comfortable.

Simone and I are very much integral parts of what goes on in here. I don't just sit in my design room and not know what goes on, with delivery, in the sales area, in the shops. And it's not out of necessity; it's because I want to. I think the girls have a clear understanding that basically they're along for the ride, and what goes on will bring a benefit to everyone, if that is the way they feel about it as well.

Simone and I have a unique relationship. We are close in all sorts of ways because we are sisters, but we also have a similar mindset about business and how to treat people. We think very similarly, which works well. It can't really be a fluke, because it's been 13 years from starting the business to where it is now, and it still works.

I think I always wanted to be involved in design, in fashion. That has always been very much a passion for me, and Simone has always been acutely aware of it because it's been the case since I was young. I've never wanted to be anywhere else, never even thought of it. Her skills lie more in the business end; really she has one job and I have another job. They blend here and there, but we can go for a day without talking to each other, from one end of the room to the other. We're very clear on what it is all about. She is very supportive of what I do and basically she runs all the business part of it.

Sometimes I regret that I haven't diversified because it means that what I do is so focused I may not get to read about other things I might be interested in doing. When I was younger I didn't get to travel, I didn't do things that make people have broad, wonderful minds. I do this, and to do it I need to stay focused. With things like getting married and having children, if I didn't concentrate on doing what I do when I am here during the day, I couldn't have the rest of it.

Focus is the main ingredient that allows you to balance your life, and I think procrastination is the great danger. It's one of the hardest things to control in your own business. Time-wasting is such a luxury for me, I can't stand it. I am a very focused person, and my work is one of my first loves, so it's not something that I would risk in any way. I am also not a procrastinator, I never have been, which means that I can come in and get more things done in two hours than most people can in two weeks. It's just because I know so much about what I am doing, and because I am particularly focused.

These days my lifestyle isn't compromised by my work. When I go home I don't take my work home with me. I never have. I don't know if my husband even knows what I do. I don't work on the weekends, I'm not interested in that; I'm interested in having my weekends as a separate part of my life. It's very important to be able to compartmentalise. I'm rarely in here past seven o'clock, which in my sort of business is kind of unusual. However, there are things that I have missed out on, probably as a younger person when it was harder and I did do those long hours. Now I've given myself a lot more to actually do than what I did back then but I don't have to do it all; I have people who help me.

Another ingredient of success is to surround yourself with talented people, people you respect for their abilities and skills, and allow them to be good at what they can be good at, because you are not the only one who can be good at something.

I think a lot of people see our industry as glamorous and fun, and everyone appears to have a lot of money and to travel a lot — these are all wrong reasons for going into it. I see people who focus only on the PR aspect, instead of setting up solid foundations for a business so that they can create something that is good; I see a lot of people with the wrong reasons for wanting to do what I do. My reason has never been ego based; it's been the passion for fashion.

My dad used to say years ago: 'There is no such thing as a free lunch.' I was never under the illusion that having your own business was about just money. You have a business for different sorts of reasons. Mine is a very personal sort of reason; I don't know if it is a control reason, like I want to control my

own life. I don't know what it is. The money becomes war-
ranted at a certain point because you work so hard, but if that
is why you're doing it, then in this industry, don't do it.

Strategies for living
YOUR DREAMS

You'll see it when you believe it See yourself at the finish line! Many of the men and women featured in this book had a clear picture in their mind of being tremendously successful in their respective fields. They knew it, they felt it.

There are entrepreneurs who pictured themselves sitting in that corner office overseeing the operations of the company; athletes who could practically hear the crowds cheering as they concluded their spectacular performances; the author who felt the weight of her completed book in her hand; they sensed and tasted the feeling of success and accomplishment.

They saw themselves receiving that medal, that award, that honour, and they heard the cheering of the thousands of excited fans. All of them had a clear and crisp picture imprinted deep within their mind of the end result. There was absolutely no question, not an ounce of doubt, that they were going to succeed — the question was when.